WAR AND CRISIS
IN THE AMERICAS

FIDEL CASTRO
SPEECHES 1984-85

WAR AND CRISIS
IN THE AMERICAS

PATHFINDER PRESS

New York   London   Sydney

Edited by Michael Taber

Library of Congress Catalog Card Number 85-61641
ISBN: cloth, 0-87348-656-0; paper, 0-87348-657-9

Printed in the United States of America
First Edition, 1985

Pathfinder Press
410 West Street
New York, NY 10014

Distributor in Britain: *Distributor in Australia:*
47 The Cut   P.O. Box 37 Leichhardt
London SE1 8LL   Sydney, NSW 2040

Contents

Introduction

On four successive evenings in February 1985, Cuban President Fidel Castro entered the homes of millions of television viewers in the United States. Answering questions directed to him by Robert MacNeil on the MacNeil/Lehrer NewsHour, Castro explained, in clear and simple terms, the views of the Cuban government on a wide range of topics.

The four-part interview, which was broadcast twice, generated considerable debate and discussion throughout the country. Castro made a positive impression on many people, and the overall effect of the interview helped undermine Washington's relentless anti-Cuba campaign. Doubts were raised in the minds of many viewers about the justifications given by the U.S. government for its current course toward war in Central America and the Caribbean.

The interview on the MacNeil/Lehrer NewsHour, which is published in this collection, is one of many speeches and interviews given by Castro between December 1983 and March 1985. Twelve of these are excerpted or reprinted in their entirety in this volume.

Two principal themes emerge from these documents. One is the enormity of the stakes in the struggle against Washington's course in Central America and the Caribbean. The other is the explosive social and political situation generated throughout Latin America by the deepening economic crisis of world capitalism and the debt burden it imposes on Latin American countries.

The revolutionary perspective that Castro outlines is in response to the U.S. government's sustained offensive in the region over the last five years. A clear picture emerges of the consequences for Washington if it invades Nicaragua or Cuba.

One of the questions dealt with in these speeches and interviews is the qualitative upgrading of the military preparedness of the Cuban people.

In May 1980, the Cuban government announced that, in addition to the armed forces and reserves, a volunteer militia would be formed for the first time since the early years of the revolution. Since then, more than one million Cuban men and women have enrolled in this Territorial Troop Militia. Organizations such as the Federation of Cuban Women, the National Association of Small Farmers, the trade unions, and the neighborhood Committees for the Defense of the Revolution have also been drawn directly into these active defense preparations.

Castro gives particular credit to the creation a decade ago of the elected organs of People's Power — representative governing bodies from the local to the national level — for making possible the breadth of these defense preparations.

The central concept in Cuba's defense policy, Castro reminded the National Assembly of People's Power in December 1984, is that "the military defense of the country, on the battlefield and in all the backup work in any form of attack — blockade, war of attrition, invasion, total or partial occupation of the country — was a task for both the armed forces and the people as a whole, so the people had to be organized and prepared for the struggle."

He illustrated what he called "people's war" by pointing to several of the most notable examples from recent history: defense of the Soviet Union against Germany's invasion during World War II, the struggle of the Vietnamese against U.S. aggression, the Algerian fight for independence from French colonialism, and the current liberation struggle in El Salvador.

Castro then added that Cuba has an advantage over even these historic struggles. This is because, he said, "In our country, it is an entire people, 10 million inhabitants, united, with a single party and army, a solid mass structure, a single government, complete unity and no bourgeoisie, a solid and coherent social system. A worker, peasant, and student people; a country where everybody, women and children included, would stand solid with a political and military doctrine, defending the country. A country like that can be exterminated with ten or more atom bombs, perhaps, although that would be another type of war and only possible in the framework of a world war."

As a result of Cuba's recent military preparations, he added, "the defensive capacity of the country has been multiplied by ten." An aggressor now knows, Castro affirmed, "that if he attacks he will have to pay a price ten times greater than he would have had to pay four or five years ago, as great a price as defeat and humiliation, that is, an unpayable price."

'We should not lower our guard'

The Cuban people's determination to defend their country and revolution is cited by Washington as evidence of Cuba's preparations to "export" revolution to other Latin American countries.

The Cuban leadership repeatedly explains that this is a slander designed to justify hostile actions against Cuba. Cuba's policy is not "an adventurist one; we are not warmongers," Castro told a December 1984 Cuban student congress in a speech excerpted for this volume. To the contrary, we "will do all that is in our hands to further détente in our area, in Cuba and in Central America."

Shortly following this speech, an agreement was reached between the Cuban and U.S. governments on immigration matters. In reporting this December 14, 1984, accord to the Cuban people on national television, Castro urged that "the same spirit that characterized these talks prevail in those that are now in progress and that will be held in the world in the weeks and months to come." Nonetheless, he cautioned, "our constructive, positive, receptive stand doesn't mean that we are overconcerned about negotiations" and "no one should harbor illusions. We, especially, should not lower our guard or in any way neglect our defense."

Castro's cautionary statement soon proved to be well-taken. On May 20, 1985, Washington demonstrated its low opinion of normalizing relations with Cuba by belligerently starting up Radio José Martí. This was eighty-three years to the day after Washington's imposition of a fake, neocolonial independence from Spain — a date etched in the consciousness of every Cuban fighter against Yankee domination. The Cuban government responded to what it called this "cynical and provocative decision" of Washington by suspending the immigration agreement. The statement of the Cuban government is reprinted as an appendix to this volume.

While the Cuban leadership has repeatedly reiterated its readiness to enter into discussions to improve relations with the United States, Castro emphasized to the student congress that "peace is not attained through weakness. Peace is attained through strength, courage, and determination of peoples. I believe this is what has characterized our revolution over these twenty-five years."

Even if détente with Washington is achieved, he stated, "defense cannot be neglected! This is very important, for what we have achieved cannot be cast aside. It is a reality imposed by our geographical location."

Nicaragua counters Washington's moves

Right now the Nicaraguan government is the central target of Washington's mounting attacks in the region; and it also, like Cuba, has been effectively parrying each move made by the North American colossus.

As in Cuba, the Sandinista government in Nicaragua is mobilizing and organizing the working class and peasantry to defend the revolution. It has been forced to allocate gigantic human and material resources to put up an effective defense against the *contras,* the U.S.-financed and -organized mercenaries. This has meant substantially strengthening the military forces. And it has imposed the burden of putting a large portion of that country's limited economic resources behind the defense effort.

In addition to the deaths and maiming of thousands of Nicaraguans, the brutal U.S.-engineered *contra* war has led to economic hardship for most of the country's citizens. Defense needs have made it impossible for the new government to continue advancing many economic and social programs at the same pace as during the first years after the 1979 victory. But the big majority of Nicaraguans recognize that if their workers' and peasants' government is overturned, all hope of further economic and social advances will be snuffed out. It is the Sandinista-led government that has made possible the gains that the Nicaraguan people have achieved. For that reason, they are resisting everything Washington is throwing at them and making big sacrifices to make sure they win.

Their determination is proving effective. They have dealt the *contra* raiders substantial defeats, inflicting many casualties and driving thousands of them out of the country. Moreover, the armed people have prevented the *contras* from establishing a foothold on Nicaraguan soil that could be used as a territorial basis for establishing a counterrevolutionary "provisional government" that Washington could rush in to recognize and support.

The victories that the Sandinista government has scored against the mercenary bands have raised the stakes for Washington. Castro pointed out to the student congress that "any adventure in Central America will not be the walkover Grenada was." The U.S. government would have to pay "an enormous political and human price" for the direct use of its troops, he said.

Castro spelled out what this would mean in an interview with the Spanish press agency EFE in February 1985. "Perhaps [Washington] would have to kill hundreds of thousands of people in full view of international opinion, in full view of the mass media, television, film," he said. "No matter how many measures they might take, they wouldn't be able to hide the magnitude of the genocide they would have to commit there with the use of their warships, bombers, tanks, and troops to kill Nicaraguans."

The majority of Nicaraguans, Castro said, are guided by the same principle as the Cuban people. "Our country can be exterminated but not defeated. That is our philosophy and the philosophy of the Nicaraguans and the Salvadorans."

Castro is often asked by interviewers whether or not there are Cuban troops in Nicaragua, and what military assistance Cuba would offer to Nicaragua in the event of a U.S. invasion. Each time, Castro explains that Cuba has some military advisers in Nicaragua, but that most of its personnel there are teachers, doctors, construction workers, and others engaged in civilian activities. He then challenges the governments of much larger and wealthier countries to match the assistance in these areas that Cuba has provided to Nicaragua.

Castro points out that in the event of a U.S. military blockade of Nicaragua, the Cuban government would be physically limited in what it could do. "We can't, just as in the case of a blockade against Cuba, break the blockade." Cuba and Nicaragua are small countries in this region, he notes, "where the United States has overwhelming superiority in conventional air and naval weapons, not to mention nuclear weapons."

From the military standpoint, both the Cuban and Nicaraguan governments are relying on the mobilization and readiness of the working people in their own countries if Washington imposes a blockade, launches an air attack, or sends in U.S. combat troops.

Look to Latin American people

In addition to their own defense preparations, the Cuban and Nicaraguan governments are also looking for international support, especially from the people of Latin America. Cuban and Nicaraguan leaders repeatedly point out that a U.S. war against Nicaragua would become a Central American war.

The explosive political situation in Latin America makes the opportunities for winning support there far better than in the early years of the Cuban revolution, when Washington had some success in isolating Cuba from other Latin American countries.

In the 1960s Washington succeeded in getting Cuba excluded from the Organization of American States (OAS) and got the OAS to urge member countries to sever diplomatic and trade relations with Cuba. By September 1964 every Latin American country had broken diplomatic relations with Cuba, with the sole exception of Mexico.

This sharply contrasts to the response in Latin America to the U.S. government's embargo against Nicaragua announced May 1, 1985. The Latin American Economic System (SELA), which includes twenty-five countries in the region, called on Washington to lift the trade sanctions. It also resolved to aid Nicaragua in countering the effects of the embargo.

Moreover, Cuba has reestablished diplomatic and trade relations with many Latin American countries. Two examples can be cited to demonstrate how much Cuba's isolation has been broken down in recent years. Cuba's volume of trade with Argentina last year surpassed that with Mexico, Cuba's largest trading partner in Latin America for more than two decades. And, in April, Ecuador's President León Febres Cordero made the first visit to Cuba by a Latin American head of state, other than from Mexico, since 1959.

Castro often points to another contrast between the 1960s and today. Twenty years ago Latin American countries were not weighed down by the mammoth debts they owe to imperialist banks today. In fact, one of the problems many Latin American countries had at that time was obtaining credit for loans. In 1961, "during the period of obsessive trauma over the Cuban revolution," Castro says, President Kennedy launched the Alliance for Progress. This was aimed at averting revolution by increasing aid and loans to the Latin American countries.

"Twenty-four years have elapsed since then," Castro explained to U.S. television reporter Robert MacNeil in February. "The population has doubled. The social problems have tripled. The debt is $360 billion. And in interest alone they must pay $40 billion per year — double the amount Kennedy thought was going to solve the problem in a certain number of years."

Kennedy's promise that the Alliance for Progress would bring prosperity for the majority of Latin Americans has proved to be hollow. Today the Latin American governments are being pressured by the big banks, through the International Monetary Fund, to apply onerous, belt-tightening measures against their working people or lose their credit. As a result, economic conditions for the great majority continue to deteriorate throughout the continent. They suffer from skyrocketing inflation, cutbacks in social services, and high unemployment. Massive numbers of peasants, driven off the land, scrape out a meager living in miserable shantytowns ringing the cities.

Castro reported to the Federation of Cuban Women in March 1985 that in the past twenty-six years "we have seen many things, but never what we're seeing now, phenomena that are reflected in the delegations that visit Cuba. Not only is there an enormous, monstrous crisis, but also a growing awareness of the situation created by that crisis."

This awareness, the Cuban leaders say, is giving rise to a very explosive situation.

"The U.S. administration may say that democracy [in Argentina, Brazil, and Uruguay] is advancing," Castro told the Spanish EFE interviewers, "but what is advancing is the crisis of the U.S. system of domination in Latin America." As a result of the debt crisis engendered by this domination, he told MacNeil a few days earlier, "I am convinced that the Latin American societies will explode, because there is a situation of despair among the workers, among the middle strata, and even in the oligarchy."

Chile, governed by a military dictatorship, is a "volcano," with the prospect for a "profound social revolution if rebellion breaks out," Castro predicted in the EFE interview. But the rulers in countries with civilian governments also face a dilemma, he told *Excelsior,* a daily paper published in Mexico City. They say they "aren't about to burden the people with the consequences of the debt" or "sacrifice their countries' development." Yet they don't say how this can be done, Castro added, "if no solution is found for the problem of the debt."

The increased militancy and political understanding that are emerging from the crisis today among tens of millions of people throughout the Americas can create a powerful ally for the struggle by the Nicaraguan and Cuban people against aggression. "An intervention in Nicaragua would cause a commotion in Latin America," Castro told EFE. "Graphically speaking," he added, "we say that to intervene in Nicaragua is to play with fire beside a powder keg. . . . It would really be a great folly on the part of the United States."

To illustrate what the response is when "a country of the Latin American family" is attacked, Castro cited the example of the British war against Argentina over the Malvinas Islands in 1982. "Despite the fact that the Argentine government was an indefensible, completely isolated, and discredited government," he said, "the Latin American nations unhesitatingly supported Argentina, that is, they supported the Argentine people. They supported the Argentine nation in its war against the British and there was a deep sense of solidarity."

It is within the framework of this political and economic situation in Latin America that the Cuban leadership proposes specific measures to alleviate the debt crisis.

When Castro was interviewed in March by *Excelsior,* he explained that the debt has grown so large that there is no way to pay it. He proposed that the debt be canceled. The imperialist governments, Castro said, should assume responsibility for the debt. He suggested that they raise the money to pay the banks by issuing ten-year government bonds. Funds for paying the interest could be obtained by reducing military expenditures 10 percent.

The response in Latin America to these proposals by the Cuban government also gains a hearing for other of its positions, including winning respect and solidarity for the struggle against Washington's aggression in Central America and the Caribbean. The Cuban leadership is pursuing every avenue of dialogue open to it to promote its proposals on the debt situation — trade unions, cultural organizations and activities, religious organizations, professional associations, political parties, liberation groups, state-to-state relations, the capitalist press, and international bodies.

For some time Castro has been explaining the source of the mounting debt crisis and how it can be overcome. This was the theme of his report to the Sixth Summit Conference of the Movement of Nonaligned Countries in Havana in 1979.

Shortly following that meeting, Castro reported to the United Nations General Assembly on behalf of the Nonaligned Movement. He stated there that "the task of helping us to emerge from underdevelopment is first and foremost a historic and moral obligation for those who benefited from the plunder of our wealth and the exploitation of our men and women for decades and for centuries."

Castro called on the imperialist countries to contribute $300 billion, above and beyond their current investments, for distribution to oppressed countries "in the form of donations and long-term moderate- and low-interest credits."

In evaluating the severe hardships that all countries oppressed by imperialism are suffering, Castro told *Excelsior* that Latin American countries "are in a better position than those of any other region in the world to tackle this problem seriously." He pointed to their political weight in the world, their enormous debts, their terrible economic and social crises, their deep community of interests, their potential for joint action.

Castro emphasized that the basis exists to unite all the peoples of Latin America to fight for a common proposal against the big bankers in North America and Western Europe. He once again cited the solidarity displayed by millions of Latin Americans against the British government during the Malvinas War.

But the current economic crisis and robbery by the imperialist banks, Castro said, have the potential to unite the Latin American countries much more than the Malvinas War did. He suggested that the Latin American governments form "a club, a committee, a group, or whatever you want to call it" that would collectively cancel their debts and present common demands on imperialism. He cited the example of the Organization of Petroleum Exporting Countries (OPEC), which in the 1970s contested the monopoly position of the big imperialist energy trusts in order to get a more just price for their oil. But the "debtors' club" that Castro proposes "would be much fairer and economically more beneficial for all countries," he explains.

Castro rejects proposals that call simply for renegotiating the loans or for short-term moratoriums. These are often motivated, he says, by the argument that the debt problem is very complicated and cannot be resolved easily. The "technical aspects mean nothing" to working people, however, because "they offer them nothing when they get up in the morning to look for work or when they see their wages shrinking while products grow more and more expensive." But the simple proposition that the Latin American countries collectively cancel their debts, and that the imperialist governments assume responsibility, makes a lot of sense to working people, he told *Excelsior*.

Castro says that canceling the debts "would be no more than the beginning. We would have to demand an end to unequal terms of trade; an end to protectionist policies; an end to the practice of dumping and to unjust, abusive monetary policies, excessive rates of interest, overvaluation of the dollar, and other diabolical procedures that make our countries' development impossible."

The Cuban leadership is directing its proposals to the Latin American governments for their consideration. At the same time, tens of millions of Latin Americans, especially the exploited workers and peasants who would most benefit from a cancelation of the debts, have heard about and are discussing the debt cancelation proposal. They have begun to press their governments to endorse it.

Castro, in refuting less far-reaching alternatives for dealing with the debt problem, stated that such formulas "don't attract, don't rally, don't persuade, don't motivate, and they don't mobilize anyone." By removing the negative, it is easy to see what the Castro proposal does accomplish. It is one that *does* attract, *does* rally, *does* persuade, *does* motivate, and *does* mobilize.

So far, the impact of Castro's proposal has been stunning to commentators. The *Excelsior* interview, for example, was run in installments in nine consecutive issues — each one featured on the front page — along with considerable commentary, both pro and con. The *Excelsior* interview was widely publicized, summarized, and excerpted in other newspapers and on television and radio throughout Latin America, and elsewhere around the world. Summaries were run in major dailies in Brazil, the South American country with the largest debt burden. The Cuban government published the section on the debt crisis in Latin America in pamphlet form in several languages, and is distributing it throughout the world. The full interview, which includes Castro's views on the situation in Central America and the Caribbean, is scheduled for publication in Cuba. The interview has also been published in Bolivia as a book by the Sergio Almaraz Center for Economic and Political Studies.

The positive response in Latin America has created consternation in the boardrooms of U.S. banks and corporations, and has been the subject of articles in the *Wall Street Journal, New York Times,* and other big-business dailies.

Tad Szulc, a journalist who covered Cuba and Latin America for many years for the *New York Times,* wrote from Havana that "there is no question that when Mr. Castro speaks Latin Americans listen."

Roger Lowenstein, writing from Havana for the *Wall Street Journal,* complained that Castro "has harped on debt in dozens of speeches and interviews, as well as in private talks with politicians, business executives and diplomats from around the world."

Lowenstein said that "Mr. Castro's meddling in debt obviously is unwelcome in Washington. And that is one reason why some Latins are pleased Mr. Castro is speaking out." He quoted an unnamed ambassador to Cuba from a Latin American country. " 'There are 20 presidents in Latin America saying the debt is unpayable. But Americans take more note of it when Fidel is saying it.' "

It is not just a single individual that people throughout Latin America and the world are listening to. They are responding to the example of the Cuban revolution — what it has accomplished, and its selfless inter-nationalism. As Castro put it in his speech to the Cuban National Assembly in December 1984, "In the field of moral values, the example, the ideas of socialism and patriotism we represent, go beyond the borders of our small island and are more powerful than the most sophisticated strategic weapons and the old capitalist ideas."

A different lending policy

An important theme of Castro's speeches and interviews is the contrast between the effects of the world capitalist crisis on socialist Cuba and on the rest of Latin America.

He points out that Cuba has the lowest hard-currency debt in Latin America, and that it continues to enjoy significant economic growth. Eighty-five percent of Cuba's trade is "with countries of the socialist community," he explains, "and, while the terms aren't the same with all of them because they have different levels of development and avail-abilities of resources, our relations are based on truly fair principles of cooperation and trade."

In its relations with the Soviet Union and Eastern Europe, Castro says, Cuba does not suffer from unequal terms of trade, protectionist measures, or the dumping of low-priced goods. It has also been able to obtain credit on easy terms.

A common charge by U.S. ruling circles is that Cuba has been able to hang on only due to massive doses of Soviet aid. Columnist James Reston bluntly stated in the *New York Times* that "Mr. Castro's so-called revolution has been a spectacular failure. He has been surviving by borrowing from the Soviet Union. . . ."

It is true that following Washington's economic embargo in the early 1960s, Cuba's trade and credit with the Soviet Union was indispensable for its economic growth. The question Reston fails to answer, however, is why Cuba — substantially dependent on economic relations with the Soviet Union and Eastern Europe — has made gigantic strides in education, health care, and industrial development, while living standards are being driven down in every other Latin American country, despite massive loans from U.S., British, and other imperialist banks.

"If the industrialized capitalist countries employed the same forms of trade and economic and financial relations that we have with the socialist community," Castro says, "the problems I have mentioned would be solved and the Third World countries' development would be guaranteed."

Not immune to world capitalist crisis

Despite Cuba's social and economic achievements, it has not been immune to the effects of the world capitalist crisis. Cuba still obtains loans from and has substantial trade with capitalist countries, trade it is working to increase. It has been hit hard by the high interest rates it must pay for hard-currency loans. The prices it must pay for imports from the world capitalist market have increased. At the same time, prices have plummeted for many of the semifinished products and many of the raw materials it exports, particularly sugar.

In December 1984, Cuba's National Assembly discussed a series of proposals to deal with these economic problems. At the meeting Castro compared these proposed economic measures to the launching of the Territorial Troop Militia and preparations for "people's war."

Cubans must also wage "the economic battle of the entire people, the economic war of the whole people," he said.

Castro explained that "the entire 1985 plan was revamped and definitive versions of the 1986-90 plan and the long-term plan for the year 2000 are being drawn up" in the realization that savings are the most immediate source of increased usable earnings.

Castro emphasized that the goal is to carry out these measures "without affecting what the population already receives." Nevertheless, he said, "we must begin with what we have and not think about new increases beyond what we have, at both the personal and social levels."

One area where a retreat must be made, Castro explained, is housing. Construction of new housing has not kept up with demand, and there is no immediate prospect of resolving the shortage. Priority, Castro pointed out, must go to production that generates exports.

Faced with this situation, the National Assembly adopted a new housing law aimed at utilizing existing dwellings more fully. The government anticipates that more housing will be made available by relaxing the policy on renting out rooms and exchanging homes, offering more incentives for repairs and maintenance of homes, and encouraging individual construction of new homes. To facilitate this, tenants in rented housing are being granted ownership titles to their dwellings.

In addition to Castro's interviews for U.S., Spanish, and Mexican publications and television, and speeches in Cuba and Nicaragua, this volume includes two speeches by the Cuban leader at an October 1984 meeting of the Council for Mutual Economic Assistance (CMEA). The CMEA is a ten-member organization that coordinates economic cooperation between the Soviet Union, many East European countries, Mongolia, Vietnam, and Cuba. Also included here is an interview with Cuban Vice-President Carlos Rafael Rodríguez given at the time of a June 1984 CMEA meeting held in Moscow.

In Castro's brief opening remarks to the October 1984 CMEA meeting in Havana, he urged that, "The countries that make up the socialist community in the CMEA must not overlook" the "threatening situation" in Central America and the Caribbean. He described the huge resources Cuba is putting into military and economic preparations, emphasizing that "all our people are preparing to defend the homeland and the revolution to the last inch of territory and the very last breath."

Both at the October and June 1984 CMEA meetings, the Cuban representatives pointed to the importance of helping Nicaragua, which is not a member of the CMEA. Castro stated in Havana that "we believe it is dramatically urgent to do our best to help Nicaraguans confront victoriously the enormous human and economic sacrifices that the Reagan administration's attacks have imposed on it. Cuba will spare no efforts to fulfill this undeferrable duty."

Underlining its commitment to help Nicaragua, the Cuban government in January 1985 canceled the $70 million debt owed to Cuba for helping to build the Victoria de Julio sugar mill in Nicaragua. This decision was announced by Castro during his speech at the dedication of the new mill, which is published in this volume. Cancelation of the debt will not only aid Nicaragua, but serves to underscore the brutal money-grubbing character of the capitalist profiteers, who, despite their vast resources, refuse to wipe the slate clean on a single debt owed to them.

The Cuban representatives at the CMEA meetings also strongly supported the special efforts of countries making up this organization to bridge the gap between its relatively more developed members, on one hand, and Cuba, Vietnam, and Mongolia, on the other.

*   *   *

The outcome of the unfolding conflict between Washington and the working people of Central America and the Caribbean will depend on many factors, especially developments in the fight against imperialism elsewhere in the world, including in the United States. The Cuban and Nicaraguan governments are prepared to confront the direct military might of the U.S. government. But they do not assume that a U.S. invasion is inevitable, that nothing can be done to help stave it off. To the contrary, they explain that their determination and the thoroughness of their defense efforts — not only military, but their entire range of international activities — can help deter the use of U.S. troops.

Castro concluded his speech to the Cuban National Assembly by stating that "one of the ways to struggle for peace is to do what we have done: be stronger. Our strength is no threat to anybody; but our strength does make a successful attack on our country virtually impossible. Our power is an element of containment."

*   *   *

This volume is part of Pathfinder Press's series entitled Fidel Castro Speeches. Other volumes include *Cuba's Internationalist Foreign Policy 1975-80* and *Building Socialism in Cuba*.

As with the earlier volumes, most of the speeches have been taken from the English-language *Granma Weekly Review*. Two of the items — Castro's interview with *Newsweek* correspondents and his speech in Nicaragua — are taken from the biweekly socialist newsmagazine *Intercontinental Press*. And Castro's television interview on the MacNeil/Lehrer NewsHour is published here for the first time in a readily accessible form.

In order to keep the book to a reasonable length, some of the contents have been excerpted. Wherever excerpts have been made, these are indicated by four ellipses. Minor editing for clarity and consistency has been done, in consultation with the Spanish-language texts.

Doug Jenness
June 1985

Cuba, Grenada, and Central America

Interview with 'Newsweek' Correspondent

Patricia Sethi: On the eve of the twenty-fifth anniversary of the Cuban revolution, what have been the major achievements of the revolution? If, as the leader of this revolution, you had the opportunity to do things all over again, would you change anything?

Fidel Castro: The Cuban people — and you can confirm this by speaking with any of our citizens — have achieved a sense of national independence that they never had before. They enjoy a personal dignity that had always been denied them. For the first time, Cubans are masters of their own country. Nothing and no one can threaten them from within their own country. No one can belittle them for being Black, or discriminate against them because they happen to be women.

Their social standing is not determined by their economic income. To find a bed in a hospital when they are ill, or to get a job, they no longer have to humiliate themselves if they are men or prostitute themselves if they are women, as often happened in the past. On the basis of that dignity, which makes us all equal, there comes all the rest — the social and economic transformations that have characterized the revolution.

Our economy has grown at an approximate annual average rate of 4.7 percent for twenty-five years, one of the highest rates in the continent, despite the U.S. blockade. In Latin America, we are the second country in terms of per capita food consumption. Moreover, our "per capitas" are better distributed than in any other country of the hemisphere.

In health, education, culture, and sports, we hold first place among Third World countries and rank higher than many industrialized countries. You will be surprised when I tell you that there are more illiterates

This interview was conducted in late December 1983 by Patricia Sethi. While Newsweek *ran less than half of the interview, the Cuban newsmagazine* Bohemia *published it in full in its February 10, 1984, issue. An English translation of the* Bohemia *version appeared in the April 30, 1984,* Intercontinental Press, *from which these excerpts are taken.*

and semiliterates in the United States, in proportion to the population, than in Cuba.

It will surprise you less, perhaps, when I say that in the United States there is drug addiction, gambling, prostitution, unemployment, extreme poverty, racial discrimination, and sexual exploitation of children, all of which make up an inseparable part of U.S. capitalist society. Such problems do not exist in Cuba. Acts of bloodshed and violence occur in the United States at a rate at least ten times higher than in Cuba. So I think we have advanced somewhat in relation to North America since the victory of the Cuban revolution.

If we were to have the chance to do things over again there are things we would do differently, such as not starting our revolutionary struggle by attacking the Moncada barracks but rather by beginning straight from guerrilla warfare in the mountains. But the strategic line we have followed in the revolutionary process and the principles underlying it would be no different.

Sethi: One often reads reports that your revolution is on the verge of collapse and that it is only a matter of time before your leadership comes to an end. But you and your revolution remain a vital force. What is the secret of this success?

Castro: The defeat and collapse of the Cuban revolution have been ceaselessly predicted throughout these past twenty-five years. And I do not believe we will soon be free of such predictions, since they form part of the policies of isolation and aggression waged against Cuba.

All the while such forecasts go on being artificially propagated, thanks to Washington's influence over the mass communications media — not only of the United States but also whole networks of international propaganda — the Cuban revolution keeps on demonstrating its vitality, even though it is besieged militarily, politically, economically, and through propaganda. This is the result of its authenticity and of the fact that, like all true revolutions, its roots lie deep among the people. If the Cuban people had not been profoundly identified with their revolution, we could have been crushed, since the powerful United States has used all possible forms of aggression against the Cuban revolution. Our people are the ones who sustain and determine the course of our revolution.

What is involved is not blind, uncritical adherence. To the contrary — if you go out on the streets and listen to the Cubans without them finding out you are not Cuban yourself, you will learn that they are quite explicit in making known everything that seems wrong to them. We know this not only through our responsibilities as leaders but also because the citizens let us know their complaints by means of the many forms of democratic communication that exist. There is also quite frequent direct contact between the leaders and the people.

We are aware that there is still much to be done. Still, we are advancing and making yearly improvements on all levels. At the beginning all we had was ideas; now we also have experience.

Sethi: Will relations between Cuba and the United States ever reach a more normal level? What must happen for that to be possible? Some observers insist that so long as Fidel is around no change will be possible — that you are too "antiestablishment," too revolutionary, to be acceptable. What do you think about this?

Castro: The current relations between Cuba and the United States are so irrational, so absurd, that I feel obliged to have a certain "historical" confidence that they must reach a more normal level someday. For this to be possible, the first thing that has to happen is for a U.S. administration to realize that the premises that led the U.S. government in 1960 to try to prevent the Cuban people from taking the political-social course they found most convenient are not justified — either in political terms or much less in terms of international law.

The time has come for U.S. rulers to grasp that the Latin America they considered for decades to be their "natural backyard," where they set up and removed governments, issued orders, and had U.S. ambassadors making decisions that properly belonged to presidents of republics, has ceased to exist. It is also time it was understood in the United States that socialism is a solid reality in a considerable portion of the world and that it can be eliminated neither by war nor by economic or military pressure.

In the years to come, and quite possibly before the year 2000, Cuba will not be the only Latin American country to adopt socialism as a system of government, even though what's involved is not the poorly labeled "Cuban model," which we in no way intend to universalize. There will also be nonsocialist governments determined nonetheless to block economic domination by the multinational corporations. The United States will have to adapt to all this, like it or not. It is a fact of history. This has nothing to do with my presence at the head of the Cuban government, since it was bound to happen sooner or later whether I existed or not.

I do not deny that I am, as you put it, very "antiestablishment." And perhaps some find me "too revolutionary." But my entire rejection of the U.S. imperialist structure — a rejection now shared by tens of millions throughout Latin America — poses very little threat to the stability of the capitalist system in the United States. I would like the capitalist system to disappear and be replaced by a more rational and humane system that Latin America could come to a better understanding with, but I can assure the U.S. people that I have no intention of fomenting a socialist revolution in the United States. I see this as still distant, and when that day comes it will have to be led by those who come forward from among the U.S. working class and people.

Sethi: Are there certain areas in which you and the United States could establish constructive ties even though a philosophical or ideological reconciliation is impossible? Would some form of dialogue with the Reagan administration be totally out of the question?

Castro: You are right when you assume that a philosophical or ideological reconciliation between us and the current U.S. administration — or even between us and other possible administrations in coming years — is out of the question. But the fact that we in Cuba go on being socialists and the United States remains the most important center of world capitalism does not mean there cannot be important areas in which both countries and governments could work constructively.

Right now, if the Reagan administration were to renounce its ideological obsession and heed the call of the Contadora group by deciding to seriously sponsor a negotiated solution to the problems that are shaking Central America today, it would be possible for Cuba and the United States to contribute along with other countries of the region to lay the basis for peace and for the democratic structural change Central America requires.

We have never rejected a dialogue with the Reagan administration. As you know, conversations were held between Secretary of State [Alexander] Haig and Vice-President Carlos Rafael Rodríguez. Later, Gen. [Vernon] Walters came to Havana, and I talked at length with him myself. But we cannot say that a dialogue was established; instead, it was a confrontation of viewpoints.

We have no hope at all of a dialogue so long as Mr. Reagan goes on thinking that what happens in Central America is the result of evil plotting between the Soviet Union and Cuba and does not grasp that these social upheavals have been going on in Central America for fifty years, even back when the Soviet Union was fighting to survive and the Cuban revolution did not exist.

Sethi: President Reagan constantly argues that your aim is to export the revolution and communism to the entire hemisphere.

Castro: I do not believe that revolution is an exportable product. I must confess that I do find the example of the Cuban revolution to have exercised important influence on the revolutionary movements of Latin America during the last twenty years, since it showed that even on a small island, subjugated and reduced to neocolonial status by the United States, it was possible to make a deepgoing and genuine revolution. Nor shall I hide the fact that revolutionary Cuba has offered its active solidarity to other Latin American revolutionaries in countries like Somoza's Nicaragua, where any democratic action and any possibility of protest outside of armed struggle had been wiped out through brutal terror. It is all too well known that Cuba was not the only one to help out in the fight against Somoza; that other governments, which I will not mention, cooperated as well.

Nor will I deny that when an important group of Latin American countries, acting under the inspiration and guidance of Washington, not only tried to isolate Cuba politically but also blockaded us economically and helped with counterrevolutionary actions (sabotage, armed infiltration, assassination attempts, and so on) aimed at defeating the revolution, we replied in self-defense by helping all those who at the time were trying to struggle against such governments. We were not the ones to initiate subversion, they were.

But in the same way I can affirm categorically — and I challenge anyone to demonstrate the contrary — that no government that has maintained correct and respectful relations with Cuba has failed to enjoy Cuba's respect in return. That has been the case with Mexico, which was the only Latin American country to refuse to apply Washington's diktat in 1964.* It has been the case since then with those other governments of Latin America and the Caribbean that reestablished normal and respectful relations with us.

The reality is that we cannot export revolution and the United States cannot prevent it.

Reagan utilizes this argument with cunning to frighten the U.S. people, stirring up primitive anticommunism like that of [Senator Joseph] McCarthy's time, which has now begun to prevail again among a considerable section of the people of the United States. Such arguments enable Reagan to carry out a policy of open intervention, as was brutally put into practice against Grenada, a tiny island of 100,000 inhabitants.

Sethi: Mr. President, what exactly was going on in Grenada? The Reagan administration recently divulged what it termed a "warm bag of evidence" and suggested that Cuba was: (a) training and organizing the armed forces and security forces of Grenada; (b) building a communications base tied in to the Soviet Sputnik satellite system; (c) building a huge airport capable of servicing Soviet transport aircraft furnished to the Cuban armed forces; (d) storing immense quantities of Soviet arms and equipment for Cuban use; and (e) preparing an antiaircraft defense system designed to protect Grenada against precisely the operation the United States carried out there last October.

Let's take these charges one by one.

Castro: That is all laughable, of course. They talk about the Grena-

---

*A July 1964 meeting of foreign ministers of the Organization of American States directed all member governments to cut off diplomatic and trade relations with Cuba. Only the Mexican government refused to apply the sanctions.

dian "armed forces" Bishop was trying to organize, for example, giving the impression that what was involved was a gigantic army capable of invading the entire eastern Caribbean. But the facts are evident.

The events in Grenada showed that the armed forces that were being set up there corresponded wholly to the dimensions of a small island constantly threatened by invasion from Miami by counterrevolutionaries sheltered by the CIA — the sympathizers of the eccentric and reactionary [Eric] Gairy, among others. The United States had also made threats and insinuated that other Caribbean countries could be utilized for an invasion.

Moreover, Washington found it necessary all of a sudden to close down its "exhibition" of the "armaments" it had seized in Grenada. According to its initial claims, these showed Bishop's intention to dominate the Caribbean. What the visitors saw was a limited number of modern weapons to which Grenada had every right as a sovereign country, along with many useless old firearms.

As for the airport, it was shown after the invasion that Grenadians had wanted to build it long before Bishop's government. It was proven also that the technical tasks had been under the direction of a well-known English company whose representatives explicitly confirmed that the airport lacked any aspect whatsoever that could have caused it to be considered a military installation. Rather, it was a civil facility designed for the modern planes that fly into Caribbean countries today. Several of the Caribbean countries have bigger airports than the one that was being built in Grenada.

Regarding what was said about Bishop storing "Soviet arms for Cuban use," our weapons are kept here for defending our country against a possible invasion. It would be absurd for 3,000 or 4,000 automatic weapons to be deposited for our use in Grenada.

Finally, it is true that we had sought to help the Grenadians to establish a communications base, but everyone knows that there are many similar bases in the Caribbean and Latin America. This is something that is required by the modern conditions of today's communications, and everyone aspires to have them.

The historical and irrefutable truth is that Reagan and his aides made nineteen false statements regarding the events in Grenada. These have been exposed by Cuba, and the U.S. government has not been able to substantiate them.* On the other hand, it has not been possible to use the facts to refute any of Cuba's statements.

The press was totally manipulated; a select group of journalists was sent in seventy-two hours after the invasion. The press was furious at

---

*Castro reviewed these nineteen lies in his speech of November 14, 1983, printed as an appendix to *Maurice Bishop Speaks* (Pathfinder Press, 1983).

first, but then it changed its stance and let itself be carried away by the wave of chauvinism. The politicians changed their position as well. Thus it was that a big crime could be committed with the unconscious complicity of U.S. public opinion. And Reagan could present his people with a victory. It is shameful, offensive.

The scope of the crime committed in Grenada is inversely proportional to the size of the island. Bishop was our friend. We respected him; he was a true revolutionary. He was the man of his people.

Our position toward the new government was well known. Relations between us and the Coard grouping were very bad. It was quite probable that in the future we would have withdrawn from the country once construction of the airport was finished. We could not cooperate with that grouping. Perhaps we would have left medical personnel in the country for humanitarian reasons, but we would have reduced our assistance.

Our assessment of the situation was that the Coard grouping could not sustain itself after having killed Bishop. The revolution had committed suicide. But this did not justify intervention. U.S. citizens were in no danger. The extremist grouping visited them and offered them guarantees, and we knew they were not in danger. We even informed the U.S. government of this seventy-two hours before the invasion.

The whole theory Reagan has utilized to try to justify the invasion is false — it is a big lie from beginning to end. It was a show of force — a cheap, opportunist political operation to take advantage of the tragedy that had taken place in the country.

There were other factors as well — Reagan recalled the fate suffered by the hostages in Iran, how the U.S. people were humiliated by that experience. He recalled that a week before 230 U.S. marines had died in Lebanon. There was also the defeat suffered in Vietnam. Reagan exploited all this to present the Grenada invasion as a great victory to the U.S. people. That's dangerous. That's an irresponsible policy that can lead to war and to new adventures in El Salvador, Nicaragua, and Cuba.

Sethi: Given the close ties between you and Bishop, how was it possible that you did not have the slightest idea of the turmoil inside his party?

Castro: Yes, it is hard to understand how, with all the personnel we had in the embassy there, we did not know the split was taking place. That is the greatest criticism that we must make of our own political, diplomatic, and military aid personnel.

We did not have any idea what was happening. And even though Bishop visited Cuba while this turmoil was going on, he said not a word to me. In a certain way, this makes me happy, because it showed the respect he felt for his own country and people. The only thing he did in that period was submit to self-criticism, stating that he felt he had not devoted full attention to work with the masses.

Now, of course, we know what was going on — there was a deep ideological contradiction between Bishop and Coard. Coard presented himself as the theoretician, the intellectual drunk on political theory. But I am convinced to the marrow of my bones that there was great personal ambition involved. A majority decision was made that Bishop and Coard share the leadership, with Bishop remaining prime minister and Coard assuming the leadership of the party.

After that, Bishop attended no further meetings of the party, but even then he did not insinuate in any way that there had been a split. I explain this in two ways: at that time he was in an absolute minority inside the party and had a defeatist attitude; thus he did not want to talk about it owing to deep pessimism. Or else he underestimated the seriousness of the situation and thought he could solve the problem.

It was only the day before his arrest that he visited our embassy and explained that there had been a serious split. He said he feared he might be killed. It was a brief conversation — he said he was only informing us.

Sethi: There was nothing you could have done to save Bishop's life?

Castro: When they arrested Bishop I sent a message that the situation could create a serious problem in international public opinion and weaken the revolution inside the country.* I asked those people to be understanding and generous. I feared that one of those radical elements might try to resolve the problem with violence. I made an appeal, but it was only when the real danger from the United States became evident that they made contact with us. It is beyond doubt that there was no coordination between their defense plans and our own.

All we could do was appeal for Bishop's life and the revolution. Besides, we were receiving reports that Bishop's friends were leading and organizing a response among the people. But that was suspended when they thought it was possible to achieve a solution.

We could not intervene in a situation where Bishop was in a minority inside his own party. When a group of conspirators is a minority there is greater room for action. But what happened in Grenada was that the Coard grouping had a majority against Bishop. This was apparently clear, and even legally in accord with democratic norms.

It is necessary to accept such a situation, even when one realizes it is an error or a grave development. We could do no more than what we did do. We show great respect for international relations with other parties. We give them opinions only when they ask us. That is the secret of our relations with all revolutionary organizations — with El Salvador and Nicaragua. We know that the peoples are sensitive regarding their independence, autonomy, and sovereignty. If we told revolutionary govern-

*This letter was printed in the April 16, 1984, issue of *Intercontinental Press*.

ments every day what was right and what was wrong, things would be impossible. Such relations are delicate.

We have great respect for the internal affairs of parties and organizations. . . .

Sethi: If I gave you a crystal ball and asked you to look into it, what would you predict for Grenada?

Castro: The people of Grenada know what independence and revolution mean, and those sentiments can never be uprooted. The people of Grenada have also been fooled, mainly by the group that murdered Bishop. There was an initial stage of confusion, but the events themselves will provide clarity, and Bishop's banner will go on flying. Sooner or later the people of Grenada will take up Bishop's banner and gain independence.

Right now Grenada is not an independent country; it is an occupied country. Some day it will again be independent and revolutionary. This is an inexorable law of history that cannot be eluded, either in Grenada or in Central America.

Sethi: But the reports on U.S. television showed the Grenadian people offering thanks to the U.S. marines for having liberated them.

Castro: It is possible that some Grenadian citizens did so. When Hitler invaded Poland, some fascist and reactionary Polish citizens welcomed him. After the invasion of the Soviet Union, some persons collaborated with the invaders and also greeted them and called them liberators, but this was not the sentiment of the majority of the peoples of Poland and the Soviet Union.

In my view, the special circumstances in which the invasion of Grenada took place, the trauma brought on by the death of Bishop, the repugnance of the Coard grouping, and the confusion that followed these events could have caused some confused Grenadians to welcome and congratulate the Yankee soldiers, and probably this was televised and photographed.

But I can assure you that this effect will not last long. In the most recent report I have received, it is said that the people are more and more irritated with the methods being used by the occupation forces and the measures being taken in Grenada. That is the news we have received. It is only a matter of time. It seems that Mr. [Alister] McIntyre refused to head the government because of the humiliating conditions; he refused to be the instrument of the occupation forces.

Sethi: Why do you consider it necessary to play a role on a world scale? Cuba is a small country with limited resources. Why do you find it necessary to send teachers, doctors, technicians, and advisers to other developing countries when they could be put to use in your own country? Why do your people have to sacrifice in this way? The day will come when the people may say to Fidel, "No more. Please, let's stay home."

Castro: That day will never come, because there is a sentiment of solidarity that is growing in our country, an internationalist spirit that keeps on growing. To live up to that internationalism is a great honor for the Cuban people.

Do you find this strange? I will explain this phenomenon. If you observe what happens in capitalist societies and industrialized societies, and even in the Third World, you will see that individualistic and egocentric attitudes prevail. That was the case in Cuba before the revolution. Then we could never have sent anyone abroad to help meet the needs of other developing countries. Now we have thousands who want to go to Yemen, Nicaragua, Vietnam, Angola.

Sethi: The secret is Fidel?

Castro: No, the secret is not Fidel, nor is it economic resources, because our economic resources are limited. The secret of that sentiment of dedication is the revolution. Our economic resources may perhaps be limited, but our human resources are unlimited.

The U.S. Peace Corps was set up and mobilized on a salary basis. Catholic missionaries have devoted their lives to work in Africa and Asia out of sentiments of charity, self-sacrifice, and vocation. But let me tell you something: when 2,000 teachers were needed in Nicaragua and we asked for volunteers, 29,000 Cubans expressed willingness to go. When a few months later they murdered a Cuban teacher in Nicaragua, 100,000 Cuban teachers expressed their willingness to go and replace that teacher. That means that we have plenty of people here ready to go teach in Nicaragua.

In Cuba we have more people willing to go to the Third World in a spirit of self-sacrifice than the missionaries of all the churches and the Peace Corps put together. We have an unlimited number of youth who are ready to go fulfill any task assigned to them because they understand the moral values of the revolution. They will be willing to go anywhere, except, perhaps, to the moon. This is the greatest treasure our revolution can offer. . . .

Sethi: The Reagan administration insists that the Grenada invasion constituted a serious blow to Cuba's prestige and to its aims in the hemisphere. How do you respond to that?

Castro: Our view is that the Grenada invasion was a blow to the United States. It was a cowardly and ridiculous action, which brought the United States no glory and only helped to intensify the fighting spirit of Nicaragua, Cuba, and the revolutionaries in El Salvador. At this moment we are in a stronger position to confront U.S. aggression. The morale of our people has risen. The revolution is stronger than ever.

Cuba's prestige in the world has grown. This event showed that we do not interfere in the internal affairs of a country and that Cuba refused to withdraw in face of Yankee military might. It showed our revolutionary spirit and our determination to struggle. Now our peoples are more convinced than ever that the Reagan administration is a government that simply does not respect international law.

Sethi: The U.S. invasion of Grenada helped you to strengthen ties with Spanish-speaking Latin America. But what were the consequences for your relations with the English-speaking Caribbean?

Castro: Before the invasion of Grenada, we had already lost an intimate and valuable friend with the death of Bishop. With that the revolutionary process was virtually liquidated. The United States, by invading the island, killed a cadaver and carried out a monstrous crime against the sovereignty and the aspirations for freedom and progress of all the peoples of the Caribbean and Latin America.

That is why I called President Reagan's victory a "Pyrrhic" one. By invading Grenada, he showed Latin America that he would not respect the commitment to nonintervention that forms part of all continental agreements and that he was determined to go on using the "big stick" of the old days. This served to bring Latin America and the United States still more into conflict; it aggravated the situation brought about by the Malvinas affair.

So the United States is not more respected now. To the contrary, the crime of Grenada has intensified the fighting spirit and will to resist of the Cubans, Nicaraguans, Salvadorans, and all revolutionaries, progressives, and democrats of our continent.

As for the English-speaking Caribbean, it is unfortunate that the two recent events that helped to strengthen the cohesion of Latin America have also served to separate a group of English-speaking Caribbean countries from Latin America as a whole. This had already occurred at the time of the Malvinas and has now been repeated in the case of Grenada.* Cuba itself does not suffer much from this drawing apart, since the governments that were complicit with Reagan's invasion of Grenada, especially those of Jamaica and of Mrs. [Eugenia] Charles of Dominica, had already been the promoters of anti-Cuban campaigns for some time.

We attribute special significance to the fact that two countries of obvious importance within the [British] Commonwealth, Guyana and Trinidad and Tobago, which could be considered the most important of that group, also took a firm stand in condemning the U.S. invasion. . . .

Sethi: How do you see the danger for Cuba?

Castro: In Cuba we cannot fail to remain constantly on guard in face of the dangers we have to confront, since Reagan continually threatens

---

*Several Caribbean governments, including those of Jamaica, Guyana, and Trinidad and Tobago, refused to condemn Britain's aggression against Argentina in the Malvinas War.

us with blockades and military aggression.

It would be a question, of course, of an irrational attack counter to all laws, but Reagan has shown that reason and law matter little to him. We cannot forget his abominable statement that the UN General Assembly vote of 122 nations condemning the United States for invading Grenada did not disturb his breakfast in the slightest.

Therefore, neither Latin American public opinion nor the support the Contadora efforts receive in Western Europe, Scandinavia, and Japan can suffice. We have to prepare ourselves, and we are preparing. We prefer negotiation to confrontation, but we also reiterate that no threat of confrontation will make us turn back. Whoever seeks to humiliate and subjugate us will have to think several times before deciding to pay the high cost involved.

It is necessary that U.S. public opinion be aware of this. We do not harbor any feelings of hostility toward the U.S. people. We want to come to an understanding with the United States, and we think that we could understand each other on a basis of equality and mutual respect. But whoever seeks to invade us will clash not only with modern, powerful, and well-organized Revolutionary Armed Forces, but also with the resistance of millions of armed, trained, and organized citizens who will go on fighting even if the country is occupied.

The resistance would never end. The United States would need millions of soldiers, which it does not have, simply to occupy Cuba, and in the end the invasion troops would have to withdraw in defeat. Conventional war is one thing, but war against an entire people is something else. No power, however mighty, will ever be able to defeat a people of 10 million inhabitants with deep combative and patriotic traditions, ready to fight to the death for their lives, their homeland, their independence, and their social achievements.

Such an invasion, moreover, would flagrantly violate the 1962 accords,* and, while we count fundamentally on our own forces for defense and therefore consider ourselves an absolutely independent country, no one can predict the consequences for world peace an invasion of Cuba would entail.

Sethi: The Reagan administration insists that you are a puppet and lackey of the Soviet Union. How do you answer such an accusation? What exactly is your relationship to the Soviet Union?

Castro: Anyone who has studied the history of our revolution and understood its origin will see that our revolution is a truly autonomous one. We made it ourselves. We did not even have relations with the Soviet

*In the agreement between the United States and the Soviet Union ending the October 1962 missile crisis, President John Kennedy pledged that the U.S. government would not invade Cuba.

Union when our revolution triumphed. Therefore, the interpretation of the doctrine of our revolution was our own interpretation. The forms and the road we followed were truly our own.

But to our good fortune, the Soviet Union did exist. What would have happened if the Soviet Union had not existed? What would have happened to Cuba when the sugar quota was suspended? The country would have died of hunger. What would have happened when oil supplies were suspended? When replacement parts could not be obtained for all the U.S.-made manufacturing equipment? When the United States imposed the blockade?

We could not have survived if we had not found another market for our sugar, if we had not had access to fuel and oil supplies for our country, if we had not had access to the weapons needed to defend ourselves against the threats of an invasion — like at Playa Girón [Bay of Pigs] — and the assassination plans and acts of sabotage. It was a privilege for us to find a friendly country that helped us face all those difficulties.

Never in twenty-five years have the Soviets tried to interfere in our affairs, in our policies, or in our behavior. They have been extremely respectful toward us. Even at certain moments when we were critical of certain conceptions — not even at those times were they tempted to affect us economically; rather, they treated us with respect. They made no public criticism of us.

Relations between the Soviet Union and Cuba have been exemplary. They have been based on a policy of independence and mutual respect. Do not forget that while we were waging our struggle against U.S. imperialism under particularly difficult conditions, the Soviet Union had relations with the United States and traded with the United States.

Reagan's statements don't bother me, since he is an absolute liar. It's a traditional charge against us. But we are not willing to become enemies of the Soviet Union or sacrifice the excellent relations we have with them just to prove we are not their puppets. We don't have a puppet complex. We consider ourselves firmly independent, masters of our own country, our fate, and our policies. Our consciences and our morale are at peace. The Soviets do not have a single piece of property in Cuba. There are mutual relations and influences, but they are as independent of us as we are of them. That is the reality. . . .

Sethi: Let's suppose the U.S. administration tells you, "O.K., President Fidel, we are going to make a deal. We lift the blockade, establish diplomatic relations, open technical and economic ties with Cuba. But in return, for your part, you will have to stop supporting the governments of Nicaragua and Angola and revolutionary movements like SWAPO."

Castro: They would be putting a very high price on our honor and our principles, in exchange for material benefits we are not very interested in. But even if we were interested in such benefits, we would not be willing nor could we ever pay such a price.

　Sethi: Everyone says that this is Fidel's revolution, that this is Fidel's Cuba, that the Cuban people are Fidel's people. Mr. President, we are all mortal, we all have to go someday. What will happen to Fidel's revolution when Fidel goes?

　Castro: There is a strange opinion abroad that this is my revolution and that when I go it will go too. Let me tell you that whether Fidel is here or passes away, the revolution will continue. Because this is the revolution of the people of Cuba. There is a collective leadership here. We are a united people, and we now have thousands of cadres with a high level of consciousness and experience, all working together in the same direction, toward the same goal. This is not Fidel's revolution. It is the people's revolution. And the future does not worry me.

Closing the Gap Between the Developed and Underdeveloped Socialist Countries

Comments by Carlos Rafael Rodríguez on CMEA Economic Summit

"An effective symbol of socialism's historical strength": this is the way Carlos Rafael Rodríguez, member of the Political Bureau of the Communist Party of Cuba and vice-president of the Councils of State and of Ministers, described the economic summit conference held in this city, with the participation of first and general secretaries of Communist and workers' parties and heads of government of CMEA member countries.

Carlos Rafael Rodríguez went on to say that the general consensus reflected in the resolutions and final declaration demonstrates socialism's unity, strength, and fortitude.

Regarding the political aspects of the conference, he said that it showed the socialist countries' unwavering position in favor of peace. "As Comrade Fidel Castro said in his message," he pointed out, "it was a response of peace and fortitude."

Carlos Rafael Rodríguez, who is also Cuba's permanent representative at the CMEA, went on to say that the essence of socialism had been unanimously demonstrated in the summit.

The Cuban leader spoke very highly of the whole conference at a meeting on the twenty-fourth floor of the CMEA building with *Granma, Juventud Rebelde,* TV morning news and TV national news special reporters, and *Prensa Latina* correspondents in Moscow.

The head of the Cuban delegation to the summit said, "The conference also demonstrated in its internal resolutions and outer views the fundamental historical contrast between capitalism and socialism

---

This article, written by Granma *correspondent José Gabriel Gumá, reports Carlos Rafael Rodríguez's comments on the June 12–14 economic summit meeting in Moscow of the countries belonging to the Council of Mutual Economic Assistance (CMEA). It is excerpted here from the June 24, 1984,* Granma Weekly Review.

as regards the developing countries.

"The problems of the underdeveloped and developing countries were discussed with a view to contributing to their development and national independence. In other words, in a manner entirely different from the capitalist approach."

Delving further into his evaluation of the conference, he ventured the opinion that it was the outcome of a process of internal analysis on the part of CMEA member countries on the activities of the organization, which has been working for many years in the economic field of member countries and which has grown in all ways, becoming more and more universal.

"This sense of universality," he said, "is provided by the presence of Mongolia, from an Asiatic standpoint; the presence of Cuba, a country that joined the council several years ago; and the presence of Vietnam, confirming the Asiatic character of the organization, which was already there with the entry of Mongolia."

Regarding the work of the organization, composed of ten countries of Europe, Asia, and Latin America, he said, "In the last few years we have made a collective effort to improve our internal activities and the external projection of the CMEA, with a view to consolidating our organization.

"Naturally, the results have been very satisfactory, but the resolution of the summit conference indicates that our efforts will continue. The resolution provides all CMEA bodies and agencies with the means to modify and improve their activities based on the experience acquired in these past few years. We are absolutely convinced that, in this regard, the results of the conference will be positive."

In response to a question put by the *Granma* reporter regarding a balanced development of CMEA member countries, Carlos Rafael Rodríguez drew attention to the fact that one of the organization's main concerns is "the balancing of member country economies, to bring the more backward up to the level of the more developed.

"In the past few years, especially since the council's meeting in Berlin, this has been of greater importance to less developed countries such as Mongolia, Cuba, and Vietnam than for the European countries. Although there are different development levels among them, there is not that gap as between a developed and an underdeveloped country."

He stressed the fact that "ever since the Berlin meeting, the council has paid special attention to balancing the economies of the most backward countries — Mongolia, Cuba, and Vietnam — with those of the more developed ones. "This was confirmed in the economic summit. A paragraph in the internal resolution guarantees those countries a process of balancing and accelerating economic levels with the cooperation of all member countries.

"In this sense, even though our countries must necessarily continue to give great importance to agricultural programs — and Cuba in particular attaches decisive importance to agriculture and the food program in all its projects through the year 2000 — industrial change is also planned.

"The economic summit conference reflects our countries' aspirations to an accelerated industrialization also, not only in regard to the primary processing of agricultural or mineral raw materials but also the machine industry and beyond that [as formulated by the Cuban delegation] to such key industries as electronics, genetics, and so forth.

"Summit agreements provide us with that possibility. Bilateral as well as multilateral cooperation is a means for accelerating our whole development process. This will be reflected, as announced at the conference, on documents to be signed with various member countries, especially the Soviet Union but also, in the immediate future, the German Democratic Republic, Bulgaria, and Romania, and later with other agreements on cooperation and integration through the year 2000."

He explained that the Central Planning Board had kept the Council of Ministers and its Executive Committee informed in this regard and that Cuba is making progress in that direction with the cooperation of the CMEA.

Asked if the conference had taken into account broadening relations with the developing countries, he said, "This was naturally a point taken up by the council. One of CMEA member countries' permanent concerns is their relations with the developing countries."

At this point he explained, "We distinguish between developing countries, giving preference to those which in one way or another are headed toward socialism; they have priority treatment. But this does not mean that overall preferential principles are not applied to the rest of the developing countries.

"The conference took time to study this issue, which is included in its internal documents. It is also included in the declaration which, as you have seen, emphasizes the critical situation of the developing countries as a result of the world capitalist crisis.

"The socialist countries have a role to play in contributing to the growth and development of the economies of developing countries. There is a whole series of agreements with developing countries seeking deepgoing change. One of the most recent agreements was the establishment of joint CMEA-Nicaragua commissions."

He went on to explain that "a CMEA special commission has just undertaken a comprehensive study of the Nicaraguan economy to enable member countries to focus on ways of contributing multilaterally to Nicaragua's development.

"Angola, Mozambique, and Ethiopia are also being given special attention by CMEA member countries. Similarly, there are agreements with such countries as Iraq, Mexico, and Finland, in the context of our attention to basic development problems in both more- and less-developed countries but within the framework of countries that have still to attain full economic development."

Regarding future economic summits, Carlos Rafael Rodríguez said, "One of the basic elements in realizing the collective objectives of CMEA member countries is coordinated economic plans as a part of the process of integrating their economies.

"Cooperation is the first stage in a process of integration, that is, a closer integration of the collective and global economic processes of CMEA member countries." He noted that "more recently this has been accompanied by a conciliation of viewpoints on each member country's economy for more effective global and collective economic efforts."

He went on to explain, "Naturally, there is a close relationship between the coordination of plans and the development of the multilateral economy of member countries. It has been found that economic summits, such as the one that has just been held, were too far removed from the last occasion on which the member countries' highest political and economic authorities met and that these meetings will be held more frequently from now on. This will also have a bearing on the process of coordination of economic plans which, as you know, is every five years.

"In addition to the study of each country's economic outlook, this will make for a progressive integration of our economies, without any of them losing their individual characteristics and, naturally, without any state having an overriding influence on the decisions to be taken. The conciliation of economies and the most perfect coordination of economic plans will be a decisive step toward integration as we see it now; that is, integration plus the preservation of the sovereignty and independence of each country, without interference in the economy and political processes of others, with full respect for each country's viewpoints."

Another topic dealt with in the press conference was the seven most developed capitalist countries' recent conference in London. Carlos Rafael Rodríguez recalled that President Mitterrand had said regarding the summit conference that the problems of contemporary life, particularly those of the so-called Third World, had not been discussed in full, and that was true.

"This reveals the nature of imperialism and the capitalist system as a whole," he said, "because Ronald Reagan, as the representative of U.S. imperialism, cannot make his ideas of military supremacy and absolute rule compatible with the ideas of respect for the sovereignty of Third World peoples and the development of their economies to ensure national independence.

"It was impossible, therefore, for the problems affecting the developing countries to be dealt with in full at the London conference.

"The problem of the foreign debt was discussed recently by the Latin American countries at the Quito conference," he said, "and a series of proposals were made designed to relieve them of their burden to a certain extent.

"The brutal response of the United States to those proposals by the Latin American countries was to raise its interest rates, and this led to the irritated response from the presidents of Argentina, Brazil, Mexico, and Colombia and the call to representatives of all Latin American countries to a meeting in Cartagena.

"I can say, and this is reflected in the conference documents and final declaration, that socialism has given the only valid response to the concerns, aspirations, and anguish of the developing countries; a response that, needless to say, is backed by the strength of socialism, by the possibilities socialism offers, since socialism alone cannot solve all the Third World's problems.

"Since part of the underdeveloped world has relations mainly with the capitalist countries, unless every country — including the most powerful capitalist countries — cooperates, the situation of the Third World will continue to be dramatic.

"The socialist countries' response to Third World aspirations is in keeping with the demand made by the Third World countries in the program for a new international economic order, which is viewed by the socialist countries meeting in Moscow as one of the programs to which attention must be paid.

"This satisfactory response is directed, first of all, to countries that have opted for socialism. It is only fair for the socialist countries to try to meet the economic needs of those countries that have opted for this system for the transformation of their own society.

"Furthermore, we believe that developing countries trying to take the capitalist road to development will never find a solution to their problems. As Comrade Fidel has said on many occasions and as our party programs state, only socialism can give a valid answer to the underdeveloped countries' greatest problem of our time, that is, their becoming developed countries.

"The CMEA socialist countries' economic summit conference has given the answer in international terms," he said, "and that shows the vast difference between what happened in London and what has just happened in Moscow."

A Grave Danger of
U.S. Military Intervention

Opening Speech to Meeting of CMEA Council

Esteemed heads of delegation and guests;
Esteemed comrades:
  The thirty-ninth session of the council is meeting at a time of great
danger to world peace and when the region of Latin America and the
Caribbean, where the meeting is taking place, is disturbed by the threat
to peace and the grave danger of armed imperialist intervention.
  Despite seemingly tranquilizing statements — which it is as yet impossible to decide whether they stem from a more realistic policy or are
merely part (as many suspect with abundant reasons) of electoral maneuvers designed to temporarily allay the fears of the very people of the
United States — that country's present administration has not altered its
course of arms buildup. It now intends to extend it to outer space. Nor
has it renounced its programs for military superiority, nor has it changed
the deeply reactionary and warlike character of its visible foreign policy
in its desire — as fanatical as it is impossible — to wipe socialism from
the face of the earth.
  The countries that make up the socialist community in the CMEA
must not overlook this threatening situation. Recently, the economic
summit conference of the member countries of our organization took
place in Moscow. The declaration of that conference was a denunciation
of the aggressive designs and the policy of confrontation conducted by
the imperialist circles, especially U.S. imperialism, as well as a firm response to those threats. It was also a clear, responsible, and serene expression of socialism's policy of peace. The European CMEA member
countries that are closest to NATO borders and that have been forced by
the nuclear threat to deploy on their territories nuclear missiles aimed at
preventing and deterring any attack, reaffirmed their desire for peace at

*This speech by Castro was given October 29, 1984, opening the thirty-ninth
meeting of the Council of Mutual Economic Assistance session, held in Havana.
It is excerpted here from the November 4, 1984,* Granma Weekly Review.

the summit. This determination for peace is unswerving and presides over our activities as a permanent principle.

Our thirty-ninth meeting is being held here in Cuba, a few miles from the airfields that harbor hundreds of combat aircraft that continuously carry out aggressive maneuvers around our small island. Cuba is near bases where the Rapid Deployment Forces are stationed and surrounded by seas in which aircraft carriers, battleships, and destroyers periodically carry out trial maneuvers against our country adding to the permanent threat represented by the Guantánamo naval base on illegally occupied territory. Despite this, it is not the intention of the Cuban delegation, however, to make these issues the topic of our meeting, which is above all devoted to economic cooperation and development.

I merely wish to state that our country is permanently vigilant, that we have responded to the aggressiveness of the threats by considerably increasing our defense capabilities, and that all our people are preparing to defend the homeland and the revolution to the last inch of territory and the very last breath. Our people are firmly determined to exact from the imperialists an unpayable price, and in the end, to inflict upon them an inevitable defeat were they to launch an aggression against Cuba. But at the same time, we are a dedicated and hardworking people that wishes to advance its just social and economic development programs which have placed our country in a salient position among all the nations of the Third World. We wish to enjoy and share with other peoples Cuba's outstanding achievements in public health, education, culture, security, social justice, and the dignification of mankind, in a future of progress and well-being for all humanity.

Therefore, Cuba very clearly states its determination to work for peace. To the same extent that on the worldwide level we support the Prague declaration in which the Warsaw Pact outlined the road to peace, and we endorse the peace policy of the Soviet Union and the statements by Comrade Chernenko ratifying it, here too, in our own region, we will do our very best to promote negotiated solutions and peace agreements.

We support the Contadora initiative and applaud Nicaragua's decision to sign the Contadora agreement, despite the aspects of the agreement that might be unfavorable to them. We will assume the obligations that commit us to peace efforts in Central America together with all the other forces that must make identical commitments, the United States among them. Neither will we decline any action that favors an honorable and worthy solution, based on mutual respect, to the differences we have had during twenty-five years with successive U.S. governments and which have been aggravated by the present administration.

It is because we are confident that peace is possible and that the peoples of the world will stay the hand of those who proclaim aggression and military supremacy as their policy that we have met here. Our basic objective is to advance and improve efforts to further develop our economies, build socialism in a world of peace as a society that will technologically surpass capitalism and leave behind its characteristic injustices, cooperate economically with countries whose social system differs from our own, and contribute to the development of the underdeveloped countries, who are the main victims of the economic crisis that originated in the capitalist system.

Thus we devote ourselves to peaceful construction amid the din of preparations for local and global wars. We shall examine the main problems on the agenda of this thirty-ninth session with the presence of guests, including some who, indeed, do not share our socioeconomic ideas. We have nothing to hide.

Esteemed comrades, in the work of the thirty-ninth session we will be guided by the successful outcome of the economic summit conference which bore witness to our unity of purpose. There the leaders of the socialist community examined our circumstantial weaknesses and our ever-widening possibilities and perspectives. The council and its Executive Committee were mandated tasks that will be fulfilled during the thirty-ninth session.

We hope the delegations will find in our country, besides the fraternal environment of our people who will welcome and accompany them, the minimal material conditions that will help and facilitate their work.

It is in this spirit that I again welcome you to our homeland and invite you to commence the work that has brought us together in this thirty-ninth session of the council.

Thank you.

Report of Cuban Delegation to CMEA Meeting

Esteemed heads of delegations;

Esteemed comrades:

I am very sorry to have to give another address after the great effort that you have made in today's historic and fruitful session, but I must follow the program. I trust you will understand. First of all I want to express our deep appreciation for the warm, fraternal, and solidary remarks by the delegations about our country in their addresses today, which encourage us greatly and which we will never forget.

Although the Executive Committee's report stresses that many aspects of our work must be improved and even require profound changes — as was pointed out at the economic summit conference of our countries held last June — its outstanding feature, as the conference itself noted, is the socialist system's sound and firm outlook in comparison with the instability and contradictions that are increasingly becoming the hallmarks of capitalism.

We are meeting here to carry out the mandate of the summit and to examine and implement the organizational measures adopted in this context by the thirty-eighth special meeting of the session. In doing so we are certain that if the world, with our socialist countries at the vanguard, is successful — as we believe it will be — in thwarting the irrational positions of the Reagan administration that would lead to nuclear devastation, we shall be able to carry out the development plans that have been outlined up to the year 2000 with a systematic improvement in the national and multilateral efficiency of our economies, which will guarantee successive increases in the standard of living of the workers and the entire population.

In my opening statement I referred to the complex international conditions that our economies must overcome and which impose upon the Soviet Union and the European member countries above all, but also

This speech was given October 29, 1984, as a report from the Cuban delegation to the CMEA's thirty-ninth session, meeting in Havana. It is reprinted here from the November 11, 1984, Granma Weekly Review.

upon the others, enormous expenditures and efforts for indispensable national defense.

Despite the considerable lag of the Cuban economy, as well as the economies of Mongolia and Vietnam, as compared to the economies of the European member countries, we too, as the rest of the community, are working to accelerate the transition of our economies to an intensive line of development. We are determined to continue working to derive the maximum benefit from our own modest scientific and technological achievements as well as from those made available to all of us, through cooperation and integration, by the potential of the CMEA member countries in this field.

To this end we have, first of all, an efficient mechanism of coordination and cooperation, namely the coordination of our national economic plans. We must thank Comrade Baibakov, chairman of the CMEA Committee on Cooperation in Planning, for his report to the session on this question. As far as Cuba is concerned, we are also satisfied with the progress made in plan coordination for the period 1986-90, although with some countries there is a delay. A number of countries have already expressed their readiness to maintain the terms of trade presently in force in our bilateral relations in the coming five-year period, as opposed to the unequal terms of trade governing relations between the developed capitalist countries and the underdeveloped and developing countries.

At the same time, the process of mutual understanding and the will toward integration between Cuba and several member countries proceeds at such a pace that the plans regarding perspectives up to the year 2000 for cooperation between Cuba and the Soviet Union, Bulgaria, the German Democratic Republic [GDR], Romania, and Hungary have already been concluded and are also advancing with other member countries.

I should like to reiterate our appreciation for the spirit of fraternal cooperation that governs relations between the developed CMEA member countries and Cuba, confirmed at the summit conference. Without this spirit, our economy, which depends mainly on sugar — whose buying power today in capitalist markets is lower than fifty years ago during the Great Depression — would be condemned to stagnation, and even to regression. When we inaugurate the Punta Gorda nickel plant, built with the cooperation of the Soviet Union, and lay the cornerstone for the CMEA 1 plant a few days from now, we will have the opportunity to see a concrete and eloquent expression of the fruitful cooperation of the USSR and the other fraternal countries of the socialist community.

We are aware that this fraternal relationship entails for us immediate responsibilities. The Executive Committee report stresses the persistence of substantial delays in the delivery of merchandise as one of the shortcomings of CMEA economic activity. Cuba is one of the member countries incurring in these delays. Not only because of adverse weather conditions and even blights introduced by the enemy in our country with sinister regularity, but also for reasons related to limitations in certain resources which we have not been able to solve and deficiencies in our own plans, Cuba's exports to the member countries — albeit increasing in all cases — are not meeting the obligations assumed in the trade agreements where several items are concerned.

I want to express our determination to work on these negative features until they are eliminated.

We endorse all the measures contained in the Executive Committee report, summarized in the resolution on machine building, the electronics industry, and others. We do not always participate as exporters and we intend to broaden our participation in CMEA integration efforts in the future and make a modest contribution in many aspects as we are already doing in the electronics industry. In any case, as importers we benefit from improved production, as in the case of the decision to build heavy tractors of 500 horsepower and over and trucks of 110 tons and over, both of which we are now obliged to import from capitalist countries under unequal terms of trade.

Our contribution to meet the rational needs of the CMEA member countries in the field of energy, fuel, and raw materials is expressed in the increased nickel output achieved through bilateral and multilateral efforts; also in geological prospecting to discover raw materials that might be useful for the socialist community. These activities are being implemented with the cooperation of the member countries. In this respect we are satisfied with the modest increase in our country's oil production with the cooperation of the Soviet Union, and with the signs of existence of fuels in other parts of the country. At the same time we are making efforts through the National Energy Commission and other agencies to economize fuel and raw materials. It is significant that in the sugar industry alone we have reduced fuel oil consumption in the production of raw sugar by half a million tons as compared to 1980, and that during the first four years of this five-year period the economy has grown at a faster pace than fuel and power consumption, something that had never occurred at any time before the revolution.

We attach equal importance to the introduction of design, especially industrial design, throughout the production process in order to save raw materials in our equipment and other manufactured products. We are certain that the program being prepared by the CMEA Committee on Cooperation in Material and Technical Supply, which will be discussed in next year's meeting of the session, will also contain measures that will be useful for us.

The use of nuclear power, which is advancing in Cuba with the construction of the Juraguá nuclear power plant, is a means for future savings of liquid fuels in power generation. We also intend to apply the experiences in depth oil refining, which the USSR and other countries are applying.

In the field of cooperation to improve the supply of foodstuffs to the member countries, we are pleased to report that one of the basic elements in our programs up to the year 2000, in addition to the prospects for industrial development which we intend to promote, is the so-called Food Program that we are preparing with the cooperation of experts from the Soviet Union. This program is aimed both at increasing our country's degree of food self-sufficiency and also at increasing food exports, in addition to sugar, as part of our relations with the member countries.

We would like, esteemed comrades, to express our support for the decisions of the summit conference on the further extension of cooperation with the developing countries.

Modestly but with the enthusiastic and, at times, necessarily heroic participation of our cooperation workers, we have been present in Angola, Mozambique, Tanzania, Ethiopia, Guinea-Bissau, the People's Republic of the Congo, the Saharan Arab Democratic Republic, the People's Democratic Republic of Yemen, People's Democratic Republic of Kampuchea, Lao People's Democratic Republic, Guyana, Nicaragua, and many other countries. In the multilateral cooperation efforts by the CMEA through joint commissions with Finland, Iraq, Mexico, and Nicaragua, we believe it is dramatically urgent to do our best to help Nicaragua confront victoriously the enormous human and economic sacrifices that the Reagan administration's attacks have imposed on it. Cuba will spare no efforts to fulfill this undeferrable duty.

Cuba endorses the draft resolution on items one, two, and three, which we examined in this plenary meeting.

I wish to inform you that Cuba's national economy has continued to progress steadily in spite of the fact that the Reagan administration's military threats forced us in the past period, and still force us today, to prepare ourselves in the military field. We are organizing, training, and arming our people and preparing the national territory and the economy, including the creation of material, food, drugs, and other product reserves that, though still modest, we deem indispensable for a strong, active, and protracted resistance in case of an aggression. This has forced us to double the defense expenditures planned for this five-year period, without cutting back our assistance in this field to other countries. All this has been done in spite of adverse natural phenomena in recent years that have harmed our agricultural production, particularly sugar. Yet sugar production now tops 8 million tons a year and we export the calories necessary to feed 40 million people.

As reported in the summit conferences, the Gross Social Product grew 2.3 percent in 1982, and in 1983 this rate was over 5 percent. Third-quarter figures show a 9.8 percent growth rate for 1984. This stands in contrast both with the tragic situation in the Asian and African countries and with the similarly dramatic negative growth of the economies of Latin American countries considered as semideveloped. In recent years these countries have experienced, as a consequence of their dependence on relations with developed capitalist countries — the United States above all — an economic regression which places them at 1976 levels, with drops of over 10 percent in industrial output. The ECLA [Economic Commission for Latin America, a United Nations agency] secretary has just illustrated this in detail.

If one considers that our relations with the capitalist camp are governed by a sharp drop in prices for sugar, nickel, and other raw materials and products of the developing countries, it is readily understood that it is Cuba's membership in the socialist community, along with our people's successful efforts to continuously raise labor productivity and make our economy more efficient and profitable, that has enabled us to advance as we are doing.

It is obvious that the international situation will not enable us to attain in the future such high growth rates as in 1984. Nevertheless, we are certain that we will ensure the preservation of material living standards and continue advancing at a steady rate in the field of health, education, culture, sports, housing construction, and other areas of social development while advancing economically at a satisfactory rate. We know that this entails great efforts, but we will make them.

We now have 20,500 doctors, over three times what we had on January 1, 1959, and six times the number of those who remained in the country when, through deceitful offers and political lies, imperialism managed to have over 3,000 doctors leave the country. Today there are medical schools in all fourteen provinces of the country, where over 20,000 young people rigorously chosen for their intellectual and moral standards are being trained. Cuban doctors are currently rendering service in over twenty-five Third World countries.

One of every three Cubans is engaged in regular and systematic studies; in higher education there is a total of 222,000 students and some 22,000 scholarship students from eighty-two countries, most of them from the Third World, who are studying in Cuba. The working class is striving so that all workers attain a ninth-grade education. In the past three years, by supplementing the efforts of the state with their own efforts, the population added 190,000 homes to those of the state plans.

This shows that in recent years, while our people have had to focus their attention on defense in view of the serious dangers implied for our country in the particularly aggressive and cynical policy of the present U.S. administration and while honorably fulfilling our internationalist obligations, we have not neglected production and services. Outdoing themselves in the face of imperialist threats and challenge, our people have doubled their efforts, raised their efficiency, and scored significant successes in all fields.

These facts, esteemed comrade heads and members of delegations, esteemed guests, once again show us what history has already confirmed many times: the endless moral wealth of our cause, the immense energy and heroism of revolutionary peoples, and the reason for our unshakable confidence in socialism as a political system and Marxism-Leninism as a political ideology, both invincible in Cuba and in all countries of the socialist community. We follow the course and the example set by Lenin and the glorious October revolution.

Thank you very much.

The Fight Against Washington's War Drive

Closing Speech to Students' Congress

The most outstanding feature of this congress is the fervor with which you express your readiness to defend the revolution and the homeland. I know that defense preparations and joining the Territorial Militia have been discussed in considerable depth in all their aspects at the congress.

I have closely heeded your watchwords, thinking to myself, "Well, there are more than 400,000 intermediate-level students in our country and with that spirit they represent a tremendous force that the enemy should take into account, has to take into account, unless it's completely out of its mind." [*Applause*] It expresses the revolutionary spirit of our youth that has truly taken up the traditions of our people, the spirit of our workers, our peasants, our women, and all our people in general.

Needless to say, we would not like to have to put that force to the test, to need to demonstrate that our enemies are out of their mind. The policy of the revolution will not be an irresponsible one; it never has been. Nor will it be an adventurist one; we are not warmongers. All that is in our hands, in the hands of our state and our party, everything possible will be done to prevent the bloodshed of the youth.

By this I mean that we will do all that is in our hands to further international détente, to foster a climate of peace; we will do all that is in our hands to further détente in our area, in Cuba and in Central America; we will do all that is in our hands to further détente even in other areas, as part of our principled policy and our awareness of the need to fight for peace. By doing so, we feel we are interpreting the finer aspirations of humanity and of our own people.

But peace is not attained through weakness. Peace is attained through strength, courage, and determination of peoples. I believe this is what has characterized our revolution over these twenty-five years.

This speech was delivered December 8, 1984, to the closing session of the Sixth Congress of the Federation of Students in Intermediate Education (FEEM), meeting in Havana. It is excerpted here from the December 23, 1984, Granma Weekly Review.

Without a firm line, without the determination to struggle, to resist, and to pay whatever price for our revolution and independence, we do not think our revolution would have survived under the difficult conditions in which it came about and developed, within a few miles of the world's most powerful imperialist country. I believe that spirit of our people has been decisive, first to the survival and later to the momentum and development of the revolution.

One day our adversaries will have to understand this: we have no interest in seeing the bloodshed of the U.S. people and the Cuban people in an imperialist adventure in our country. This is why we will always be on the alert for any sign or indication of U.S. leaders veering toward a policy of respect or a policy of aggression toward our country.

What's more, there have been contacts made in the past few months in regard to what is called normalization of migratory relations between the two countries. This is the only point that is being discussed, a question of interest to both sides. They have their set interests and we will have to yield a little and they will have to yield a little. But if these contacts bear fruit, they will, without a doubt, point to the real fact that problems can be resolved through dialogue and that, with us, no problem can be resolved through force. [*Applause*]

I would say that a large part of the world and the world's statesmen are waiting to see what is to be the main course chartered by the U.S. government — that is, the current administration — in its second term of office. That's the unknown, the question that is being asked in all corners of the world, on all continents. We do not believe that the people of the United States want war. It is evident that the immense majority of the people of the United States reject the idea of war, of any war, but most of all a world war.

It is already known that scientists, thousands of scientists in all fields have carried out computer studies and used mathematical models to determine what would happen in the event of a nuclear war. They have all reached the same conclusion: nuclear war means an end to human life, at the very least, and perhaps to other forms of life, although it is said that cockroaches may be able to survive a nuclear war. [*Laughter*]

They know what they are talking about. They are mathematically certain of all phenomena, not only contamination but ecological change, fallout, the drop in solar radiation, the drastic drop in temperature, to say nothing of land and water pollution that would make survival impossible. The men who have in their hands the possibilities of carrying through or averting this type of war bear on their shoulders a tremendous responsibility.

We know that socialism doesn't want war, has no interest in war, and makes no business out of war or weaponry. Wars and the arms race have always been the business of capitalists, of imperialists, not of socialism, which has no economic reason for investing huge resources in destructive weapons when there are so many needs to be met, so many aspirations to social and economic development for the well-being of man that must be made a reality.

And so wars, the arms race, and the arms business are inherent to capitalist society and diametrically opposed to the nature, concept, philosophy, and needs of a socialist society. For the socialist countries, arming themselves is a bitter necessity, a costly necessity, which they do without hesitation because they have no alternative.

It is our conclusion, therefore, that the main danger of whether or not there is war in the world and the danger of nuclear war comes largely from the United States. There are even those who dream of military supremacy and space weapons capable of creating an invulnerable shield, fantasies that could only lead to an increase in the arms race and in the danger of war.

But we know that the people of the United States do not want war. They can be fooled in regard to certain things and through the skillful use of the mass media. They can be skillfully manipulated into certain prejudices, false conceptions, and lies, and on certain occasions a large part of U.S. public opinion has been led to support criminal acts for which there can be no defense or jusification, as for example in the case of the invasion of Grenada over a year ago.

The students, who, it was said, were in danger and would have been held as hostages, arrived in the United States after the invasion, kissing the ground. All this was shown on TV in totally artificial, preconceived, melodramatic, theatrical fashion, calculated to make an impact and demonstrate that it was thanks to the action that those students had not shared the same fate of the U.S. embassy officials in Iran, who had been held as hostages for many months.

In the minds of many U.S. people, the one was associated with the other, and [they had] the idea that the operation had saved the lives of those students who were never in any danger whatsoever. And who could know this better than us? No one there, not even the extremist group who with their atrocious actions practically opened the doors to invasion, ever had the idea of even bothering the U.S. students in any way and, in fact, offered them all kinds of guarantees.

Cuba's cooperation with Grenada was associated with the idea of ominous plans for continent-wide subversion. And the tourist airport that was being built with the cooperation of several countries, including Britain, Western European countries, and Canada, was made out to be an extremely dangerous military airport, when it was almost finished and did not have a single military brick in its construction. That was another of the big lies.

Now they've finished the airport, and followers of Bishop, those who remained loyal to Bishop and his ideas, sent a cable to Cuba recently saying that they wanted it to be called Maurice Bishop Airport and thanking the Cuban people for the airport.

I firmly belive that the airport will be called Maurice Bishop Airport, that our people will always know it as Maurice Bishop Airport. Grenadian revolutionaries will call it Maurice Bishop Airport, and revolutionary, progressive, honest people everywhere will also call it Maurice Bishop Airport, no matter what other name it is given. [*Applause*] The airport will have two names: the official and the popular.

They associated events in Grenada with other events, with the Vietnam War, the humiliation that meant, etc. And that attack on a small country, one of the world's smallest countries, with an area of some 400 square kilometers and a population of 120,000, was presented as a great deed, a great victory, a great demonstration of the power, greatness, and glory of the United States. It was all orchestrated with the mass media, to make an impact on U.S. public opinion, and in part it succeeded, because many people were taken in. These are the facts, and only history and time will make episodes such as this completely understood in all objectivity.

However, and this is the truth, these manipulations have failed to arouse a war spirit among the people of the United States. The U.S. people do not want a world war, and that includes the tens of millions who voted for the current president of the United States and who could be influenced by conjunctural factors, for example, a certain economic growth on the tail of a profound crisis for which the system is to blame, because the preceding administration cannot be specifically held to blame.

The crisis had been developing for many years as a result of the fabulous expenditures of the Vietnam War, financed with the issuing of currency, and the contradictions and problems inherent to the system, but there had also been a marked increase in unemployment and a big increase in inflation.

All these factors made a big impact on public opinion, and in the last two years there has been a conjunctural growth of the economy and a drop in unemployment. We say conjunctural because many specialists predict a new crisis — and relatively soon — if there's a continuation of the high interest rates, budget deficits of around $200 billion, and a trade balance deficit of $100 billion, all of which may lead to an even greater crisis of the U.S. economy than before.

On July 26, in Cienfuegos, I took the opportunity to explain how the economy of the other capitalist countries and, above all, the economy of Third World countries, has had to pay the price of that increase in the U.S. economy over the last two years.

This conjunctural increase was the result of mechanisms that enabled the United States to freely dispose of money from other countries in its economic sphere. Money was brought in from Europe, from Japan, from all parts, especially the Third World, through high interest rates and a partial confrontation of the problems but without any sound foundations for the future. Most of those resources have been invested in armaments, with a military budget of over $300 billion.

These arms expenditures do not help develop the economy. Precisely one of the benefits enjoyed by the Japanese economy after World War II was that, by virtue of the treaties established at the end of the war, Japan was not allowed to invest in armaments. As a result, most of the investments went into industry, new technology, much more productive branches, while many sectors of U.S. industry lagged behind — steel, for example, whose products cannot compete with those of Japan or even those of European countries.

This forced the United States to levy quota restrictions in its free enterprise, free trade system, for its steelworks to survive. All that enormous arms investment does not create a solid base for the economy; it bankrupts it.

The real fact is that in the last few years of the present U.S. administration there was economic growth and a drop in inflation and unemployment and, in our opinion, these were very important, basic, decisive factors. Familiar as we are with U.S. voter patterns, we never had the slightest doubt as to the result of the election. It was clear on analyzing all these factors.

But the people of the United States, I insist, do not want a war. They can be cajoled to a certain extent by telling them that theirs is a powerful country, that it continues to be a great power and will become an even greater one. Certain nationalistic chords can be touched, even certain chauvinistic feelings can be developed.

But for the last 120 years the people of the United States have not experienced war in their own country. They had the Civil War in the middle of the last century, a costly and bloody war, but the people of the United States never experienced the destruction of either World War I or II, as the Soviet people did.

The Soviet people know what war means, because they experienced it at close quarters, between 1914 and 1917, and especially after the revolution, with foreign intervention leading to the occupation of a large part of the country in the wake of great destruction. Years later, they were the object of fascist attack with a toll of 20 million lives and the destruction of thousands of cities. The Soviet people know what that means and are much more aware of what war is like.

But in spite of the difference, the people of the United States, too, are against war; they have the intelligence, understanding, and knowledge to realize what a war means. They are not only against a world war —

which nobody wants — but also against any local war.

We can say that the people of the United States are against intervention in Nicaragua; and this is reflected in the congressional opposition to the allocation of funds to mercenary bands. U.S. public opinion rejects a military venture in Central America, and none of the efforts of the U.S. administration have been able to really change that.

U.S. public opinion does not want a war in Cuba. They have not been persuaded that an attack on Cuba would be convenient. There may be a number of extremist groups — they exist everywhere — made up of extreme reactionaries, impassioned advocates of the use of force, but the majority of U.S. public opinion, while realizing that the danger involved is not that of a nuclear world war, is against local wars.

People have not been persuaded of that and know that any adventure in Central America will not be the walkover Grenada was. Many people realize this, many intelligent people who believe that this would take many lives, apart from the fact that such an unjustifiable act, the responsibility for the virtual genocide that world public opinion refuses to accept, would discredit the nation. And that would be an enormous political and human price for the United States to pay. They also know, of course, that in the case of our country, it would be much worse and of unforeseeable consequences.

How the people of the United States think is important, because, even though sometimes their leaders might forget what the whole world thinks, it's not so easy for them to forget what the people of the United States think.

The intervention in Vietnam, a grievous war that took so many lives, was one that initially was given scant attention by world public opinion. As the years went by, greater attention was paid and there was greater international condemnation. As the years went by and the casualties started, when the mass media also began to reveal the atrocities in that war — and there are those who think that television is to blame for the defeat in Vietnam, because the people should never have been informed about what was going on there — when U.S. public opinion took a firm antiwar stand, that was decisive to the end of the war.

We must take all these factors into account. And I believe they will also have to be taken into account by the U.S. administration. They know that a $200 billion budget deficit is untenable and that they will have to either levy high taxes, which would be both unpopular and hard to justify, or put a limit on that fabulous military spending.

Mention is already being made about measures, further restrictive social measures, to try to cut down on the deficit. Those measures will also be unpopular. A worsening of the international climate is not good for the U.S. economy. What it needs is a certain détente.

The way things stand, there seems to be no solution to these problems, and everybody is watching and waiting, wondering whether apocalypse is around the corner, whether there is a fatalism to this administration as to the end of the world having come or whether, on the contrary, the time has come to reflect on these questions.

There are those who think that perhaps the concern is another: whether this administration will go down in history as an administration that fought for peace or an administration that led to war.

Of course, the outcome is relative. If the course is one of peace, it will go down in history; but if it is one of war, then there will most probably be no more history, history will come to an end.

This is why world public opinion is closely charting the events and any signs that can appear. There have been some positive signs. For example, we could mention the interest shown in continuing the talks on migratory questions, even after the elections. Although the talks are strictly limited to that, this is in our opinion a positive sign. The meeting between U.S. Secretary of State [George] Shultz and Comrade [Andrei] Gromyko, the Soviet foreign minister, next month is unquestionably another positive sign.

This doesn't give anybody the right to harbor illusions. The course of events must be observed and analyzed.

I believe that our people's knowledge of international politics is greater than it ever was. I remember that several years ago, when the international agreements on arms control, etc., were signed by the Soviet Union and the United States charting an era of détente, our party wrote a series of editorials to explain to our people what détente meant. This was because our people, a militant, harassed, irate people under attack, were naturally not the most psychologically prepared to understand détente.

Several years have passed since then, and our people have attained a cultural level and concrete knowledge of international economic problems and political problems and have a much more solid and clearer awareness to understand these problems much better and to follow closely what is happening and what might happen.

The next few months will be decisive, and 1985 will be an important year. We will have to see how these factors work in conjunction and what the outcome will be, and whether or not the world can harbor any hope for peace. This is important. Whether there can be hope for peace in our area is very important, and also what course the international situation will take in the next few years.

Peoples driven to desperation by underdevelopment and hunger — and you have heard the news about the famine in Africa — by ecological phenomena on top of the problems of underdevelopment and technological backwardness that have shaken the world, know that in a climate of international tension and arms buildup there isn't the remotest possibility of solutions being found to Latin America's $350 billion debt and the even higher figure in the rest of the world, bringing the total up to about $800 billion.

Until now, the increase in the foreign debt and military expenditures has been roughly on a par, but now military expenditure has shot ahead. According to recent data, it runs to a million million dollars, at least what I was taught was a billion. In the United States, a billion means 1,000 million. In the language of that country, it is 1,000 billion; in Spanish one billion. That is, world military expenditure at this moment runs to a million million dollars.

And those countries whose situation is desperate, irrespective of ideology — we've seen this in the Movement of Nonaligned Countries: left-wing governments, middle-of-the-road governments, right-wing governments — have many problems in common, including unequal exchange, foreign debt, and underdevelopment, which are a source of concern to them all. They know that without détente, that unless a stop is put to the arms buildup, there isn't the remotest possibility of funds being found for a solution to their problems, that is, if they are ever to be found.

There are situations of entire continents, like Africa, where the desert is advancing steadily southwards, while the population is growing everywhere, even in the desert area. It has taken a tragedy like this for world public opinion to be made more aware of the problem. But just imagine how much it will cost to take the pertinent measures to check the desert's advance and make the land fertile again, apart from the agricultural development and hydraulic resources the continent needs in order to solve its food problems.

That is why the world is very much watching and waiting to see what is going to happen everywhere in the world in the next few months. For us, that's important. Yes, because we're prepared for any eventuality. We're prepared for war and for peace. [*Applause*]

I think that the efforts of our country, its fortitude, calm, courage, organizational capacity, and revolutionary and patriotic fervor, have made for greater possibilities for peace, whatever the U.S. line may be. Because over the past four years, every day, every week, every month that has passed has made us stronger.

The threats against our country have served only to multiply our forces, over and over again, because not only the number of organized, armed, and trained men and women has multiplied, but so also have the ideas. There is now a greater sense of awareness and knowledge of defense, taking in major experiences in the world over recent decades that have enabled us to develop our defense potential on the basis of people's participation, and this has made us much stronger, much more invincible than ever before, and this effort must be kept up.

Clearly we prefer peace to war. This is a basic duty of every revolutionary, of every Marxist-Leninist, and, above all, of every party in power, every responsible government.

It's very important for every citizen — every mother, father, brother, sister, and child — to know what the revolutionary government's stand is on this, to know that the government does not act on impulse or pride but is rather characterized, and must always be characterized, by calm, deliberation, and cool-headedness, because the responsibility for the life and destiny of an entire nation falls on our party and government. This obliges us to look ahead, to take every measure, and make every effort to be strong and, at the same time, calm.

Even should a situation of détente emerge — and that's what we would want — defense cannot be neglected — cannot be neglected! This is very important, for what we have achieved cannot be cast aside. It is a reality imposed by our geographical location.

The difference in the political, economic, and social system between us and our most powerful neighbor forces us to always give maximum attention to defense. Even if someday the United States were to have a socialist system, we couldn't neglect defense because, well Vietnam is bordered by China, the two countries are socialist, and Vietnam cannot neglect its defense! [*Applause*]

Sweden is a neutral country; it doesn't belong to any military bloc. It's in northern Europe and, nevertheless, despite the fact that it was not involved in World War I or World War II — which is one of the factors that has contributed to its economic and social development — it doesn't neglect defense, or arms, or the training of the population, or fortifications.

We need, therefore, to understand the importance of the efforts we have made to date and the importance of always being on the alert, always strong, even in a situation of détente on international and regional levels. There can even be a certain international détente and no regional détente — this is one of the possibilities — although international détente clearly benefits the whole world in one way or another and establishes a logic which differs from that of an aggressive, warlike policy.

Tonight seemed like a good opportunity to explain this, especially given the enthusiastic response demonstrated by the students with regard to the country's defense. I also take this opportunity to convey these ideas, which I think are very important, to public opinion in the country, to the rest of our people.

The U.S.-Cuba Accord on Migratory Relations

Address to the Cuban People

Fellow citizens:

A few days ago, during the closing session of the congress of the Federation of Students in Intermediate Education, I announced that talks between Cuba and the United States on migratory issues were advancing. Today, I can report that those talks have concluded and that an agreement was reached this afternoon.

I would have preferred to announce this TV appearance, held to inform the people, earlier, but the agreement was reached at 1:40 this afternoon. Besides, we agreed to make it public at 4:00 p.m., so there was little time to announce this appearance.

Today, I have been really busy with the delegation headed by Comrade Mengistu [Haile Mariam, chairman of the Provisional Military Administrative Council of Ethiopia], a close friend. I'm dressed this way not because this is a special occasion but because from here I'm going straight to a reception in honor of the visiting delegation. However, in view of the importance of this question, I wanted to explain it personally to the people.

I will begin by reading the communiqué which the representatives of the Republic of Cuba and of the United States signed this afternoon. It reads as follows:

"Discussions between representatives of the United States of America and of the Republic of Cuba on immigration matters concluded today with the adoption of agreements for the normalization of immigration procedures between the two countries and to put an end to the abnormal situation which has existed since 1980.

"The United States will resume issuance of preference immigrant visas to Cuban nationals residing in Cuba up to the number of 20,000

This speech was given December 14, 1984, and was broadcast live over Cuban television. It is reprinted here from the December 23, 1984, Granma Weekly Review. *On May 19, 1985, Cuba suspended the migration agreement in response to Washington's launching of "Radio José Martí" against Cuba.*

each year, in particular to close family relatives of United States citizens and of Cuban permanent residents in the United States.

"The United States side expressed its willingness to implement — with the cooperation of the Cuban authorities — all necessary measures to ensure that Cuban nationals residing in Cuba wishing to emigrate to the United States and who qualify under United States law to receive immigrant visas, may enter the United States, taking maximum advantage of the number of up to 20,000 immigrants per year.

"For its part, the United States will continue granting immigrant visas to residents of Cuba who are parents, spouses, and unmarried children under twenty-one years of age of United States citizens. These immigrants will not be counted against the annual limit indicated above.

"Cuba will accept the return of those Cuban nationals who came to the United States in 1980 via the port of Mariel and who have been declared ineligible to enter the United States legally. The number of such persons is 2,746, and their names appear on an approved list.

"The return of these persons will be carried out by means of an orderly program of returns with the cooperation of the immigration authorities of both countries. The returns will proceed in a phased and orderly manner until all the identified individuals who appear on the approved list have been returned.

"The returns will be effected at a rate of 100 each calendar month, but if the figue of 100 is not met in a given month, the remaining numbers may be used in subsequent months, provided that no more than 150 will be returned in any calendar month.

"The United States stated that measures were being taken so that the Cuban nationals who came to the United States in 1980 via the port of Mariel may acquire, beginning now and with retroactive effect of approximately thirty months, legal status as permanent residents of the United States.

"Both delegations expressed their concern in regard to the situation of those persons who, having been released after serving sentences for acts which Cuban penal legislation defines as 'offenses against the security of the state,' wish to reside permanently in the United States. The United States will facilitate the admission of such persons and their immediate family members by means of a program to be carried out under applicable United States law.

"The United States delegation stated that to this end the necessary steps have been taken for admission during fiscal year 1985 of up to 3,000 such persons, including immediate family members. The size of the program and any possible increase in subsequent fiscal years will be determined in the light of experience with the process and the desire expressed by both parties to carry out this program in such a way as to allow for its ongoing implementation until fully completed in the shortest possible time.

"The representatives of the United States of America and of the Republic of Cuba decided to meet again within six months in order to analyze progress in the implementation of these agreements."

I would like to examine the background of the agreement.

The question of normalizing migratory relations between the two countries was first examined with the Carter administration after the happenings at the port of Mariel, in December 1980.

The first contacts and talks on this issue were held in December and in January 1981, but the time frame was very short. The new administration was inaugurated early that year, and the contacts and exchanges on this issue were interrupted until May 1983, when we received a note from the U.S. government asking our country to accept the return of such Cuban citizens who had arrived in the United States via the port of Mariel who, according to its criteria and legislation, were inadmissible.

At that time, we were sent a list of approximately 800 names, and it was announced that, of course, the final figure would be several times as high and that as long as the Cuban government didn't accept such citizens regarded by the United States as inadmissible or excludable, the United States would be unable to issue immigration visas to other Cuban citizens, enabling them to enter the country, since its legislation stated that acceptance of the principle of the return of the so-called excludables was prerequisite.

At that time, the Cuban government replied that it was willing to examine this question, together with all other migratory issues that had a bearing on the relations between the United States and Cuba. That is, we couldn't accept the principle of simply agreeing to the return of the excludables without discussing, examining, and solving the other migratory problems.

In March this year, the U.S. government sent the Cuban government a note expressing its willingness to discuss the question of the excludables and the other issues related to migratory relations between the United States and Cuba. I repeat, this took place in March of this year.

The Cuban government analyzed the proposal bearing in mind that the election campaign was being launched in the United States. Concerned over the possibility that this complex and sensitive question might become an election issue in that country and that a reasonable solution could be jeopardized, we agreed to initiate the examination and discussion of this subject but added that we would rather do so after the election in the United States, for the reasons I have already given.

Later, when [Jesse] Jackson visited Cuba, in the meetings that were held on June 26, this problem was included in the ten points that Jackson considered to be important issues for improving relations between the United States and Cuba.

We told Jackson that in March the U.S. government had proposed to the Cuban government that these talks be held and that we had agreed, suggesting that they be postponed until after the election, for the reasons I gave. We stated, however, that if both parties agreed and if the United States and its people wanted to find a solution to this problem, we would be ready to discuss it even before the election.

During the press conference held that same evening, on the twenty-sixth, I explained what our position was regarding this problem and publicly stated our willingness to discuss it if both parties agreed. In a matter of hours — perhaps twenty-four or forty-eight hours — before Jackson left Cuba, the U.S. government expressed its willingness to discuss the problem immediately, just as we had suggested.

The answer wasn't immediate; it took a few days, for we had asked Jackson to contact [Walter] Mondale, the most likely opposition candidate at the time, to find out what he thought and get his approval, since we had stated that we were ready to go forward on a bilateral basis.

Naturally, Jackson agreed to do this, and, as soon as he contacted Mondale, informed him about the subject, and obtained his approval, he let us know. As soon as this had been done — which we considered an essential prerequisite — we contacted the U.S. government expressing our readiness to discuss the issue immediately.

The United States proposed a first meeting of delegations from the two countries for July 12. We immediately formed our delegation, headed by Deputy Minister [Ricardo] Alarcón, and it traveled to the United States.

The question of where the talks were to be held — in Havana, New York, Washington, or elsewhere — was discussed. We didn't feel that this was an essential problem. We raised no objections, stating that we were ready to go wherever it would be easiest to hold the discussions. We weren't going to start arguing about whether they ought to be held here or there; we said that we weren't at all concerned about this.

The talks on this subject began on July 12. The delegations met on the twelfth and thirteenth and set forth their positions — I won't go into details — and work began.

The second meeting took place some time later, on July 31 and August 1. The U.S. delegation was headed by Mr. [Michael] Kozak — I'm told he's a legal adviser at the State Department.

Progress was made in that second meeting, even though the subjects discussed were complex. Both delegations worked very hard. Comrade Alarcón told me that each point was discussed exhaustively, for many hours, almost nonstop. The members of the Cuban delegation returned to our country in early August.

Progress had been made, but, in the first half of August, some difficulties arose which interrupted the negotiations. This interruption lasted for approximately two months: the rest of August, September, and part of October.

In October, as a result of the exchange of messages between the two countries, it was decided to resume the talks in November. The United States proposed November 28 and 29. Our delegation left for New York, and, on November 28, the third round of talks began. This round lasted until December 5. The participants in the talks worked very hard for almost a week.

Our delegation was in constant communication with our country, and each of the points, each of the questions, was carefully analyzed. During that period, remarkable headway was made, and some draft agreements were even prepared.

The delegation returned to Cuba, and a fourth meeting was scheduled for December 13 — that is, yesterday. The members of the delegations worked all day yesterday. This time, too, our delegation kept in constant contact with our country. Details, the wording of the draft agreement, were analyzed. The delegations worked almost through the night — later, I will explain why it took so long — until, at 1:40 p.m., an agreement was reached.

Both delegations are to be congratulated for having worked hard, carefully, and diligently. Some points required long discussion: first of all, the concept of excludables because, if we analyze the legislation, the fact that somebody entered the country illegally already constitutes grounds for his inclusion in that category. Well, all those who left via Mariel could be considered excludables. The first point, then, was to determine who were the excludables.

I don't want to go into too much detail, I don't want to be indiscreet, but this was an important point: the U.S. party expressed its intention to settle the legal status of the vast majority of those who had arrived via Mariel and to limit the number of the excludables, according to the criteria of the U.S. authorities. Then it became necessary to identify and determine the exact number of these excludables.

In the course of this process, several lists were presented — a first, a second, and a third. Our delegation worked on those lists, and we also worked on them in our country, employing the criterion that the most important thing was to verify that the person had really left via Mariel.

Even during the period when negotiations were suspended, an exchange of information about the lists was kept up. Our staff analyzed those lists carefully, and, thanks to the work done during those months, considerable headway was made in identifying all those people. Sometimes all we had was a first name; sometimes, only a last name; there wasn't much information. There were instances in which a name was repeated by mistake.

In this way, the lists — the first list, the second, and the third — were gradually screened. And this work continued until the wee hours this morning. When all the other points had already been agreed on, the lists had to be screened to avoid any possible repetition of error, and it was in this that the comrades worked through last night and this morning in New York.

This was to have ended at midnight and to have been announced at 3:00 a.m., but it wasn't until nearly 2:00 p.m. that the exact figure, the exact number of people, was determined. The lists, the definition, and the identification of the excludables took a lot of work and a lot of time.

Another point that was discussed at length concerned the period of time over which those people should return. The U.S. view was that they should return within six months. Our view was that, if their return and adjustment were to be effected in an orderly and careful manner, it would take longer. We felt that even the United States needed more time to take all the legal measures that those persons' return implied.

Therefore, we proposed that approximately 50 return each month. Finally, we arrived at the figure of 100 per month, and if, in one month, 100 people didn't arrive — if, for example, only 70 came — then the remainder could come the following month, or as many as were pending, up to a maximum of 150. An agreement was also reached on this point.

Another question was that, although there was talk of 20,000 migrants a year, we raised the need to establish a minimum — or, rather, a maximum — of 20,000. This is apart from the relatives of U.S. citizens (parents, husbands, wives, and unmarried children under twenty-one) and from those who would leave, under a program, for having been counterrevolutionary prisoners.

After making a very careful analysis, we found that it was impossible to establish a minimum; according to the laws, no exact figure could be given, since each case had to be examined. We felt that this argument was reasonable, which is why, in one paragraph, we agreed that both parties would do their utmost to see to it that full use was made of the quota. An agreement was reached on this point.

Moreover, everything had to be carefully studied, because, if anything in the agreement was contrary to U.S. law, this would seriously hinder its implementation, for it would require changes in laws, congressional approval — a long and complex process.

Therefore, it was necessary to analyze each point in the light of U.S. laws, since those people are there, in the United States, and it is the United States that is going to accept the people that are going to join their relatives or who are going to emigrate from our country. Since it is involved in this question, we had to pay close attention to all U.S. laws.

Finally, an agreement was reached, and it was drafted in a form that was satisfactory to both parties.

It should be kept in mind that these migratory problems have existed under abnormal conditions for nearly twenty-six years — not just since 1980. Of course, a particularly abnormal situation has existed since 1980, but it really dates back to 1959.

We were very careful to maintain the utmost discretion regarding the content of the talks. In the United States, there were some leaks about what was being discussed, and the press and the wire services placed special emphasis on the return of the excludables, claiming that they were mentally ill or criminals. I feel that I should explain, objectively, something that all our people know.

Regarding these two myths, I think that international propaganda has deliberately placed a lot of emphasis on the mentally ill and criminals. It speaks of patients who were taken out of the hospital and sent via Mariel.

I would like to reiterate, once again, that no mental patients left any hospital in our country to travel to the United States via Mariel — first of all, because our country takes excellent care of our people's health and has made enormous efforts to care for every citizen in this country, without payment, whatever the cost, whoever it may be. We would never do such an absurd thing as to take a patient from a mental hospital and send him to the United States or any other country.

We feel too much respect for patients to do this. A patient of any kind is sacred to us, and such an action would go against an essential part of our philosophy, our conduct, and the history of our revolution. No one in our country would be capable of, would have dared to accept such a thing.

All of this is part of the campaign, the lies, the malice, and the myths; but that was one of the points that was greatly emphasized and propagandized abroad.

If any mental patients left here, it was because their relatives claimed them and nobody was aware of their illness. The relatives said: We want so-and-so and so-and-so. If any did leave, they must have been exceptions, and no one noticed, because they weren't in the category of those who left via Mariel.

A few of those who left may have become ill in the United States during the past four years — more than four years. As a matter of fact, we have heard that some of the ones who were imprisoned there later had problems of this sort, and, in a contingent of more than 125,000 persons, anywhere in the world, mental problems can crop up in some people in a period of four years.

That is why I say that those who are in that category are there because their relatives claimed them and no one noticed, or because they became ill in the United States afterwards. That is the historic, objective, and strict truth: no one left any mental hospital here to be sent to the United States. I want to make this perfectly clear.

Second, no one guilty of bloody crimes left via Mariel — everyone knows this, too. If any did leave they must have been very exceptional cases, because no one was aware of it; no one noticed; it was a mistake, a confusion — never because we had considered the idea of sending people guilty of bloody crimes to the United States.

This was so, also, for an elementary reason: the safety of our country and our society makes it impossible to exonerate those who are guilty of bloody crimes and give them the pleasure of traveling to another country, to the United States.

So, if there are any such cases, they can only be very exceptional and are the result of no one's noticing, for that was one of the guidelines that was laid down: that category of person wouldn't be authorized to travel to the United States — I repeat — to protect our people's safety.

If this weren't so, an attempted homicide or homicide would be taken lightly, with no further implications or consequences, but these crimes are much too serious and are too severely punished by our laws for us to incur the irresponsibility of exonerating such persons.

Several categories of persons left via Mariel. Some of them had relatives abroad with whom they wanted to be reunited, but people of the type who forced their way into the Peruvian embassy also left via Mariel. As a matter of fact, many of the people who forced their way into the Peruvian embassy left via Mariel.

I remember the applause, the solidarity, and the international campaign that was launched in support of the people who forced their way into the Peruvian embassy following the incident that cost the life of a guard. We are all familiar with that story. They said they were dissidents, but we said: They aren't dissidents; don't be confused. Those people didn't force their way in there for political or ideological reasons. For the most part, those people are antisocial elements — we said this and explained why — or individuals who don't want to work or who haven't adapted themselves to the people's laws, discipline, and spirit of sacrifice.

No ideological questions were involved. Rather than political dissidents, they were antisocial elements, but some went ahead and fabricated the story about the dissidents. It was a worldwide campaign.

We said: Fantastic! Anybody who wants them can have them, and various countries responded. A UN commission even became involved, and Costa Rica said, send them, and Peru said, send them, and Spain said the same. We couldn't have been more delighted; we sent them all they wanted.

Well, the facts showed that we were right. Moreover, those individuals didn't want to go to the Dominican Republic or to Central America or South America; they wanted to go to the United States, to paradise, to the ideal. Really, they were that kind of people. I'm not going to say that they were all the same; there were others that I can't classify as antisocial elements.

What I can say is that they may be insensitive to the revolution, to their homeland, and are self-centered, people who think only of their own personal interests and who have no spirit of sacrifice or who are afraid of the risks of living in Cuba. As a matter of fact, this factor has had some weight; there are people who have been afraid.

We know that at the beginning of the revolution many families sent their children to the United States because they believed the stupid rumor that they were going to be deprived of their parental authority. All of those factors have had an influence, apart from the fact that living here means struggling and working in a developing or underdeveloped country that was subjected to colonialism for centuries and to neocolonialism for decades, while the United States is a country with much greater economic development than ours.

There have always been people all over the world who have wanted to emigrate from countries whose wealth had yet to be developed to another with better material conditions or more wealth.

These people didn't want to go to a Third World country; they wanted to go to the United States. And those who went to Peru were welcomed with applause — not the people's, of course, but that of the authorities, who paid their travel expenses; lodged them in a park; played the role of humanitarians, of the civilized who were saving them from socialism, saving them from Cuba. And they had four years of experience with them — enough to bear out what we had said: that those people, those "heroes," were not dissidents but were antisocial elements.

Later, they began to run wild: they destroyed that park; none of them wanted to stay in Peru; and they did everything possible to leave for the United States. In the end, they held demonstrations, stirred up conflicts, made demands, and engaged in blackmail, saying they didn't want to leave the park and wouldn't go, after four years, unless they were given visas so they could go to the United States.

Many of the people who wanted to leave and did leave via Mariel were of that type, with that spirit and that mentality, people who considered themselves heroes and were given worldwide publicity.

In addition, there are other circumstances. Some actions are considered crimes in Cuba but not in the United States. For example, prostitution is punished by law in Cuba, but not in the United States; gambling is punished by law in Cuba, but not in the United States; the use of drugs is punished by law in Cuba, but not in the United States.

There are people who do things that are crimes according to Cuban law but not according to U.S. law. People of that kind left via Mariel, but they weren't in the category of the mentally ill or of those who had committed bloody crimes.

Some of them may have committed bloody crimes later on, in the United States — as may happen anywhere. People who have never committed bloody crimes may do so one day, anywhere in the world. There may be people of that type there, people who have committed that type of crime. But the category of people who had committed bloody crimes was not included among those who left via Mariel. That is the historic truth.

This situation has a long history. As I was saying, the abnormal situation surrounding the migratory relations between the United States and Cuba dates back nearly twenty-six years. It began on January 1, 1959, when dozens — hundreds — of torturers and murderers who committed atrocities against thousands of citizens of this country and committed crimes of all sorts — some killed twenty, forty, or fifty people — went to the United States.

Where did the Venturas, the Carratalás, and all those people go? To the United States — hundreds of them, fleeing from revolutionary justice. Those people had committed acts of genocide in our country, and they were welcomed in the United States; they were given refuge and abetted right from the first. Those people were indeed the real criminals.

Criminals did leave here, but they left on January 1 — real criminals, dangerous criminals, hundreds of them, by ship and by plane. Those people didn't have any difficulties — and there were thieves and embezzlers of all types, real thieves.

I'm not talking about an individual who may have stolen a piece of furniture or a suitcase — no, not that. It's not that I justify it; I don't mean to say it's right. But the ones who stole tens of millions of pesos in this country left immediately for the United States on January 1.

Those indeed were real thieves, not petty thieves. The owners of the casinos, of the gambling dens, of the lottery, of the drug traffic — all of them went to the United States and were welcomed there. Those people, objectively and unquestionably, were worse than the ones who left via Mariel. And that began on January 1.

Later, even though people were being authorized to leave legally, anyone who stole a boat and went to the United States was welcomed — both he and the boat — and anyone who skyjacked an airplane was, too — he and the plane. Dozens of Cuban planes of various types were stolen from this country.

The fact is, the history of skyjacking started in Cuba, against Cuba. Skyjacking was something totally unknown in the world. It was after the triumph of the revolution, when anyone who skyjacked a plane was given a hero's welcome in the United States, that the nefarious business of skyjacking began. It happened at that time and for those reasons.

At that time, no one could foresee the consequences of this phenomenon that was just beginning. They even offered rewards of thousands of dollars to anyone who skyjacked a Cuban plane and took it to the United States. They not only welcomed all those persons I mentioned before, but they started encouraging others to leave our country.

Before the revolution, there was a limited entry quota to the United States — a few thousand — and many people were waiting to go there to work; they had no jobs. Before, jobless people were the ones who emigrated; now, the ones wanting to emigrate were the ones who just didn't want to work, which is something quite different.

Some time afterwards began the counterrevolutionary subversive actions against Cuba — a long period of recruitment of individuals who had left Cuba, training them in the use of explosives and weapons. They started smuggling weapons and explosives into our country by air and sea; the sabotage schemes; the counterrevolutionary bands in the Escambray and in Pinar del Río and other provinces of the country.

And not only that, they embarked on plans of economic sabotage — I'm not making this up; they've written about these things, they were verified by the U.S. Senate committees that investigated that period.

That was the time when assassination plans against leaders of the revolution began; they tried to kill me by all means available: chemical products, poisons, diseases, rifles with telescopic sights, explosives, by all methods. And it's not I who says so; Congress said it, the U.S. Senate.

It was an extended period. They encouraged the establishment of organizations; hundreds of counterrevolutionary organizations were created. Whenever any Tom, Dick, and Harry got together, they made up an acronym, a name, and asked for U.S. help.

Later we had the Girón [Bay of Pigs] invasion — men armed to the teeth, with bombers, artillery, and tanks, invading the country on behalf of a foreign power. Those were really dangerous persons; they were indeed criminals in the worst sense of the word, because they murdered children and entire families.

What would have happened, how many would they have murdered? Don't forget that Calviño — one of Batista's most notorious henchmen — was among them. How many more would they have tortured and murdered? Thousands! Those were really dangerous men. And we sent them back. They were given a warm welcome, with all honors and pomp. And, later on, there was a protracted period of irregularities.

I said that there was a small quota. After the triumph of the revolution, they opened their doors to all who wished to leave — it didn't matter whether there were 50,000 or 100,000.

They wanted to drain us of technicians, engineers, teachers, professors, doctors. They took away half of our doctors, and we overcame that hardship. We started to train more technicians, more doctors. Our struggle to develop our universities started then.

They took away our intelligentsia that couldn't adjust to the sacrifices and struggles of a revolution. Yes, at the beginning they took many such people from our country. And we warned them — after the events at the Peruvian embassy and Mariel — that, whereas they had taken technicians and intellectuals before, now they were taking antisocials, which was quite different. We warned them.

Later, during the Missile Crisis of October 1962, they canceled all flights to the United States. At a time when tens of thousands of families had been granted exit permits, they were stranded here de facto. They didn't authorize flights. No one could leave; since we had been blockaded everywhere in Latin America except Mexico, they had no country through which they could travel.

Many people were encouraged to leave the country illegally. Any time anyone landed in a small boat or fishing vessel — and they hijacked dozens of such vessels — the publicity and news coverage were tremendous. All this led to Camarioca and to a solution, and all those people who were stranded were able to leave.* Afterwards, everything was stopped once again.

The policy of encouraging people to leave the country illegally continued. We warned them many, many times that this policy was being used as a political weapon and that antisocial elements were doing all kinds of things — murdering people to steal boats, hijacking boats — and, when they reached the United States, they went unpunished.

We warned them many, many times that measures had to be taken against that policy, that something had to be done to stop this situation and that it was going to lead to trouble, until finally it led to the Mariel episode.

I believe that these problems should have begun to be solved twenty years ago. It was lack of maturity, deliberation, common sense, and responsibility, lack of foresight with regard to future problems, which allowed such a policy to be pursued for so long. That is the objective truth.

Now then, what changes have come about? An important change. We all remember that mercenaries were organized and trained not only to commit acts of sabotage and other crimes in Cuba but to perpetrate them in foreign countries against Cuban facilities and against Cuban officials at the United Nations, in Canada, in Mexico. They departed from the United States and murdered our comrades; afterwards those same individuals strolled freely in the streets of the United States.

---

*In 1965 Cuba opened the port of Camarioca for those who wished to leave. This compelled Washington to again accept Cuban émigrés.

Let us recall that those who perpetrated the atrocious assassination of the passengers on the plane that was blown up off the coast of Barbados [in 1976] were individuals who had — at a given moment — received training in those techniques in the United States. That is the truth. That policy claimed many lives. No measures were ever adopted.

An important, real, and objective change has taken place during the last four years: the present U.S. administration — whose hostility to our revolution is well known — nonetheless adopted measures against groups, once trained by the CIA, that engaged in terrorist attacks on Cuban personnel in the United States.

For the first time, effective measures were adopted, and, in recent months, one of the most notorious ringleaders [Eduardo Arocena] was arrested, tried, and convicted. That is, it may be stated that those persons no longer operate freely in the United States, which has had the elemental common sense of trying to guarantee law and order within its own borders.

If the precedent that anyone can start doing whatever he wants to were to be set, all sorts of situations would be unleashed. That is a fact.

A second fact: for the first time in this long period, measures have been adopted to curb illegal departures from Cuba in order to enter the United States illegally. We know that measures have been adopted, though with some hesitation at times.

Recently, a group of traitors hijacked a boat in Varadero to go to the United States and threw the skipper overboard several miles offshore, but, miraculously, he was saved. They were interned in some camp in the United States and there was some publicity about the event, but measures were taken. We stated the case; they said the skipper should go there to file charges. The skipper has already gone to the United States once and will go there again.

This occurred several months ago, in addition to a few other cases. We know that at present the United States isn't interested in encouraging people to leave Cuba illegally. That is a second fact, and it was one of the factors we took into account when we were working out this agreement.

A third fact, and this merit belongs to Cuba: for our part — due to strict measures adopted in our country against skyjackers — we have virtually solved this problem, which was one of the problems that most concerned the people of the United States, because they feared that anyone with a bottle of gasoline, or a bottle of water, could say that he was going to blow up a plane, so he could skyjack it to Havana.

Even though the official agreement between our two countries was no longer in effect after the plane was blown up off Barbados, we have adopted increasingly strict measures against skyjackers during the last few years.

In 1981, there were two skyjackings; the skyjackers were sentenced to ten years' imprisonment. In 1982, five skyjackings; the skyjackers were sentenced to twelve, fifteen, and twenty years' imprisonment. In 1983, eleven skyjackings, ten of which came from the United States; the skyjackers were sentenced to ten, fifteen, and twenty years' imprisonment. In 1984, four: one from Brazil, one from the United States, and two from Colombia; one group is awaiting trial, and the rest have been sentenced to fifteen years.

It is Cuba that has solved the skyjacking problem — a diabolical invention that has been aimed against Cuba since the beginning of the revolution — in the United States. This is an irrefutable fact.

Later, measures were adopted — for the first time in the past twenty-six years — to guarantee normal migratory relations between two neighboring countries. By virtue of the measures adopted and in conformity with this agreement, steps have been taken for the first time to put an end to skyjacking — something that is more beneficial to them than to us, since they own far more planes than we do.

The fact that no skyjacker goes unpunished has discouraged them, and skyjacking has almost disappeared. In case anyone doesn't know it or doesn't understand it and goes ahead and skyjacks a plane, he'd better learn that in this country, far from getting a hero's welcome, he will be severely punished.

Measures have been taken to eradicate illegal departures or attempts to leave illegally and tolerance of and a hero's welcome for the hijackers of vessels and for those who try to enter the United States illegally. I imagine that they will be interested in backing up these measures and discouraging illegal departures at all costs, since twenty-five years of bitter experience are more than enough.

Measures have been taken to put an end to the unpunished terrorist attacks on the lives of Cuban officials and on Cuban facilities. Many things have changed since the times when motorboats left Miami to attack refineries, warehouses, ports, and ships in our country. We have come a long way. Measures have been adopted to normalize migratory relations.

On the above grounds, for those who have relatives in the United States and want to join them, the possibility of leaving is in keeping with our policies and our traditions of the past twenty-five years.

We have stated that making a revolution and building socialism is a task for free and conscious people. Of all voluntary things, the most voluntary is the construction of socialism in full awareness.

We have never been interested in those who fantasize about consumer society or about vice or whatever in capitalist society. We have never been interested in them, and our doors have always been open for them to leave the country. This situation has been normalized, so to speak, and it is well within our tradition.

If it is a question of someone who holds a very important post and has no immediate replacement, all right — we delay his departure as long as necessary until we find a substitute. That doesn't worry us. But the doors are open.

Of course, this has to do mainly with those who have relatives, because they are given priority. I believe that this will be good news for those who find themselves in this situation — and for us, too — and they will be able to join their relatives.

Unfortunately, we can't offer them reunification here, because our country is struggling for its development and is in need of housing, and it is logical that we give priority to those who are here working. For the time being, we can't propose reunification here — it must be reunification in the United States.

As for those who have been in prison for counterrevolutionary activities — I have already said that here, initially, there were 300 organizations. These had thousands of members — not as many as they said (30,000 or 50,000), but they did total some 15,000 members in the early years of the revolution — most of whom left the country by virtue of the plans of the revolution or the generosity of the revolution, which in one way or another arranged for their departure by reducing their prison terms or by some other means.

We are aware that the population in general rejects or mistrusts people who are involved in counterrevolutionary activities, and this is logical. Only in some instances, with much effort, can this be overcome.

For some time we have expressed our readiness to authorize all those who have been convicted of counterrevolutionary activities, together with their families, to go to the United States and stay there. All of them, naturally, think that the United States has some obligation to them because it encouraged them to carry out counterrevolutionary activities.

They feel they have the right to go to that country and to receive some compensation and have their merits recognized in some way. I think this will be very good news for them — and for us, too. This is aside from the question of those who are relatives of U.S. citizens, which is another category.

Our part of the bargain is to accept, in a reasonable period of time, the 2,746 who are considered inadmissible, or excludable, by the U.S. authorities.

In the United States, many may have thought that we couldn't — that we wouldn't be able to or wouldn't dare — discuss and find a solution for this subject, since they know the revolutionary fervor of the people and their profound rejection of those individuals who, in one way or another, left the country. However, those who think this aren't taking into consideration the people's identification with, closeness to, and confidence in the leadership of the party and the party leadership's confidence in the people.

They may be much taken aback and say: What a catastrophe! For us, this is very simple. We have performed tasks and tackled problems which have been much more difficult, and we have the moral courage to say: Yes, we will accept them.

They made the people of the United States believe that those individuals were some sort of Draculas and fearsome. In fact, they weren't so fearsome. I've already said that the really fearsome ones, the ones who committed atrocities and who embezzled fabulous amounts, had already gone to the United States and were welcomed with applause and all honors.

These individuals — I say it, and I sincerely believe it — are only a little bit dangerous, just a bit; they are no big leaguers or anything of the sort, nor are they the cream of the crop. They constitute no danger for our country.

What are we going to do with these individuals who are coming back, who will return little by little, over a period of time? We intend to honor all the agreements, not resort to any subterfuge or create any obstacles — nothing at all. We are serious. One of the characteristics of the revolution is its seriousness in doing the things it sets out to do and fulfilling its commitments.

First of all, as they arrive, we will place them in quarantine, for health considerations, since there are diseases in the United States that we don't have here — AIDS [Acquired Immune Deficiency Syndrome], for example.

Obviously, the possibility of importing any of those diseases that exist in the Western world is much greater via the thousands of people who come to Cuba and then return to the United States and the thousands who come as tourists from the Western world. But still we don't want to run the risk of acquiring them in this way.

All the medical experience gained in our country shows that the first thing is quarantine, with a rigorous medical checkup to see if there are any cases, and then adequate therapeutic measures — isolation, if necessary — health measures. We have time, and we can do it. If 1,000 were to arrive at once, we couldn't, but if 100 at the most arrive at one time, we can take all these measures.

The policy we intend to follow is that if the individual was a sick person who by chance traveled to the United States without anyone realizing it or if he got sick there — which is the most probable thing — we'll be able to ascertain everything when we have the information. We haven't been able to obtain all the information yet, because many of those people are in different places in the United States, and one of the most difficult things was the list; we wanted concrete cases, all the details, but this wasn't possible.

We, of course, were interested first of all in whether or not the person left via Mariel and whether or not he is Cuban. We even decided that if there was an agreement and someone had changed his name and by chance came but wasn't in this category he would be returned to the United States. That was agreed on in the "Minute on Implementation."

People who are mentally or otherwise ill will be sent to a hospital and receive the best care, as do all patients.

Our hospitals have worldwide prestige. It is no burden for us to accept people, even if they became ill there, and care for them in our hospitals. We are sure that they will be better cared for here than in the United States, and it won't cost them anything.

If there is a possibility of curing them, they will be cured. Many mental patients have been cured in our hospitals. I'm not talking just about citizens who left the country and became ill. We wouldn't even mind caring for U.S. citizens in our hospitals in Cuba; they would receive the best care we can provide.

Those who have been in prison ever since they arrived in the United States — there is a group of people who have been in prison for more than four years, in the Atlanta penitentiary and elsewhere — if they haven't committed any crimes in the United States and come back, after going through the physical examination, they will be given jobs. An effort will be made to reincorporate them in society, and they will have no difficulties if this is done successfully.

If they have committed any crimes in the United States or any other part of the world — any serious crime, especially bloody crimes — respect for basic ethics and for our own safety demands that they not go unpunished. We cannot allow an individual who has committed a bloody crime to return here and go free; that would be inconceivable. Therefore, even though there is no treaty or agreement on this, that person would have to serve his sentence in our country.

Cases of misdemeanors could be analyzed, but as a matter of principle, whoever has committed a crime that is punishable here will have to serve his sentence: either the one that has been imposed or the one that is stipulated by our laws.

We still have to analyze the legal aspects of the matter, but that is our intention, and it is, in fact, being applied with regard to many countries with which we have agreements: if someone commits a crime abroad, he is tried here. We don't have that commitment, but, for ethical reasons, that would be the policy we would follow in such cases. There will be no impunity for any of those crimes.

The U.S. authorities have promised to send us all the documents, details, and evidence concerning those cases; whatever crimes are proved, there will be no impunity. That is the line we intend to follow.

Mention has been made of 2,746 persons. This doesn't mean that they can send all of them back. I imagine that many of those who have been in prison for four years will choose to return if they haven't committed crimes in the United States and can, therefore, obtain their freedom in our country.

I don't think they can feel much enthusiasm for consumer society after having spent four years in a maximum security penitentiary. But, in any case, this is apart from their inclination, apart from their ideology; if they haven't committed any crimes there, we will simply follow the policy I have outlined with regard to them.

The United States may face some difficulties in sending them; many different types of legal arguments, diverse pretexts, may be employed. Some have said that if they come they will be made to suffer here and be treated as political pariahs.

The fact that they are being sent here, however, shows that they don't really have any political or ideological contradictions with the revolution, and they will be treated with a maximum of humanity and in line with the principles of the revolution, following the policy I have stated.

How many may come? We will see that in practice, but we will keep our part of the agreement. And, if they can't come, the moral and historical fact will remain for the people of the United States to see that if those people who are considered fearsome, dangerous, don't come, it isn't because we aren't willing to accept them on a rational basis, through fair and equitable agreements. We are willing to accept them, and this isn't a task that the revolution — which is accustomed to tackling difficult tasks — can't solve, employing all of its authority and moral principles.

Objectively, the discussions were characterized by a spirit of hard work. Both delegations worked intensively, and the discussions were serious, responsible, and respectful, showing a willingness to find solutions.

Several days ago, in the meeting with the students I went over and explained the current world situation and a large part of humanity's great concern over what awaits it in the coming years — especially what is going to be decided about the future in the next few months. I'm not going to repeat here what I said and those lines of reasoning.

In the coming weeks, talks that are much more important and far-reaching than these will be held.

These were limited to a specific problem: that of migration. We had no intention whatsoever of bringing up any other problems, nor are we impatient in this regard. We are calm, serene, firm, and strong. We won't implore anybody for anything; our constructive, positive, receptive stand doesn't mean that we are overconcerned about negotiations. I would like to make this clear.

There will be far more important talks, which the world is awaiting to see whether or not a ray of hope appears.

There are the talks with the Contadora group regarding Central America; the talks between the revolutionary forces and the Salvadoran government; the talks between the United States and Nicaragua in Manzanillo [Mexico]; and the very important talks that will be held in Geneva in January between Foreign Minister Gromyko of the Soviet Union and U.S. Secretary of State Shultz on matters of the utmost importance. There are the talks regarding southern Africa and the talks in other parts of the world on various topics related to peace or the world economy.

May the same spirit that characterized these talks prevail in those that are now in progress and in those that will be held in the world in the weeks and months to come. May rational results be obtained. This is possible — I repeat — if matters are discussed calmly, without arrogance, seriously, and responsibly, with a real desire to find solutions.

As I said when I spoke to the students, we have no right to harbor illusions; we must understand and bear in mind that the present world situation is a very dangerous and critical one and there are difficult and complex problems. Therefore — I repeat — no one should harbor illusions. We, especially, should not lower our guard or in any way neglect our defense, but — I repeat — these talks, on a very specific topic, on a difficult and complex problem, have been positive and constructive.

Thank you very much.

Cuba's Revolutions in Economy and Defense

Speech to National Assembly of People's Power

Two events in my opinion have led to two genuine revolutions recently: one in the field of defense and the other in the economic field. The dangers, the tense international situation and the threat of imperialist aggression, led to a revolution in defense concepts. From the time when it seemed that the task of national defense was strictly a military problem for the armed forces up until now, there has been a big change. It's not that people didn't participate in defense, they did right from the start: the workers', peasants', and students' militia, the struggle against the counterrevolutionary bandits, the Escambray [Mountain war against counterrevolutionary bands in the early 1960s], and Girón. Then came compulsory military service, and we created considerable reserves which gradually replaced the initial militia contingents. Our defense potential increased — it's not that it didn't increase before, it grew a great deal year after year in experience, cadres, and efficiency.

But there was a widely held view that defense was strictly a problem for the armed forces, just as public health is a task for the Ministry of Public Health and education for the Ministry of Education, although there has always been mass participation in all those fields: vaccination campaigns, literacy drives, worker-farmer education, etc., just as there has been mass participation in defense.

It was in the face of a situation of threats and growing danger that we started thinking and meditating on the issue in depth, fervent as ever in our readiness to defend the revolution and our country. We reached new and revolutionary ideas in the concept of defense. We went from the old idea to the idea that the military defense of the country, on the battlefield and in all the backup work in any form of attack — blockade, war of attrition, invasion, total or partial occupation of the country — was a task for both the armed forces and the people as a whole, so the people had

This speech was delivered December 28, 1984, at the close of the Seventh Session of the National Assembly of People's Power, held in Havana. It is excerpted here from the January 13, 1985, Granma Weekly Review.

to be organized and prepared for that struggle.

From the moment we came to that conclusion four years ago, just before the Second Congress of the party [in December 1980] and when the United States had elected a new president, whose policy we knew about and whose programs we knew about, we started to broaden and implement these ideas.

Can we say how much stronger we are now? If we consider the number of troops and weapons, we can say in mathematical terms that we are three times stronger. But that would be wrong, because that is something that can't be measured by the number of weapons. Weapons have been multiplied by three but the defensive capacity of the country has been multiplied by ten; we have come from being a country which theoretically could be defeated by a stronger army, with many more weapons and many planes, aircraft carriers, and tanks — from a country which theoretically could be defeated, to a country which can't be defeated either in theory or practice! [*Prolonged applause*] Because it is no longer a case of so many divisions, regiments, battalions, tanks, planes, or other units and weapons; it is a case of all the people, everywhere, for any kind of war. Modern experience has shown there is no way of defeating a country in those conditions.

This is not Europe, let us say, or some countries in this hemisphere with a brave fighting tradition. There armored divisions entered and in a matter of days, or weeks at most, they were defeated. They entered and encircled an army and the fighting stopped. Of course, with our revolutionary army, the fighting wouldn't stop. It was demonstrated in the Soviet Union; in spite of the surprise, the concentration of weapons and men with which the fascists attacked the Soviet Union, the army did not fall apart and continued fighting. The same was not the case for other places. In many places, when they would say "tanks in the rear," the white flag would go up and panic, dismay, and demoralization set in. That was the psychological basis for the famed blitzkrieg.

Well, a bourgeois regime can fight. It all depends on morale and circumstance. But in the last world war it was shown that the fighting morale of bourgeois societies was very weak. On the other hand, the fighting morale of socialism in the USSR proved to be invincible. At first, many thought it was a matter of three months, or that in three months Moscow would fall, and this would be repeated in other places, but this did not prove to be the case. What happened was that the Soviets reached Berlin and beyond in a matter of time.

There are many examples. Vietnam is an admirable and extraordinary example of a people's ability to resist. I could mention other peoples: the Salvadorans, who have been fighting in a tiny country for five years with tremendous courage and growing experience and effectiveness. There are the Saharans out in the desert, fighting so bravely and firmly. There are hundreds of thousands of Moroccan soldiers there who have built walls and invented all sorts of tactics, using sophisticated U.S. equipment, radar that can spot when a person moves, and yet the patriots attack the radar and the walls, because sometimes sophisticated equipment can't tell the difference between a man and a goat and things like that can happen. [*Laughter*] I don't want to discuss Saharan tactics, but what I mean is that sophisticated equipment can be vulnerable.

The Vietnamese demonstrated this, and the Algerians I think should be mentioned for their brave struggle for independence against one of the most powerful armies in Europe. In the desert and other difficult areas they resisted and won.

I mentioned the Soviets. We could also mention the Yugoslavs, who under Communist leadership organized the resistance and kept many German divisions at bay.

If we want, we can go further back and look at our own history, our *mambí* fighters who spent ten years [1868-78] fighting the most powerful army in Europe at the time! We were the Vietnam of last century: a population of one million, 300,000 Spanish soldiers, and a few thousand barefoot Cubans without clothing or bullets held the Spanish army at bay. And in less than fifteen years another war in 1895, and they didn't stop trying even though the country was exhausted.

Conditions in Cuba are not those of Algeria. In Algeria it was the people, a national liberation party, but part of the people fighting. I won't go into Yugoslavia, where it was also part of the people, because there were also reactionary elements that collaborated with the Germans. In El Salvador, the patriotic movement is made up of several revolutionary organizations. In our country, it is an entire people, 10 million inhabitants, united, with a single party and army, a solid mass structure, a single government; complete unity and no bourgeoisie, a solid and coherent social system. [*Applause*] A worker, peasant, and student people; a country where everybody, women and children included, would stand solid with a political and military doctrine, defending the country. A country like that can be exterminated with ten or more atom bombs, perhaps, although that would be another type of war and only possible in the framework of a world war. But twenty-two years ago, when something like that could have been possible, nobody was very worried or frightened, there was no panic or demoralization.

We have acquired an extraordinary defense potential with the participation of all the people, of the masses. And during all these years, especially in the last year, the levels of organization we possess have been demonstrated: all factories and farms are organized; the party is organized and prepared; the mass organizations, the defense zones in every corner of the country, in the mountains and plains, the cane fields and rice plantations, the swamps and the rocks, the whole state and

People's Power, every municipality and province — all are organized and prepared, and more so every day since we will continue to be prepared.

As I said when we talked with the students, even if the United States became socialist, we would have to be armed and keep our guard up, so nobody would be tempted to intimidate us, just in case there were to be a cultural revolution or some such thing in that neighboring socialist state. I won't go on, I think you understand what I mean. [*Laughter and applause*] These ideas and concepts must be definitive and we will not lower our guard, even if the policy of our powerful neighbor were to change one day, capitalist, imperialist, or even — as I say in the extreme — socialist. We will never abandon these ideas and concepts. We can coexist if they want, live in peace and mutual respect. But our people must be the ones who assure our right to exist as an independent country and with a just revolution. [*Applause*]

We can now feel more secure, more confident in the indestructible force we have created and will continue to develop; but here too we will introduce the principle of optimizing material and economic resources, energy, and everything else! We must continue doing this while at the same time applying in this field, as in all others, the principle of the conservation and optimum use of resources.

Comrades of the Ministry of the Revolutionary Armed Forces have been studying this and have made an important contribution to this economic concept and to this policy we propose to implement. The same holds for the Ministry of the Interior; they have made important savings in their field, which have by no means weakened us, simply by determining what is most important, what has priority, and what can wait. That is another principle: fortifications have top priority, the material base can wait, in line with the principle of rationalization and optimization.

In the economic field, the international crisis, the world economic disaster, the intensified imperialist blockade of our country, maneuvers to drive down the price of sugar, have all led us to another profound revolution of ideas and concepts. [*Applause*] And let me say on this that the same was happening as in the military field when, on other occasions, awhile back we would say, "our people will fight," but our people were not fully organized to fight; in theory, yes, since we already thought in terms of a people's war, but this idea had not been put into practice.

In the economic field, there was also talk of certain ideas and concepts but, as I said, there was no collective awareness, no collective will, no total determination to implement the idea. We have been carried along by the situation, and I think just as the revolution in defense concepts has gained ground, so will the revolution in economic concepts, in the long term. But everyone must make these concepts their own, absolutely everyone, the entire people! That was a people's war and this must be the economic battle of the entire people, the economic war of the whole people. [*Applause*]

The concepts are clear. We outlined them at the Forum on Energy and the Federation of Students in Intermediate Education congress.* We are making them even clearer in this assembly, and they are included in the 1985 economic plan, the long-term plan and the 1985 plan. We decided we had to start now. The entire 1985 plan was revamped and definitive versions of the 1986-90 plan and the long-term plan for the year 2000 are being drawn up on the basis of the ideas outlined in the energy forum.

Savings are our most immediate resources available, our most immediate possible source of increased earnings. The objectives can be said to be threefold: first, to solve the long-standing hard currency problem, to cope with the debt problem in this area — as I explained, our hard currency debt is the lowest in Latin America — and to meet our international commitments, as we have so far.

We said on that occasion that we're the only [underdeveloped] country that can pay the debt, that we want to pay it, that we have the will and the possibility of paying it. As the other countries, there are so many cases that really I have no idea how they're going to solve the problem. We must guarantee the amount of convertible currency our country needs every year in order to draw up our plans in a rational fashion, to add to some of the raw materials we acquire from the socialist countries those we need from the convertible currency area, which, as I said before, could be 15 percent, at the most between 17 and 18 percent as our country continues to develop. Therefore, we do need the hard currency.

Of course, the U.S. blockade makes it harder for us to carry out a policy in that direction, because they pursue us in all our commercial dealings anywhere in the world. If we sell nickel to Italy, the U.S. government sends a message putting on the pressure for them not to buy nickel from us. If we send nickel to Japan or any other country, the warning from the United States follows immediately. It seems as if they have an army of officials dedicated specifically to pressuring every Western government not to buy our nickel. And it's not a question of pressure alone.

---

*Castro's December 4, 1984, speech to the First National Forum on Energy, and the second part of his December 8, 1984, speech to the Federation of Students in Intermediate Education congress (not included in the excerpts published in this collection) reviewed the social gains of the Cuban revolution, the valuable economic relationship with the Soviet Union and Eastern European countries, and the need for Cuba to maintain economic relations with capitalist countries. Castro then laid out the need, in particular, to boost earnings from exports while reducing unnecessary imports in hard-currency exchange with the capitalist countries, and to meet economic obligations to the Soviet Union and other CMEA member countries.

They also take measures and ban the entry into the United States of any steel or equipment that contains Cuban nickel. Thus, they meticulously try to impede our nickel sales by resorting not only to diplomatic, political, and economic pressure but they also take actual measures. Whether we sell rum, tobacco, or any other article, they spend their time putting on the pressure to keep us from selling anything. Well, anyway, we've had years of experience in this matter, and we've been able to sell. In fact, we don't sell more because we have no more to sell. When we have it we sell it, that's for sure. . . .

Therefore, we have prospects. And even though things may be more difficult for us, we shouldn't be discouraged. We've never been discouraged by difficult tasks; and in this endeavor to economize, to develop quality products for export in quantity, and to find substitutes for imports, we can accomplish a great deal. We have studied a series of measures and we are going to continue putting them into effect no matter what persecuting action the imperialists take against us in this regard. We will thank them for having helped us to reflect on and revolutionize our economic conceptions. All right, that's one part of the problem.

I've been quite clear already about the second part: we must meet our commitments with the socialist countries. We have no financial problems with the socialist countries, mainly with the Soviet Union, which is our main creditor. During the renegotiation of our debt, the capitalist countries, egged on by the United States, wanted to know how much we owed to the Soviet Union. We said that that had nothing to do with it, that we had never had financial problems with the Soviet Union. They've always given us every facility, have renegotiated the debt almost automatically; they have extended it, have granted long-term no-interest postponement. They have given us billions in credits every five-year period and provided us with an increasing flow of supplies on credit.

We're working on large and important economic projects with Soviet cooperation, technology, and credits: the new refinery in Cienfuegos; the nickel processing plant in Punta Gorda, now in the completion stage; large thermoelectric projects; the plant in Santa Clara for making sugar mill components; the expansion of the Antillana de Acero steelworks; and the nuclear power plant in Cienfuegos. When this plant's four generators go into operation it will mean a $500 million savings of oil. We're already thinking of building another plant of this type in eastern Cuba and a third later in the western part of the island. In addition to many other economic projects, the Soviet Union is cooperating with us in very large measure in prospecting for oil, gas, and minerals and in the construction of pipelines for our oil. When we start producing two million tons of oil, we won't be able to transport it in trailer tanks. They are also helping us to build the port for supertankers, which also calls for the installation of pipelines to bring the crude oil to the refineries and from there to the large consumption areas. Thus, the Soviet Union is cooperating with us on many projects under construction, in planning, with all the credits and facilities we've needed.

As a matter of elementary honor, of elementary interest to our country, of consideration and respect for the socialist community — because they also need our products — we must strictly comply with the sacred principle of meeting our commitments to the socialist countries. [*Applause*] If we have a bad harvest due to hurricanes, catastrophes, drought, blights, or whatever, we will not deprive the Soviet Union of part of its sugar to sell it on the world market. If we need hard currency then we must find it some other way instead of through the easy, comfortable — and I might add somewhat irresponsible — procedure of taking part of the sugar earmarked for the Soviet people and exporting it to the hard currency area. That is not the way to solve hard currency problems. This is the second basic point we have raised.

Now we come to the third point, as important or perhaps more important than the others: our development programs. What shall we do with the resources we have? We have abundant resources. What we receive from the Soviet Union alone in a five-year period, from merchandise and cargo to credits, runs to over 20 billion rubles. More than 20 billion rubles' worth of equipment, plant, fuel, wheat, foodstuffs, raw materials, lumber, steel. We have already studied, discussed, and agreed on what we are going to receive in the next five years. There was an excellent CMEA meeting held here at the end of October that made for an excellent opportunity to seriously analyze and discuss problems, prospects, the relations of cooperation among all the countries of the socialist community and ourselves as part of that community, the great privilege enjoyed by this revolution.

How many Third World countries can say today that they have the privilege to belong to the socialist community and have an unlimited market for their exports? Finding markets was always a nightmare for Cuba and the Third World countries and now we have an unlimited market and excellent prices in the socialist community.

We have solved the problem of trade relations — the Third World countries' terrible problem of unequal trade with the industrialized capitalist countries — in our trade with the socialist community. These are things the underdeveloped world is clamoring for. We have all these resources and this privilege, plus a united people, a revolution, and a level of general knowledge higher than that of the Third World countries and even some industrialized countries.

If you visit some of the European industrialized countries and even the United States you'll find in some areas an illiteracy and semiliteracy rate that no longer exists here. We have tens of thousands of technicians who are university trained, engineers, doctors, economists, and teachers, and hundreds of thousands of intermediate-level technicians and skilled workers. You'll find dozens of veterinarians, agronomists, and irrigation specialists in any one of our state farms. That goes for any branch. In the oil industry all we had in the past, I believe, was one geologist. Now we have hundreds of specialists who are university graduates. And the same goes for all fields. Over 240,000 students are enrolled in higher education courses; close to 100,000 of them are full-time students. In other words, we have an inexhaustible source of talent. In addition to our own technicians, we have technicians from the socialist area, and every time we have requested their cooperation they have given it. In every field, in electricity, steel, agriculture, they have always been at our disposal.

Can we or can't we make optimal and rational use of these resources and potential? Can we or can't we find definitive strategic solutions to the problems of our economy and development? That's what we were talking about. That is the task that will not take a year or even five years. It will take at least fifteen years, from now through the year 2000. And we must go about it painstakingly, rigorously, intelligently, and seriously for those fifteen years.

This is what we talked about a month ago when we met to analyze these problems. The members of the [Communist Party] Political Bureau and the Secretariat met with all the vice-presidents of the Executive Committee, the ministers in all areas of the economy and the other areas, the first secretaries of the party in the provinces, the leaders of the mass organizations, and the presidents of People's Power in the provinces. We met for three days, November 22, 23, and 24, and spent more than thirty hours analyzing and making some decisions. Many ideas were put forth and most of them will have to be studied, but we've already adopted the first one: the plan for 1985, what we should do in 1985. In the light of these ideas, a central working group was set up, headed by Comrade Osmany [Cienfuegos] and with Humberto [Pérez] as vice-president. The group is already working with the participation of all the vice-presidents of the Council of Ministers, all the ministers and the heads of party departments. They were given the task of working on an emergency basis, in permanent session, in order to apply those ideas to the 1985 plan. The presidents of People's Power provincial assemblies also took part in this work.

The plan was studied and rewritten on the basis of these new ideas, and investments were also prioritized on the basis of the ideas I've explained. First, those that will yield export products in the hard currency area, substitute imports, guarantee exports to the socialist area, or have to do with social projects of great importance to the population, and after that, the rest. The principle of absolute priority for those economic objectives must be strictly observed. This is our policy regarding investments.

The most immediate task we could tackle was the policy and plan to be followed regarding economizing on fuel and materials. A study of all stocks was made, along with the adoption of a series of measures that were explained here this afternoon. The effort really bore fruit. First of all, it aroused great enthusiasm and great interest among all the comrades, because the conceptual revolution also revolutionized the idea, the way the plan should be drawn up, how it should be implemented, and how it should be supervised with the participation of all the sectors of the economy, of the entire government, as a task involving the whole government. Thus, the plan has become a task for the entire government and, I might add, for all the people, because it has to be a plan embraced by all the people. . . .

What were some of the things we did? We reduced by 320 million the construction program that had been prepared for 1985. This meant a savings of about $70 million in fuel and materials that can be exported and materials that won't be imported. By this way alone, I repeat, there was a $70 million reduction in hard currency expenditure in the construction sector alone.

Now then, no fundamental project was sacrificed, not even the major projects that involve big investments over many years. We will continue our major projects: the nuclear plant, as fast as possible, with the plans and the imported equipment that we have there awaiting installation; the oil refinery, Punta Gorda, CMEA 1, all these investments in cooperation with the Soviet Union that lead to exports to the socialist camp or to important savings. Investments that earn hard currency have been left untouched as have all the fundamental social projects — some have been mentioned here — such as the cardiovascular surgery service for children and the program designed for this purpose.

In my opinion, this is very important because it is estimated that one out of every 100 children is born with congenital heart problems. Since the total number of births in the country is 150,000-160,000, there would be 1,500-1,600 such infants. Without special care, 80 percent of half of them — as a noted Czech specialist explained to me and according to the international experience upon which these data are based — die in the first year of life. While others may not die in the first year, many do so afterwards. We are in the process of developing a modern cardiovascular surgery service for adults in the western, central, and eastern parts of the country and at the William Soler Hospital for children. The latter will be the national center that will support and draw support from other services in the interior. This will reduce infant mortality. Given the level we have achieved, it won't be easy to lower. There must be very special programs to lower it, but I think these services can reduce the rate — these are preliminary estimates that must be followed up — by three points, that is, if we have reached 15 this year, then it can drop to 12 in the future. There is prenatal genetics that we are starting to apply and this will reduce the rate even more. A one point drop will become increasingly difficult from then on. The rate for 1984 appears to be about 15 or slightly less or slightly more. Pinar del Río, previously one of the most backward — "Cinderella" — is about 13.7 and the other provinces are around 13.0.

Then we will have to see what areas have higher rates. A rigorous and tenacious struggle will be required to continue advancing after the progress that has been made. That's how we must struggle in all fields — painstakingly in this and everything else.

That is a very important social program, which is of interest to all families in this country and the people as a whole. It is more important than any other project. I think all are important; it isn't easy to draw comparisons. Let's say this cardiovascular service we are developing is more important than a recreational center. And so on.

Important research centers have been included; important and very significant health projects are on the list, such as the program for medical schools, because of its importance in the future and in order to meet the needs of the thousands of students who have enrolled in the last three years. We have also included the development of the schools of technology because we plan to reach an enrollment of about 50,000 students in the field of advanced technology, which involves personnel training in electronics, computers, machinery construction — engineers of all kinds, highly skilled personnel. We are creating both wealth and a solid economic foundation. This program has great intermediate-term economic and social importance.

If we had to sacrifice one of them to give priority to investments that earn hard currency, we would have done it; it would have had to be that way. Of course, we knew that with judicious use of available resources we could handle both the top-priority economic projects and the most important ones of a social nature. A certain percentage of investments will go for objectives in the hard currency area and the other for those in the socialist camp. Some of the latter, such as nickel, also lead to hard currency earnings or save imports that require hard currency spending. Between the two, they account for 40 percent of investments.

Ah, but there's enough left to attend to those projects of great social importance and to follow other plans, even the housing program. There is a housing program, which includes around 19,000 dwellings which, when added to those built by agencies with their own means, can run to 35,000 for which the state is responsible. This amount, plus the dwellings that the people on their own can build, could reach 75,000 in all. It's not a bad little program for housing construction. I think we should take these details into account. In reality, we have seen that construction resources give us certain scope, but we have to use them rationally. The proposed plan for 1985 had to be decreased by 320 million.

There are some things that interest us, that we like, but that simply have to wait, as I was telling the comrades on the Central Committee. We all have projects that we like, all of us. There's no one here who doesn't have a project that he likes. I have several; many are related to education, health, research centers, even sports. All of us would like to improve sports and have more swimming pools, for example, to develop swimming in which we are far behind. We've said: no more personal preferences! No one here has a project. No more subjectivism, regardless of the situation; everyone must guide themselves according to the indicated criteria. I began by renouncing all those I used to defend. Then I asked if a certain center still remained and it did, and if another thing was still left, and it was, but others weren't. I myself said: I'm very interested in the children's hospitals of Bayamo, Ciego [de Avila], Sancti Spíritus, and the one here in Marianao, in Havana.

I remember that this idea came up during the dengue epidemic [of 1981], when we saw the need for these specialized facilities for children and the plans were made and the work was begun. Now I say: there's no hurry. We can continue to make do with what we have; we have expanded and improved all the children's hospitals in recent years and we've built intensive care units in them all. If we have to wait one, two, or three years to move ahead with the construction of these hospitals we can wait. I am tremendously concerned about these hospitals, on such a high-quality blueprint as that which has been drawn up, being built. They are going to be better than those that we now have, because many of our children's hospitals are old hospitals that have been adapted for pediatrics. Nevertheless, we must wait. Regarding the research centers, I said that there are some that seem fundamental to me: the genetic engineering and biotechnology center, for example, which is of enormous long-term economic and medical interest. So in that we are moving ahead and our center is being built as rapidly as possible. That is one which falls in the category of great scientific, social, and economic importance. We'll look at the others, one by one, to see which have acquired equipment that is already here and the importance each has.

The plan was thus worked out according to these criteria; 1985 investments were analyzed in this way. I can't say that it's perfect. Something could have been left out which might be a little more important than something else, but what was achieved in such a short time was a great deal. I think that it will be better next year. I think that if we work with the work force that we have, the resources that the country has, the existing production of materials, we can attend to all spheres, following an order; sticking to the priorities we can continue to advance in the social sphere. . . .

It may be that there are things we want right now that we can't do, but within ten or fifteen years we may be able to take on many more projects which otherwise we would never have been able to do. We are going to set aside some of our wants and aspirations for the time being, but we are going to multiply our capacity to do things in the future, things which are much better, more stimulating, and more encouraging than those we can do now. We are going to multiply our capacity on solid foundations, on the basis of solid programs and a solid economy. These are, shall we say, the ideas. I've gone into detail, taking advantage of the occasion to inform the population, because this must be everyone's battle.

Some measures for economizing are strong. In two words, the economy grew by 7.4 percent in 1984; in 1985 it will grow by a further 4 to 5 percent. I repeat once again, the percentages do not matter; what we have to examine and analyze here next year in the assembly and everywhere is in what areas is there growth and what does this 4 to 5 percent mean. The measures for saving are strong. The 1985 plan calls for from 4 to 5 percent more than what was achieved this year, and, moreover, with less fuel and less electricity than in 1984, as has been presented. The fuel oil for electricity even is set at 0.1 percent less than 1983, diesel fuel and gasoline at less than 1984, all the fuels at less than 1984.

Comrades know, especially all those in the sugar industry, how fuel can be saved. They began by saving a half million tons alone in the production of raw sugar, thanks to a sustained effort over several years. This coming year they are going to save considerable amounts in refining sugar, and in other areas, keeping the bagasse [sugar residue] and using it as fuel. Nevertheless, the 1985 plan, in general, is tight. The goals are tight and demand effort and real saving. Don't think: let's see what someone else is saving; but rather let's see what I can save, what each one of us can save.

It's not so easy in some cases, as a worker explained who won a prize in the Forum on Energy, who had saved hundreds of tons of fuel at the Santiago de Cuba refinery. He said: I've saved a certain amount but that was after already having saved a lot, after the great savings we'd previously made. This was as if to say: it's increasingly more difficult to save a ton. In other words, we're already beginning at important levels of savings.

Another principle which was established and which was especially fought for was: we have to solve the problem without affecting the population's standards. In other words, we have to move forward with this policy without affecting what the population already receives. The plan has been developed on this basis. Some gratuities which persist and which must end were mentioned here with a view to saving. They involve a few items such as cigarettes and cigars whose greatest saving is very advantageous because they comprise export funds. Population consumption levels will essentially be maintained and there will even be some increases in certain lines.

Nevertheless, as I put it to the students and in the Forum on Energy, we must begin with what we have and not think about new increases beyond what we have, at both the personal and social levels. There will always inevitably be some improvements beyond what we already have, and basic strategic problems will be solved in the next fifteen years.

Were we in Haiti, the truth is that it would be a little hard to say to the people: we'll make do with what we have. The same would be the case in many other places in Latin America where people are dying of starvation, where there is huge unemployment, poverty, children begging, illiteracy, high infant mortality, low life expectancy, lack of health care, in essence, where everything is lacking. It would be hard to say: make do.

I truly wonder if for us to put forward this policy is something intolerable or impossible. That's why I said to the young: you have to take up these ideas, this strategy, because this is the world that we are leaving to you, that our generation is going to leave to the students who are now between fifteen and twenty years old.

At current life expectancy rates it's estimated that they will be less than halfway through life in the year 2000. They have to think: What kind of world are we going to inherit or what kind of world are we going to build? This is not only the concern of intermediate-level students; it is the concern of all young people, of everyone who is at present less than twenty-five or thirty years of age.

There are two problems then. Our generation has a responsibility to future generations, which is what kind of country are we going to hand over to them in a world which we know to be complex, which has problems unsolved. We say: What kind of country are we going to hand over to you in fifteen years? And the young people must also pose the problem: What kind of country are we going to have in the year 2000? What kind of country are we going to be fighting for? Because this will be your country, your resources, your economic, technical, scientific, and material possibilities. It will be their duty and ours, our responsibility and theirs. That's why I think that the young must also take up these ideas. And we must also, because it is our responsibility.

Is it difficult? No, because fortunately, over all these years we have really avoided the calamities which befall other Third World countries. A huge amount of effort and resources has gone into solving these problems over the years. Why were we able to do this? Logically, it should be the reverse: let's devote everything to development and then we'll attend to these problems. Well, because we had international solidarity;

because we had the cooperation of the socialist countries. The path of the revolution was not such a great sacrifice for us. From the very beginning, we were able to devote many resources to social development.

First we began with the country's defense which was, is, and will be the absolute priority. Then came literacy, the first rural hospitals, the struggle against unemployment, the beginnings of reforestation programs, the sending of teachers and doctors to all corners of the country, to all the provinces. Cultural and sports activities began to be developed and great social reforms were made. Urban reform came into being in that period, and the reduction of rents by almost half of what used to be paid had important economic implications. What we are doing now means nothing; it affects virtually nothing in the country's economic sphere. But what we did in 1959 put many millions of pesos into circulation; it liberated or took away income from the bourgeoisie and gave it to the people. The present Housing Law does not imply any immediate increase in circulation.*

The Agrarian Reform released peasants from the payment of rent, from all that, even taxes; it also put many millions into circulation. Then came the nationalization of large enterprises, the banks, foreign trade, and the country's mining resources; structural changes; and, above all, the survival of the revolution. The country demonstrated its capacity to survive and embark on economic and social development.

There was really very little economic progress during the early years; there couldn't be. Rather, existing wealth was redistributed and many problems were solved: educational opportunities for everyone, the beginning of scholarship programs that would later benefit hundreds of thousands of young people, work opportunities for everyone, and unemployment was eradicated. And then, social ills such as begging, prostitution, gambling, drugs, all that disappeared. Health services and education were made available to all. Minimum pensions were increased and social security was extended to all workers. When the revolution triumphed, all the retirement funds had been embezzled. There were sugar workers who were given six pesos as retirement pay and now almost one billion is invested every year in social security. Much later thousands of elementary and junior and senior high schools were built in the countryside and in the cities, as well as technical, vocational, and teacher-training schools, and schools for sports and physical education instructors, and for training athletes, vocational military schools, art

---

*A new housing law was approved at this meeting of the National Assembly of People's Power, granting all Cubans who did not currently own their apartment or house the legal title to it, to be paid in monthly installments set at the same rate as their current rent. The new law was designed to help relieve the effects of Cuba's housing shortage.

schools, and schools for intermediate-level health workers, etc. Hundreds of polyclinics and other health facilities were built. University education was extended to all the provinces.

With accumulated experience the revolution became strong and was institutionalized, the socialist constitution was enacted and People's Power was established. This was a tremendous advance. Errors were rectified and correct criteria adopted in the economic sphere, in management and planning methods. The socialist formula of to each according to his work — an unavoidable principle in the phase of socialist construction which we had ignored for a time — was applied. The First Congress of the party was held and the Programmatic Platform was drawn up.

There has been considerable progress over the last ten years. People's Power has demonstrated its strength not only in that which concerns the population, development, and in solving the country's problems, but also right now in the military sphere. In other words, we have made constant progress, at times more slowly, at other times more rapidly, leading up to these last years in which, as I say, we are coming to a culminating point in the accumulation of experience and knowledge of the revolution, the party, and cadres, which is reflected in these two great revolutions in the concepts of defense and the economy. And we've come this far with tremendous accumulated resources, with tremendous social progress! The figures demonstrate this: school enrollment for ages six to sixteen is more than 90 percent; more than 240,000 university students; 258,000 professors and teachers; 20,500 doctors; tens of thousands of engineers, architects, economists, and higher-level technicians; and hundreds of thousands of intermediate-level technicians trained by the revolution; a solid and organized vanguard party; experienced party members, a youth that is demonstrably strong, enthusiastic, and revolutionary; excellent young people and magnificent students.

Well, they are an inestimable force; put to good, optimal use, this force can set itself any goal and achieve it.

Given what has been achieved, I think our people can easily take this decision: we are going to devote ourselves to development, to intelligent and strategic development as something fundamental.

Referring to the reports given here on the situation of health and doctors, what is our misfortune? Are there such bad problems in store for us when, in 1983, we had one doctor for every 526 inhabitants; and now, in 1984, we have one for every 486 inhabitants; and for 1985, with all this effort, all this rationalization and this policy of austerity which I am outlining, we'll have one doctor for every 445 inhabitants. It won't be long before we have one for less than every 400, and already direct medical care is being extended to families in their neighborhoods. More than 200 new doctors began this year to work directly with more than 25,000 families. We will graduate 2,400 doctors in 1985 and no less than 500 will be involved in that program. Look at the possibilities offered by what we have, and these family doctors do not cost us hard currency!

They are going to care for and give security and well-being to the people. These doctors are going to fight to reduce infant mortality, mortality in the first year of life, and to prolong the life of adults. They are demonstrating this where they are working, evidencing a really extraordinary and promising experience.

The Ministry of Education is already beginning to graduate the first thousands of college-degree elementary school teachers who will work with first-graders on up. We are already talking about how we are going to improve on university admissions.

We have been talking about the cultural sphere in the Central Committee meeting. Our newspapers, which are included in the investment plan, will have an excellent and modern material base allowing our national papers to be simultaneously printed in the western, central, and eastern parts of the country, thus saving on costly transportation.

This program that I am outlining does not mean that there'll be a social status quo, far from it. We'll be able to make extraordinary progress with what we've established and accumulated, especially in qualitative terms. I have no doubt that every year we'll continue to lower the infant mortality rate, even if only by a fraction of a point, and that every year we'll lengthen our people's life expectancy. I have no doubt that we'll have better health, educational, cultural, recreational, and sports conditions and that we'll also have better material conditions. But material improvement is not the heart of the matter. The philosophy behind our strategy involves prioritizing economic development and not consumption. Once we've prioritized the objectives and made optimal use of resources to ensure the future, what remains available will be distributed in the most appropriate and beneficial way for our people. This involves an austere, far-sighted, intelligent program that we can develop under social conditions which are better than in any other Third World country and any other Latin American country. It is a program with a clear and secure path forward, closely linked to the socialist community and to the Soviet Union. This is the future — let there be no doubt about it — because socialism is the future.

The imperialists, the reactionaries, launch a growing campaign against socialism, about whether it is having problems and crises. Those who have problems and crises in reality are the capitalists. I hear talk about capitalist plans. Here, for example, we can now analyze how many doctors, teachers, college graduates in elementary education, education and sports instructors, cultural workers, engineers, and intermediate- and higher-level technicians and skilled workers we are going to have in 1990, and in 1995, and in the year 2000. We can analyze what each one will be doing and what material production and service levels we'll be able to achieve. But what I see the capitalists planning is the unemployment they are going to have and whether a certain country will have so many unemployed in 1985, 1986, and 1990. What's interesting, and amazing, is that they continue as if all were well! They have planned unemployment; they can also plan the debt and social problems. I think they can plan them well. What problems they are going to have in the year 2000 and which ones the Third World and Latin America are going to have can be said because they are huge problems, with no solution in sight.

I think that we also have a duty and a very big responsibility in the economic terrain. We have to deepen our economic awareness. We cannot rest on our laurels and our glories because we have achieved many things. In terms of the economy, our cadres, all of us have generally had an approach, an idea that we must rectify. Once and for all. Everyone knew what was needed when the revolution triumphed. Jobs were needed for everyone, yes, jobs for everyone in one thing or another. So many schools and 20,000 teachers were needed. So many doctors and hospital facilities were needed. So many tractors were needed, as well as buses for transportation. So much of this and so much of that.

We spent the last twenty-five years listening to all comrades speak about what they need and request what they need; but what is more incredible, receive what they need over these twenty-five years: education, public health, culture, the universities, science, technology, sports, and social security. It used to be said: I have so many about to retire, I'm going to spend 250 million this year, and another, since there are more, 300 million. How much is needed for the aqueduct and sewage systems that service the towns and how much for the maintenance of cities, roads, and highways? I am no longer talking about economic but social development — that's the way it always was before People's Power. After People's Power was set up, it was added to the national agencies and the demand grew.

Now I'm going to pose a question: Were any of you, any province or any municipality, ever denied the funds requested for the annual budget to pay doctors, teachers, and nurses? Before the triumph of the revolution, I think that there were some 800 nurses; now we have 35,000 and another 30,000-plus intermediate-level health workers. There are around 650,000 workers alone in education and health. I have almost lost count of the budgets for these two activities, but it's around two billion–plus. They always had all the resources they requested for all the services. They may not have had certain equipment that could not be acquired, but they had the funds, the facilities, the material resources, and the food they requested — for the day-care centers, cultural complexes, everything, for all the good, fine things that came about here. No one ever lacked the resources! If they had transportation or other problems, everything possible was done to solve them. That is a reality. It's not that I don't understand the fine spirit, the love for the people, and the desire to solve age-old problems that inspire these efforts. I myself personally pushed for many of these programs.

In these twenty-five years there was never anyone who asked where the money came from, where the resources came from, what a mystery, what a miracle — or as I was saying in the Central Committee — what an Aladdin's lamp it was; everything could be requested and it never ran out!

It must be said that all the national agencies, the provinces, the municipalities, and the mass organizations behaved in the same way: we want to launch a campaign for the sixth grade, we need so many teachers; if we have 80,000 cultural groups, a million Pioneers, we need school cafeterias, boarding schools, university scholarships. I think there are something like 50,000 among the regular students — 50,000 university scholarship students! There weren't any when the revolution began, nor were there any boarding schools. I don't know if there was a little orphans' home. Yes, there was the charity orphanage and some rural civic institute or other from previous times. At present, we have more than a million students who have school lunches, and some have breakfast, lunch, and dinner in the schools — more than a million!

There were virtually no workers' dining rooms in this country. How many such dining rooms do we now have in the services and factories and farms! How many workers have lunch at their work place! This is in addition to the midmorning and midafternoon snacks in many centers, with the usual loss of time and disorganization they generally create. These are considerable figures. We have done all this over these years, virtually everything that everyone requested. How was this miracle possible? But it has been a fact, and no one ever wondered where the resources came from.

I'm going to say that the resources, in part, came from the efforts of our people, but what essentially made possible these advances and the solution of all these problems was international solidarity, the solidarity of the socialist camp and primarily the Soviet Union. That is the truth. We achieved certain prices for our sugar and for our nickel and other products, in addition to the loans, and they always met their commitments to us, although many times we did not meet ours, when a plan didn't work out or a production goal was not met. We are able to rely on tremendous resources, not only for our economic development but also for considerable social development.

It's true that in our efforts to meet our obligations with the socialist camp, on occasions we set goals that were beyond our potential, like the idea to achieve ten million tons of sugar in 1970. The price we were receiving at that time was six cents, 50 percent higher than the world market price. The goal of achieving such production levels was inspired by the objective of having resources to be able to acquire merchandise from the Soviet Union, including the fuel to meet our country's growing needs. Despite our efforts, we did not achieve the ten million; we failed to meet the sugar commitments that had been contracted on the basis of that program. Nevertheless, the Soviet Union continued to meet all their export commitments to Cuba.

After 1970, sugarcane production dropped and later, when recovery was consistent and the country was meeting its contract commitments each year, sugarcane smut inflicted severe losses. What I want to point out is simply that none of these factors directly affected us. None of the problems that on several occasions damaged sugar production and export plans — a cane blight, or drought, or problems of any kind, subjective or objective — lowered the rate of expenditures in education. These grew annually, as did those in public health, culture, and social security. Everything continued to be done. Everything continued to advance throughout the twenty-six years. The Soviet Union never failed in its cooperation.

That was our privilege, but it also created a mentality among us. Everything was solved; everything was secure. No one ever asked: Did exports to the socialist countries increase? Did hard currency exports increase? Everyone drew up a plan, with its demands and requests, but never asked if production increased, if exports increased. This is the reality. And that habit must also be eradicated with this revolution in economic conceptions. We already have sufficient maturity, experience, and wisdom to understand and be concerned about things. When the price of sugar on the world market dropped and lowered our hard currency income — and this happened many times — never were any of the programs I mentioned affected; never did the people suffer the consequences of any of these junctures. Because of our seriousness, the country gained credits and, by way of credits, maintained the population's living standards in many circumstances such as these, with low sugar prices. We have to take a close look at these issues: assembly delegates, all delegates at the [local People's Power] circumscription level and all the people. Because I know that it's you who are constantly asked: When will this street be repaired? When will there be water here? How will this be solved? You will have to educate the voters and explain to them what can be done and what cannot be done in each place to solve each problem. . . .

I'm not denying in the least the extraordinary virtues evidenced by our people and our cadres in many respects. Nonetheless, I can't rightfully say they have been excellent managers, that they have been economy-minded. I should rather say we have consumed a lot, even if we have done excellent things. The stone and cement we put into building factories, dams, roads, schools, and hospitals, in our country's economic and social development — all that was an excellent thing. But I believe that had we invested these resources better, we would have accomplished a lot more. I believe that had we known then what we know today, had we had the experience earlier, had we arrived at these concepts sooner, we could have accomplished a lot more.

Many things we discovered as we went along, but others we've discovered now are the result of meditation. The enemy has actually helped us both in our defense and our economy, what with the blockade, the growing blockade and the crisis, which is a crisis of the world capitalist system. It is not simply a passing crisis, since they are up against many insoluble problems, ranging from growing environmental pollution to chronic and growing unemployment in the developed capitalist societies, the huge foreign debt and the ruin of the Third World — composed of their former colonies — the poverty and recurring starvation of billions of people in the world.

But we in particular must be thankful to them for what we have learned. With what we now have, and the strength, the experience, and the organization we have achieved, we are going to work hard and with renewed enthusiasm in the years ahead.

We have grown stronger. We have increased the security of the country. We shall be observing what goes on in the world — I already spoke about this to the students, explaining our stand, the importance we attached to the need for achieving a climate of détente and peace in the world, how vital that was. For us, there are great hopes for development, for progress; we've already attained in a short period of time many social goals that other nations propose to attain in the next twenty or thirty years.

As we listen to the United Nations speaking about "health for all in the year 2000," we can't help but think that such a goal, which is set for the Third World, is already behind what we have accomplished. It could also be said education for all in the year 2000 or, more realistically, education for all in the year 2020. Because already the educational levels achieved by Cuba have exceeded what the Third World can perhaps achieve by the year 2020, if they can be achieved at all — something highly questionable unless they perform a revolutionary and social miracle and put an end to the exploitation, unequal exchange, and injustice prevailing in a great part of the world. That's a fact.

What goals can we set ourselves in the next fifteen years? What we have done in these twenty-six may be nothing compared to what we can do, especially if we measure what we do not in quantitative but in qualitative terms, in terms of good sense and our good effort. We can make the next fifteen years qualitatively much more fruitful than the last twenty-six, of this I am sure. We have a great multiplier effect, and have accumulated notable human and intellectual resources. We have not used our economic and material resources in the best possible way, nor have we made the best use of our human resources — we also said this at the Central Committee meeting. Of course, this is not the most pressing thing for the moment, because now the greatest objective limitations on economic growth are raw materials, this or that material or imported good. But what I said was: If a service can function with 1,000 workers, why have 1,500? When we have 500 more, we need dining rooms and rations for 500 more, transportation and homes for 500 more, and salaries for 500 more. We can discover huge reserves when we delve into the use made of human resources. As I said, this is not something which is a problem for the moment; it will take time because, among other things, the problem of moving people from one sector to another takes time.

We don't want to have anybody jobless, but I think that in the next fifteen years we can transfer many improperly used human resources to necessary services and activities. If there are twenty-five people in a place and ten too many, wouldn't it be better for those ten to render a useful service in a necessary economic activity, as community health workers or helping build homes or in new industrial centers or solving problems of services, that is, in socially useful activity? We will have huge reserves of human resources when used properly, but this is not a task for the moment. What we must do is study this well and take great care not to incur in useless labor force expenditure.

I repeat, the reserves are enormous, and I think that in the next fifteen years we can do much better than we have done so far in rationalizing our efforts and optimizing our material and human resources; it is not only a duty to our country, it is a duty to the world, to the progressive movement, and to socialism because — I repeat — socialism has possibilities which capitalism will never have. Socialism advances. It has problems, of course, but it will overcome them. Its future is certain and it can safely and realistically set itself economic goals for 1990, 1995, or the year 2000, which the capitalist system can't do. The capitalist system is in crisis and will have to resign itself to philosophizing and answering a certain question as to whether such a system can survive much longer and whether the Third World can survive with the system that has been imposed on it. In response to those who open their mouth to slander and speak of crisis in the socialist camp, at the meeting of the Central Committee I used certain data which, to conclude, I would like to repeat here.

For example, in 1981 the USSR — after the war! — raised industrial output to a par with that of the whole world in 1950. In 1950, world energy output was 988 billion kilowatt–hours; that of the USSR in 1981 was 1.326 trillion, and that was four years ago. World oil production, including condensed gas, was 521 million tons in 1950; in 1981, the USSR produced 608.8 million tons. In natural gas, world production for 1950 was 191 billion cubic meters, while in 1981 the USSR produced 434 billion cubic meters. World synthetic and plastic resin production in 1950 was 1.6 million tons, while in the USSR in 1981 it was 4.1 million tons. The world figure for 100 percent nutritive mineral fertilizer was 15 million tons in 1950; the figure was 26 million for the USSR in 1981. Cement: 134 million for the whole world in 1950 and 127.2 million for the USSR in 1981. The figures for the whole world include the United States as the main industrial power.

The cities, the economic and social infrastructure of the United States, and its factories were untouched by World War II. The destruction of war did not affect them. Their deaths on the battlefield were only a few hundred thousand. The most industrialized part of Europe suffered losses which were much less severe than those in the USSR. On the other hand, the USSR had 20 million killed and who knows how many wounded or incapacitated. Two out of every five persons killed in World War II were from the Soviet Union. Their agriculture, livestock, main communications links, and industry were virtually destroyed.

I wonder if any society or people have ever carried out a similar feat under those conditions. But is that the only feat of the USSR and the Soviet people? I think an opportunity such as this is a very good one for our revolutionary learning process, for deepening our revolutionary awareness and understanding realities, recalling how the Soviet people made their revolution.

They were not one of the most industrialized countries. On the contrary, Germany, England, France, and the United States were far superior to the old tsarist empire in industrial development at the start of World War I. Then came the fighting, the destruction, the October revolution, and intervention. Only a small section of that huge country was left under revolutionary control at times; the rest was occupied. And yet they were capable of resisting amidst hunger and the worst of conditions. They won and started to build socialism under those incredibly unfavorable circumstances. It actually can't even be said that they were building socialism in 1920, 1921, and 1922; they started by trying to regain prewar production levels with no aid of any kind, none at all, with their own resources, exporting the wheat needed to feed themselves and fight hunger, to buy some machinery and equipment; exporting the cotton they needed for clothing and the leather they needed for shoes. Amidst those terrible conditions and with no foreign aid, in a devastated and backward country, with severe winters, with an illiteracy rate of 80 percent, they started to build socialism.

The first five-year plan started in 1928. By the end of three five-year periods, they had virtually industrialized that country, and with what sacrifice! The third five-year plan had not concluded when again there was aggression from abroad, attack from fascist Germany, destroying thousands of villages, cities, and factories. In the midst of war, they proved capable of moving factories and reorganizing production, increasing arms production, and even developing new equipment. The Western world has always exaggerated the aid they provided at that time with certain raw materials and a limited amount of transportation and military equipment. But it was from Soviet tank, cannon, airplane, machine gun, and rifle factories that the weapons which decided the war came.

The country was destroyed again. In less than twenty years the reactionaries, the capitalist invaders, and the fascists destroyed the country twice. Only a revolutionary country such as that could have resisted and defeated the fascist hordes, in spite of the surprise, absolutely surprise attack. We could go into why it was a surprise, what mistakes were made, but that's not the point. The important thing is to analyze the nature of the attack, the losses, the casualties, the destruction it caused, and how once again, without any help, they rebuilt the country and in just thirty-one years, in 1981, reached the 1950 level of world industrial production. Let capitalism come up with a similar example, in any other period of history, or in any capitalist country. Not only that, they wiped out centuries of ignorance and poverty, of backwardness, in just a few decades, starting in October 1917. What a tremendous effort! How they did it with their own resources!

It is good to recall this because we have the economic privilege of the existence of the socialist camp. When we were without oil, they sent the oil; and when nobody wanted to sell us even a bullet, they sent us the arms and ammunition we needed. When we lost our traditional sugar markets, they purchased our sugar. When the United States subjected us to an economic blockade and desperately tried to prevent anybody from selling us food, medicine, raw materials, or equipment, they supplied us with all they could.

Thanks to all this, not only have we made great economic and social gains but we are now building things like the nuclear power plant, the new oil refinery, big nickel plants, and other factories, which require an investment of billions of pesos.

We were very privileged. We did not have to pay the price in sacrifice that was paid by the Soviet people. That is the truth. We could even allow ourselves the unconscious luxury of not worrying too much about using up supplies of fuel and material resources. Now the party, the party leadership, and the government are aware of all this, as are the comrades of the National Assembly and, I think, the people as a whole. That is why I have spoken at length and gone into detail, explaining things in my characteristic frankness, confident as always in the moral value and importance of truth, certain that we will attain our goals.

I do not underestimate what we have done so far — we have done a great deal — but I think we can and should do more and do it better. That is what it is all about and that is the strategy we have been discussing and discussing in detail at that meeting of the party and government, at that last three-day meeting of the Central Committee, and now here today. We have a year ahead of us to work in this direction, and a year before our party congress, a year to prepare our program. We will present the first party program, after the platform which was passed at the First Congress. What an excellent thing that all these ideas, well thought out and analyzed, can be included in the party program and we can promote them at the congress! If we go to the congress with the strength of the revolution in all fields, in defense, as I already said, in the political field, because we have developed enormously in both political and moral terms; if we go with those ideas and our program on the basis of them, and hold our congress, then we can really say we have gone to the congress. In part, it will be because we were brave, fearless, and firm; because we fortified ourselves and were determined to win the right to continue advancing with our revolution; and because we were willing to pay whatever the price.

If there is peace in the world, better still. We are watching the Geneva Soviet-USA talks with great interest to see what emerges.

The world needs détente and needs peace. Otherwise, billions of human beings in the Third World won't have the slightest hope of a solution. For Africa, where an apocalyptic situation is developing with the growing drought, one that requires a worldwide effort if an entire continent is to be saved from extermination by drought and hunger, the only hope is that there be peace.

If there is no peace, the dangers in our region will grow. That doesn't mean we will be discouraged; we will continue our program. The enemy must know that if he attacks he will have to pay a price ten times greater than he would have had to pay four or five years ago, as great a price as defeat and humiliation, that is, an unpayable price.

We trust that they have realized this. We don't want to have to pass that test, of course, but I think we have increased our level of security with our own forces, and to a considerable degree. For us, there is a greater outlook for a future of peace and respect. I believe this, but we are also prepared for any other course of circumstance.

We have no illusions; we have said there is no room for illusions. We are prepared for everything, for peace and for struggle. [*Applause*] If we have peace, we can implement the development strategy outlined here, and we will strive for peace. One of the ways to struggle for peace is to do what we have done: be stronger. Our strength is no threat to anybody;

but our strength does make a successful attack on our country virtually impossible. Our power is an element of containment. It is militarily defensive, not offensive. In the field of moral values, the example, the ideas of socialism and patriotism we represent, go beyond the borders of our small island and are more powerful than the most sophisticated strategic weapons and the old capitalist ideas. Being strong and increasingly stronger in defense, in the economy, and in our ideas, we will be better able to build that future.

Today, we can really say we are prepared for anything. What must we do if destiny leads us to confrontation? I think we will know well what to do. What must we do if there is peace? I think we will know well what to do.

I think these principles are basic and are those which will shape the destiny and future of our people. They give us great security in all fields, and I sincerely hope that there will be peace for the world and for us.

Patria o muerte! [Homeland or death!]

Venceremos! [We will win!] [*Ovation*]

Cuba's Cooperation with Nicaragua

Speech at Inauguration of Nicaraguan Sugar Mill

Dear Compañero Daniel Ortega, president of the Republic of Nicaragua;
Dear compañeros of the FSLN National Directorate;
Distinguished members of the guest delegations;
Compañero Nicaraguan and Cuban workers:

Since the Augusto César Sandino Order was created, the compañeros of the Nicaraguan leadership and of the FSLN, probably taking into account the ties of affection and brotherhood that have existed between us throughout the years, have had the idea of conferring the order upon me and have proposed this to me on many occasions. They invited me to Nicaragua for that purpose on many occasions.

I considered this such an overwhelming honor that I could not accept it. On several occasions, I asked them to postpone it for the future. I resisted on many occasions until today, when I could no longer resist, [*Applause*] and at last they have impressed, in both senses of the word, the honor upon me. [*Applause*]

Imperialism claims that the Central American problems, the revolutionary struggles of these peoples, are the result of an alleged international conspiracy of so-called subversion from abroad. What would the colonialists have said when all the peoples of America became involved in the struggle to win independence until they were successful? What would those who invaded Latin American countries in the past have said?

They wrested huge geographical tracts from these countries, as oc-

---

This speech was given January 11, 1985, in Nicaragua, at the inauguration ceremony for the Victoria de Julio Sugar Mill, built with Cuban assistance; also addressing the gathering were Sandinista leaders Jaime Wheelock and Daniel Ortega. At the ceremony Castro was awarded the Order of Augusto César Sandino in recognition of his contributions to the revolutionary movement in Latin America and throughout the world and for his solidarity with the Nicaraguan people. The speech was translated and published in the April 1, 1985, Intercontinental Press, *from which it is reprinted here.*

curred with the sister Republic of Mexico that lost half of its territory. What would they have said to justify the actions and to explain the heroic struggle of the Mexican people against the invaders? What would they have said to explain that unforgettable historic action by the heroic cadets of Chapultepec, who hurled themselves from the heights of the castle [*Applause*] and preferred to die wrapped in the flag rather than yield the flag to the invaders?

What would they have said in those times to explain the struggle of the Central American peoples in 1855 against the invading filibusters who occupied Central American territory and, moreover, named themselves the rulers of Central America? What would they have said in 1902, after the first U.S. military occupation of Nicaragua, to explain the people's resistance?

Since the October revolution [in Russia] had not yet occurred, who would they have blamed for that? How would they explain the Mexican revolution, which was so hard fought and so heroic between 1911 and 1920, since the Mexican revolution also took place before the revolution of October 1917?

Who would they have blamed for Sandino's struggles? For that heroic battle waged by the Nicaraguan people against the U.S. invaders in 1928 or 1927? What would they say? Who would be blamed for that subversion? Who would be blamed for that revolutionary struggle? We Cubans? Can the Cuban revolution be blamed for Sandino's struggle?

When Sandino began his historic, glorious struggle on May 4, 1927, against the U.S. occupiers, I was not yet a year old. [*Laughter*] I wasn't even nine months. [*Laughter*] Sandino struggled for six long years with a tiny army against the immense power of the invaders. Who was to be blamed for that?

We know the rest of the story: negotiations; betrayals; the installation of an army of occupation that replaced the invading troops; Somoza; fifty years of the Somozaist dynasty until the children of Nicaragua, again taking up arms as they had done so often in history, destroyed the tyranny at an enormous cost in blood and won the definitive independence of their homeland. [*Applause*]

Sandino was certainly, by his example, an inspiration for all peoples of America. Many of us grew up inspired by Sandino's example, by Sandino's teachings. Therefore, his influence was not limited to Nicaragua. It was felt in Cuba and throughout the entire hemisphere. We grew up under that influence.

However, Sandino also showed us our people's patriotism, our people's valor, our people's indomitable spirit, and their capacity for struggle regardless of how powerful the adversary. Sandino became an eternal symbol that emerged when it was so greatly needed in that period.

The proof of the value of that example, of the value of that symbol, is this revolution which carries his name: the Sandinista revolution. [*Applause*]

That is why I say that this is a very great honor. I receive this decoration as a tribute to our people, as a tribute to the thousands of my compatriots who have been here over the past five years as teachers, doctors, health technicians, construction workers, and assistants in many fields, giving their sweat and some of whom, as Daniel [Ortega] pointed out, also giving their blood and their lives. [*Applause*]

Many of them worked under difficult conditions. Our teachers lived alongside the peasants. They lived with them. They ate what the peasants ate in the most isolated corners of Nicaragua.

Cuba was often criticized for sending teachers. Every year they taught tens of thousands of children. Did Nicaragua, perchance, refuse teachers from any other country? Instead of teachers from Cuba alone, why didn't teachers come from all of the sister countries of Latin America and even from the United States? What stopped them from doing this? They and we all knew that there were children without teachers and that was our only motivation, not prestige or honors.

We have done only what we would have been happy to share with everyone. All of the other Cuban helpers worked in the same spirit. On their behalf I receive this honor, which is not only in recognition of those who worked here, but also for those over there who always made every effort to collaborate and help produce things for Nicaragua. [*Applause*]

On behalf of our people, their internationalist spirit, and their love for the Nicaraguan people, we receive this acknowledgment. [*Applause*] Compañero [Jaime] Wheelock explained the history and the significance of this project that has united us here today. I had not even dreamed or thought of the privilege of inaugurating this project on a date such as today, in the presence of so many fraternal representatives from several countries, in the presence of the FSLN, their most prestigious authorities, Nicaraguan workers, the fighters of the Sandinista People's Army and the Ministry of the Interior, and in the presence of Cuban workers and collaborators.

Wheelock's statements save me from having to explain many things about this project. Initially, I want to point out that this industry is the product of Nicaraguan initiative and was conceived by Nicaragua, an integral conception, as has already been explained, in all aspects, especially in a project as important as the saving and development of new energy resources. I want to point out that this will involve increased production, a 50 percent increase in current Nicaraguan sugar production, and 30 percent of the future production when the projected enlargements have been carried out in other facilities in the sugar industry.

I must say something, objectively. This sugar industry, this project, is the most complete in the sugar production industry. It is the best conceived and the most complete of those existing in any country in the world, even in our country. [*Applause*]

With the triumph of the revolution, we inherited many sugar mills from all eras, of all models, and with machinery from all over the world. For this reason, the maintenance and development of these mills was very complicated until after the revolution, when we enlarged and modernized many of them.

Moreover, in the past few years we have constructed several mills that are identical to this one. I speak of the industry. These are standardized mills with the same production capacity and with the same type of equipment, which helps a lot. We have approximately ten, fifteen, or twenty mills that are similar.

We contributed the conception of the mill, but Nicaraguans contributed the complete conception. This is why I am convinced that this industry, this agroindustrial complex, will become a point of reference and a model for the sugar industry. I have spoken to many persons who visited Nicaragua; they knew of this place and this project when it was under construction. They were impressed by this project, which was constructed in such a brief time with such passion and with such effort.

Wheelock explained the economic significance. While he spoke, I thought of another fact. When the construction of this industry began, it was for the people. Because this industry will not belong to any transnational or any foreign company. [*Applause*] No one is going to take a single cent from this industry, which is the result of the workers' effort. No one will take its capital and send it to the corporate headquarters. Not one cent. The entire mill is Nicaraguan and belongs to the Nicaraguan people. [*Applause*] All that is produced, saved, and all profits are for the Nicaraguan people. [*Applause*]

In reality, when we arrived here we did not meet any "misters." [*Laughter*] I remember when I was seven years old — six, eight, ten, a long time — not a long time ago, but a long time afterwards [*Laughter*] — I heard people talk about "mister" this and "mister" that. I saw all of the factories administered by the "misters." They gave the orders, they earned large salaries, and the firms earned huge profits.

When I arrived here I did not find, I repeat, any "misters," but rather some young men. They told us: here is the "investor," a Nicaraguan; here is the director of industry, a young, well-prepared Nicaraguan who is the chief. What a difference! If we think about all of this, the conclusion is that in reality this means great changes, great social changes, and great revolutionary changes.

I do not know, then, what is considered fair. Would it be fair if the mill belonged to Somoza? He had many industries, and we never heard a word of protest. If the mill belonged to sugar companies? Is that, perchance, what is just? Is it possible to convince the people that this is just? Was the past just, or is the present just?

Ah, but while the construction of this mill was starting, something else had also started in 1981. The dirty war against Nicaragua had started. The dirty war was called covert operations. What is left of this covert nature, if all the U.S. newspapers discuss all the resources, budgets, and credits approved to carry out this dirty war against Nicaragua?

What has been the meaning of this dirty war and how can it be justified? It has cost so many lives; the lives of no fewer than 4,000 Nicaraguan patriots and humble citizens. Most of them were civilians, and many of them were women, elderly people, and even children.

However, it is not just a matter of the lives that it cost. For the first time in this country's history, Nicaraguans were involved in a literacy campaign in which hundreds of thousands of humble citizens, workers, laborers, and peasants were being taught to read and write. While schools were being established, hospitals were being opened, medical services were being promoted, and vaccination campaigns were being carried out to save the lives of children by reducing the rates of illness and mortality and increasing their life expectancy.

While all this was under way, a dirty war was being unleashed that was taking the lives of children and women: 4,000 lives.

Not only did it take lives. While the Nicaraguans were trying to promote agriculture, industry, and products for export, while they were carrying out projects like these as well as other projects, that dirty war was destroying farms, agricultural installations, and schools. It was destroying the country's economy. It had a considerable adverse effect on Nicaragua's production of lumber, one of the country's most important export products. That product is also needed by the people to build houses, to have wood to build their houses. They destroyed equipment; they destroyed sawmills.

While the Nicaraguans were building roads for communications among towns, the dirty war was destroying bridges and construction equipment and killing construction workers who were promoting the country's development.

The dirty war, with its pirate attacks, mining of ports, and constant harassment, considerably undermined the country's fishing production, another important source of income.

The dirty war undermined coffee production, the country's most important source of income and foreign exchange, which helps to purchase foodstuffs, medicines, and essential products for the people. It cost the country hundreds of millions of dollars a year.

That is why today, while we are here inaugurating this plant, somewhere else they may be destroying an agricultural installation, a school, or some other social installation.

In the light of human conscience, in the light of ethics, can there possibly be any justification for this? Can it be justified? Is there any justification for sending mercenaries to destroy a people's peace, a people's wealth, a people's work? Perhaps the significance of a project like this is better understood when it is contrasted with those actions.

Have we come to such a pass, have we seen so much pretension and arrogance that it is necessary to justify and explain a project like this one, to show that it is not a great crime? Have we come to such a time that we even have to give reasons for a visit to Nicaragua? We have not visited Nicaragua very often. This is the second time in five and a half years, counting anniversaries. I have actually been invited very often, but do I have the right to be taking up the Sandinista compañeros' time? Do I have a lot of time to travel?

But is it perhaps a violation of international law to extend an invitation? If so, imagine how many violations have been committed at this time on the occasion of the inauguration of Compañero Daniel [Ortega]. Have we reached such extremes of trying to curtail the sovereignty of states that it is necessary to ask permission and even to apologize for inviting someone and, moreover, for the guest to apologize for visiting a brother country? [*Applause*]

Amazingly, yesterday a U.S. State Department spokesman said that he was very annoyed about Mr. Castro's visit to Nicaragua. [*Applause*] The friendship between Nicaragua and Cuba is a problem. Since when? It is as if we were to begin to tell another country that we are displeased when they invite a friend.

I believe that no other country receives more delegations than the United States. Yet I have never heard anyone in any part of the world protest because it has invited someone, even if that someone was Somoza or [Chilean dictator Augusto] Pinochet, or the fascist prime minister of South Africa, where horrendous racial segregation prevails. No. All kinds of personalities, citizens of the world of all kinds are usually invited, usually invited. I have never heard a word of protest from anyone.

Ah, but Nicaragua cannot invite us, and I, a citizen of the world, a modest citizen of the world, cannot visit Nicaragua without a protest. [*Applause*] Some of the news dispatches said: "Castro's surprising visit," "Castro's unexpected visit." Castro cannot do anything that is not surprising or unexpected. Or else they said: "Castro's unannounced visit."

If Castro does not announce his visits, who knows better that the United States why I cannot enjoy the luxury of announcing many visits, [*Applause*] of announcing visits?

One can go to the U.S. Senate's archives to analyze and study all the investigations they have carried out and the statements they have made about just a small part of the attack plans they have prepared: dozens of attempts, plans for attempts inside and outside Cuba. One might be called the right to ban visits, and another might be called the right to hunt down a revolutionary internationally. This is what has been done against my country, and this is what is practiced against my modest person. The situation is such that not even the right to air travel exists.

We know that many things have happened, and we remember for example that a mine exploded in the port of Corinto one day, another one exploded in Bluefields, and another somewhere else, and another in yet another place.

The puppet mercenaries then came out and said: "Yes, we are responsible for these mines; we are the patriots! And we will continue to lay these mines to blow up more ships." A few weeks later it was revealed that no mine had been laid by any puppet counterrevolutionary organization. A relatively advanced technology was needed to manufacture these mines; sophisticated systems are necessary to lay these mines.

It was then discovered who had really laid these mines; this created a great international scandal. The CIA had laid these mines. Can we place any trust in the morality and ethics of such a policy?

Well, I regret it very much. I would like to travel like any other citizen, but I cannot announce my visits. I do not like to collaborate with the enemy. [*Laughter and applause*] This explains the mystery of the "surprise" and the "unexpected."

If one wants a clearer explanation, it is a preventive measure to avoid running into one of the SR-71s [U.S. spy planes] that are flying throughout the Caribbean, violating all borders. They violate Nicaraguan airspace and have violated many other airspaces, including ours. I was seeking to avoid air accidents. [*Laughter*]

I wanted to explain something about Cuba's cooperation in this project. Compañero Wheelock gave many details, and, moreover, he spoke with such affection for Cuba that you could say, and I was thinking, that if Cuba's participation in this project can be described as generous, much more generous have been the words of recognition expressed here this afternoon by Compañero Wheelock. We were truly moved by those words.

We consider cooperation with Nicaragua and other countries a basic duty. Other countries help us, countries that have more resources than we do. We have more resources than Nicaragua. The least we can do is cooperate with Nicaragua and many other peoples, brothers and friends of the Third World, who have fewer resources than we do.

Thus, there are Cuban doctors in over twenty-five Third World countries; and we even have 22,000 foreigners from eighty-two countries on scholarships in our country. [*Applause*] That is why we have said on other occasions that to be internationalist is to pay off our own debt, our homeland's debt, to humanity. [*Applause*]

I wanted to give a few figures, not to bore you, because that is not my intent, but for a reason that I will explain later. Incidentally, I noted that some of the figures that I brought from Cuba do not coincide 100 percent with those given by Wheelock. Something happened — perhaps a typing error [*Laughter*] by the Cuban Ministry of the Sugar Industry or the Cuban Cooperation Committee, or by Nicaragua. In some cases the figures are higher, and in others they are a little lower.

I would like to point out what our cooperation consisted of. In technological equipment produced in Cuba, 34,161,000 pesos; technical equipment acquired by Cuba in the socialist world, 11.2 million pesos; metal structures built in Cuba, 170 tons worth 63,000 pesos; 7,800 tons of sheet metal — I think that Wheelock gave a higher figure, and it could be that some other equipment was listed in the steel section, but we have a figure of 7,800 tons of steel, worth $1.95 million; 219 units of pumping equipment and engines, 525,600 — was I saying "dollars"? Ah no, pesos, and it should not be forgotten that we consider our peso worth more than the dollar. [*Laughter and applause*]*

Well, in Cuba a peso has much greater purchasing power than a dollar in New York. I can give you examples. In Cuba, with a peso you can make twenty trips on a bus; in New York, a dollar pays for less than two trips. You can make more bus trips and do more things with a peso in Cuba than with a dollar in New York.

Agricultural equipment, 44 units — I think that this includes the combines, right? — 1.9 million pesos. In total — and here we do not agree, Wheelock — the value of these items is 49,810,000 pesos. I think you said 48 million. Might it not be in another currency, that of the eagle?

Now for total tonnage: Tonnage sent from Cuba was 31,500 tons. Volume was 77,680 cubic meters. That might not be a very important figure, but the compañeros who gathered the data will probably be encouraged to have their data used.

The number of packages was 22,350. It was probably stated that these were weapons being sent to Nicaragua. As for the number of sea voyages, you said 29, and my figures say 33. There were probably some other trips that you do not have listed. Shipment by air: 210 tons. Estimated number of critical, basic spare parts sent, as of June 30, 1985, 1,500 tons. We still owe another 1,500 tons.

In addition, as Wheelock said, some 400 Cuban workers and technicians worked on the project. A few hundred more, some 700, came for brief periods according to their respective skills and then left. There is a contingent of workers that is helping to put the mill into operation.

*The Cuban peso is worth approximately US$1.25.

Perhaps I should mention, regarding our cooperation personnel, that throughout these years since the unleashing of the dirty war, Cuban workers have run the same risks as the Nicaraguan people. In the face of the incessant threat of an invasion or an attack, our cooperation personnel have faced the same risks alongside the people. In other words, they are making their contribution under conditions of real and potential danger.

You may wonder why I am referring to the data on Cuba's contribution. You might think I was gaining propaganda, publicity, with that contribution. I would not have dared to speak if Wheelock had not spoken first, but he did speak, and to excess, not to excess in content but in generosity, in what was moreover a brilliant work of oratory, with data, a difficult feat, leaving out nothing and no one who made this collective project, as he called it, possible.

I speak of these specific figures for the following reasons: Our cooperation with Nicaragua throughout the five and a half years since the Sandinista people's revolution triumphed has been based on absolutely free cooperation in all areas. [*Applause*] In education, health, agriculture, construction, the merchant marine, fishing, and many other areas, at various levels of teaching, in transportation, and on occasions of natural disasters. We have contributed material, cement, and steel. We have also contributed construction equipment; in other words, everything that has been at hand, and always, of course, we have tried to give some assistance to our many needy friends here.

I have been noting that some people have become specialists in presenting their needs objectively. We do what we can with pleasure. In general, it has not been difficult for them to obtain some assistance from Cuba, because they have many other friends besides me, many other advocates in the country who greatly desire to help the Nicaraguans. I note this subjective factor among our compañeros.

All of this cooperation has been given without charge, with the exception of this project. When they proposed that we cooperate in this project they asked for a loan. Well, this was a large-scale industrial project, and although we have reached some degree of development and we already produce, as Wheelock said, over 60 percent of the equipment needed for a mill of this kind, we do not have a lot of resources.

They said: We want this on the basis of a loan, and we agreed to cooperate on that basis. It is what is called a soft loan, at low interest. We offered a credit payable in twelve years at 6 percent interest, which is less than half of the current interest rate on the world market.

If one adds up all the materials, work force, projects, transportation, and so on, plus the interest, the amount Nicaragua would pay, according to our estimates — I don't know whether Wheelock's figures are higher or lower — is $73.8 million. We have figured it in dollars in this instance.

These estimates are based on cost prices. Some projects of this type, construction cooperation, or what could be called commercial operations in worldwide practice, could be calculated — as Wheelock and I estimated — if they were carried out or supplied by a transnational company or the like — and we know this because we purchase a great deal of industrial equipment — the value of this cooperation could be estimated at some $100 million, and that would be conservative.

Well, none of this is important. The essential, fundamental reason for my explanation of these figures is as follows: The leadership of our party and of our government has been analyzing, on the occasion of the inauguration of the project, everything related to this agreement, this convention. We have also been analyzing what is happening in Nicaragua, as I was explaining.

While colossal efforts are being made to increase production and services, a dirty war is being waged against the country. It is costing lives and hundreds of millions.

In addition, Nicaragua inherited the legacy of Somoza: an enormous debt, a country that was destroyed twice in a short time, by an earthquake and by Somozaism — the Somozaist repression and Somozaist bombing. It is facing problems: high interest rates, low prices for its products on the market, and problems of the international economic crisis.

Cuba has reached the decision to cancel this debt owed by Nicaragua. [*Prolonged applause and chants of "Fidel, Fidel, Fidel!"*]

Therefore, we are donating all the equipment, material, labor, the value of the projects, and the physical and mental effort to Nicaragua. Thus, in the name of the Cuban people, we donate to Nicaragua the cooperation that we have carried out in the construction of this project, including the 1,500 tons of equipment that remains to be delivered. [*Prolonged applause*]

Actually, it is my profound conviction that the solution to the problems of our Third World countries, which are presently burdened and strangled by enormous debts and which have few resources, is the cancellation of their debts. [*Applause*] We proposed this at the last summit meeting of the Nonaligned countries, in principle, not to resolve the problems but simply to begin modestly to solve the problems related to those Third World countries that are less developed and have fewer resources. Similarly, I am convinced that for the Third World countries of greater development and more resources, the only solution is an extension of the payment period to many years with grace periods and low interest rates.

This is not an absurd demand. It is the only possible solution to begin to resolve the Third World's present problems. It is true that at times the debts are owed to private banks, but the states, especially the rich industrialized states, should assume responsibility for that debt. For example, the internal debt of the United States is $1.6 trillion. Can you comprehend that? It is not easy. It is not easy to explain to yourself. I will say it another way, as I did recently in Cuba: $1 trillion, plus $650 billion, is the U.S. internal debt.

What is spent on weapons yearly in the United States, in the United States alone, is a figure almost as large as the foreign debt of all Latin America. It is not impossible for the economy of the rich industrialized countries to assume that debt and to assume it all. In our discussions we established a difference between the countries of less development with greater difficulties and fewer resources, and those which have a higher level of development and more resour ~s, for which we proposed a longer period for paying off their debts, with low interest rates.

This is consistent with the decision adopted by our party and our government. If you permit me — I realize that I am not in Cuba and that I do not have the right to speak for such a long time [*Applause*] — but I think it is necessary, if you will permit me, to speak on the international situation on this occasion. It is related to Nicaragua and our position, and I want to go into it.

In order to justify the imperialist attacks on Nicaragua, it is stated that Nicaragua wants to export its revolution to Central America, and it is stated insistently that Nicaragua wants to export its revolution to El Salvador. In fact, if one thinks about it a little, it is not necessary to turn to the historical facts that I mentioned previously, but just to remember that in the 1930s, before the Cuban revolution and long before the Nicaraguan revolution, there were great uprisings and great struggles in El Salvador, and that tens of thousands of people were killed. Some 30,000 peasants were reportedly killed.

Anyone who is a little informed knows that at least ten years before the Sandinista triumph, Salvadorans had been fighting against the genocidal, repressive regime. I know quite well that it began many years before the triumph of the Sandinista revolution and that it had gained great strength by the time the Sandinista revolution triumphed.

How can Nicaragua be accused of wanting to export revolution to El Salvador or any other country? One thing we are totally convinced of, it could be called a principle that can be summarized in a few words. Revolutions can neither be exported nor avoided. This has been demonstrated by life, by history, and by revolutionary theory and practice throughout the centuries.

If necessary, we can go back to the French Revolution, or the Mexican revolution, or the Russian revolution of 1917, or any revolution, even ours. If we had wanted to import our revolution, we had nowhere to place an order. We did not know anyone. We did not know where to place an order for a revolution as an import. That argument is so ridiculous, so absurd, so simplistic.

We can say: Who can export the present international economic crisis that is creating so many social problems and so much instability in many countries? Who can export that enormous Latin American foreign debt of $360 billion?

We can remember the era of the Alliance for Progress, when it was said that Latin America's problems would be solved with $20 billion loans. Now Latin America, twenty-four years later, has twice as many problems, twice as many people, twice as many social problems, and an enormous and intolerable debt of $360 billion. Who can export that situation? Who can export the growing underdevelopment and misery in Latin America and the hunger, the real fact that tens of millions of people are hungry?

The statistics on average nutrition in each country are known, and averages mean that the figures are much lower for the majority and much higher for a minority. The figures on health are known. All international organizations report on this constantly. Who can export these conditions, which are the source of the peoples' struggles and revolutions?

Who can export this selfish policy of the capitalist, industrialized countries, whose protectionist policies strangle the economies of the developing countries? Who can export the unequal trade under which every year we must deliver more products to pay for the same amount of equipment that we import? Who can create those conditions artificially? Who can export those conditions? They result from numerous, varied, different historical factors and the accumulation of the problems that those factors have created.

They resort to the misused argument that Nicaragua is trying to export the revolution, as they have done with Cuba. Let me say what I think, my inner conviction — the truth is that the main, the essential, and the surefire agent of the revolution in this hemisphere is the International Monetary Fund. We saw this in some countries; we saw the measures applied, the social restrictions enforced, and the brutal damage inflicted on the people's standard of living, especially the workers. In some places, like in Santo Domingo recently, this provoked a rebellion among the people against the IMF measures. The police and the army had to be sent out to kill citizens, and they killed dozens of citizens.

The enormous foreign debt and high interest rates, the underdevelopment, poverty, protectionist measures, unequal trade, and exploitation against our people are creating unbearable conditions for our countries.

If we are going to talk seriously, these are, I repeat, the surefire factors of subversion and revolution. Subversion is a word invented by them to blame someone else for this, and revolution is our word.

If no solution is sought for these problems, and if, for example, no solution is sought to the foreign-debt problem, then the conditions of political instability in Latin American countries will become increasingly worse. If we want to achieve stability, we must start by overcoming this problem.

The world needs peace and the need for peace is currently a universal call, more than ever, because humanity has become fully aware that with modern weapons and technology you cannot conceivably solve international problems through war. For many centuries, the powerful warmongering states, the colonialist powers and then the imperialist powers, had this luxury.

Nowadays, no one can afford the luxury of thinking that the solution to problems lies in a war because, I repeat, humanity has become aware of this fact. Humanity is aware of this; leaders are aware of this; statesmen are aware of this; scientists are aware of this; and anyone with a minimum level of education — and there are many in the world — is aware of the fact that a world war nowadays would represent the extinction of humankind and many other species; possibly every species.

Some scientists say that only cockroaches and other similar insects would be able to survive a nuclear war, a world war; apparently they have a strong defense against radioactivity. This is very well known.

There is a generalized clamor for peace and we give a lot of thought to these problems. Thus, the international public, the whole world, welcomed with satisfaction the news and communiqués regarding the meeting in Geneva between the U.S. and Soviet representatives. The whole world awaited the communiqué about this meeting, because it is a very important event.

The communiqué talks about the two countries' willingness to discuss matters related to the so-called space war, space weapons, strategic nuclear weapons, the long- and medium-range strategic nuclear weapons. The communiqué talks about negotiating to curb and reduce the arms race and, for the first time in a communiqué of this nature, it mentions the destruction of all the nuclear weapons as its final goal.

This is the first time in this critical period — which was, is, and will continue to be highly dangerous — that such a complex and dangerous problem like no other ever faced by mankind is discussed and this objective is mentioned as the final goal. Naturally, this was welcomed with pleasure by all countries. This is fundamental for Third World countries because if we do not have peace, if this incredible arms buildup is continued, there will not be a single ray of hope for them to solve this other type of nuclear weapons: hunger, underdevelopment, poverty, loss of natural resources — as is happening in African countries.

These countries are facing a veritable apocalypse: the growth of their desert. Millions of people are dying of hunger, and the industrialized world has seen scenes on television screens that recall the Nazi concentration camps after the war. The world has become aware of this problem, because there would not be the remotest hope for Third World countries if this problem is not solved.

Industrialized countries, which are aware of these weapons' power, also consider it vital, fundamental, essential, and a priority to avoid a nuclear war. This concern is shared by all the statesmen, leaders, even the closest U.S. allies.

Southern African countries want peace; the southern African peoples need peace. The Southeast Asian peoples want and need peace; the Middle Eastern peoples want and need peace; the European peoples want and need peace. The peoples in our region want and need peace and they have the right to achieve peace.

I think that all of the peoples of the Caribbean and Central America want peace. Mexico wants peace in the region and works for peace in the region. We always mention Mexico with great respect, with great gratitude, because Mexico's conduct in this hemisphere has been exceptional regarding Cuba. It has been exceptional not only regarding Cuba. It has also been exceptional regarding Nicaragua. Mexico is one of the countries that has aided Nicaragua economically the most during these years. We know this. [*Applause*] However, Mexico did not only help Nicaragua; it, along with Venezuela — as a result of the brutal rise in oil prices — promoted agreements to supply the Central American and Caribbean countries with oil based on the possibility of receiving part of the price of oil as credits. Oil increased from $20 a ton to more than $200.

Mexico promoted and supported a policy of supplying approximately one-third of that price as credit to be paid under certain more favorable conditions if these resources were destined to investments in energy. Good, it was an effort, even though all the countries of the area would have to pay in cash more than $150 per ton or thereabouts, which was practically unbearable. But at least it was an effort, it helped. We can say that Mexico has been very generous in its economic cooperation with the countries of Central America and the Caribbean. Mexico has made an effort to create formulas of negotiations and peace in the region, and it is one of the pillars of the Contadora group.

Panama wants peace and needs peace, in Panama and in the region. The Panamanians struggled for a very long time to recover their rights over the canal and for the restitution of the territories occupied by military bases. For a period of years, in order to carry out their independent policies and in order to complement their aspirations of achieving total recovery of their sovereign rights over their canal and their territory, that country needs peace. It is one of the countries that along with Mexico has made a great effort to find political solutions to the problems of the area.

Colombia, the third country of the Contadora group, wants peace. Venezuela wants peace. These four countries have formed the internationally known group — with ample international support — the Contadora group, which has been struggling to achieve solutions to the problems.

Nicaragua needs and wants peace. All of the Central American countries need peace. All of the countries in the Caribbean, including Cuba, want and need peace. This is a reality.

However, I believe even more that the people of the United States want and need peace, on the international level as well as on the regional level. The U.S. economy cannot endure much longer under these colossal military expenditures. At least, it cannot endure the increase of these expenses, as it cannot continue to endure a budget deficit of more than $200 billion, a trade deficit that already reaches $120 billion annually. It cannot endure without the economy breaking down. They have done this but at the expense of the economies of the rest of the Third World countries and those of their own capitalist allies.

Objectively, the U.S. economy needs peace. This would be not only in the interests of the countries of the region and the continent, but also in the interests of the American people. No one is capable of calculating the consequences of an armed invasion by the United States of any Central American or Latin American country. It would be such a great offense and such a deep wound to the Latin American peoples' feelings that it would take who knows how long to erase it, if it could ever be erased.

We are not living in 1927 or 1912, when there were no radios or other media, nor the awareness that exists today in the world.

Today there are more than 150 independent states, an ample and powerful international opinion, not only in the world, but in the United States itself, and this was demonstrated at the time of the Vietnam war.

Regarding the invasion of a Latin American country, we only have to recall the hemisphere's reaction to the Malvinas War, even though a repressive military junta was ruling the country [Argentina]. However, this was not an obstacle to the expressions of support for the Argentine people. In view of the current level of awareness of our peoples, I really think that it would be an inconceivable mistake.

Furthermore, our peoples are not at all defenseless, and they should not be underestimated. I am absolutely sure that an intervention in Nicaragua would generate a totally invincible resistance from the Nicaraguan people. [*Applause*] This is based on realities, not wishful thinking. An intervention in Nicaragua would give rise to an endless people's war. It would develop into real genocide that the world would consider intolerable, and a war in which the invaders would have to pull out in the end.

The situation is exactly the same as in our country. We have prepared our people to resist. We are absolutely and totally sure of this, no matter how many millions of soldiers are used.

But there is nothing extraordinary about this, as we have seen in recent times, even facing the most sophisticated technologies, the most perfected weapons. I recently gave a few examples at the Cuban National Assembly.

For instance, I mentioned the Saharan Arab Democratic Republic, whose representative is here among us. [*Applause*] A small country, with a very small population, located in a desert region, is fighting for its independence against the occupation of foreign troops. It is fighting against hundreds of thousands of Moroccan soldiers, supported by the United States, with highly sophisticated weapons and equipment. That country is victoriously fighting back the occupation, and has kept the Moroccan army under control. There is no way of destroying that movement, that struggle. The Saharan people cannot be defeated.

I also mentioned the case of Algeria when it fought against one of the strongest, best equipped, and most experienced powers in colonial wars: France. The Algerians fought against hundreds of thousands of soldiers for many years and achieved victory.

In Yugoslavia, whose representative is also here among us, [*Applause*] during the Nazi occupation, the people rose in arms, under the leadership of the Communist Party. They were not really ready for that, as they were practically without any weapons when they started, but they fought against dozens of the best German divisions and against dozens of Italian divisions, against dozens, perhaps hundreds of thousands of collaborators, and gave a lesson of what people can do.

Ah, but after that we had the Vietnam lesson. For years the United States, the most powerful imperialist country, sent 500,000 soldiers, its best divisions, thousands of planes and helicopters, its best experts against the small, poor, economically poor country Vietnam. The Vietnamese people fought for years, developed extraordinary experience, and defeated the most powerful imperialist power, giving the world the example of an invaluable experience.

Near Nicaragua, Salvadorans have been fighting for five years on a small piece of land, against tens of thousands of soldiers trained, armed, and equipped by the United States, against dozens of planes, helicopters, all kinds of technologies, but the Salvadorans persist under these conditions. They have experience and strength; they are an example of what people can do and are doing.

This cannot be neutralized by any military technology, regardless of how sophisticated it may be. In other words, our people have the capacity, determination, courage, and fighting spirit. In other words, any military adventure against a Latin American country will not only generate colossal political problems, but also the invincible resistance of our peoples.

However, our peoples do not want these victories, this glory, that would cost many U.S. lives on the one hand, and countless Latin American lives on the other. No one wants that bloodshed, no one ever wants this kind of war to begin. This is why we can say with profound conviction — not only with a realistic but with a political and revolutionary conviction — that our peoples, and this includes the North American people, want peace, need peace.

I have seen many North Americans, professors, technicians, and youth, whose feeling of sympathy leads them to collaborate with Nicaragua, because they are ashamed of the dirty war. They are collaborating in different fields of agriculture. There are many in the United States who feel the same way. The way the North American people feel is very important.

We are also aware of the efforts being made to change the way the North American people feel, to fool them, writing articles, documents. Last night I read a dispatch on a book to be published in the United States in which the U.S. government uses tremendous arguments supposedly to explain and justify new funds from Congress for the dirty war. It contained some facts that astonished me. They began talking about tons of arms and ships with arms. I do not know where the agency obtained the information, but apparently the book talks about how it increased every year. And that this year, they talked of thirty-three ships loaded with arms for Nicaragua. Well, that is more ships loaded with arms than the number I was told brought the equipment for the sugar mill for Nicaragua. Thirty-three ships! It is incredible, absurd, an invention from top to bottom.

I recently read a dispatch that mentioned seven Soviet ships loaded with arms. However, I knew that the seven Soviet ships were loaded with supplies for Nicaragua and not one single weapon. I closely followed the developments.

A few days later, they said the seven ships arrived but they did not carry heavy arms, they transported light arms. I do not know if a bag of wheat, or an oil barrel, is a light arm, if foodstuffs, agricultural equipment, and transportation equipment are light arms. It is the first time in my life that I heard such a thing.

We know the truth about those ships. They did not bring one single weapon. Evidently there is a deliberate campaign to try to prove that what Nicaragua says is not the truth, and that reality and truth don't count.

A campaign has been unleashed because Nicaragua has armed itself and has tried to obtain arms that are not offensive, arms that are of a purely defensive nature. An armored vehicle or any other weapon that can be used offensively can be called an offensive weapon.

The fundamental arms that make Nicaragua powerful are the light arms. Definitely. They are very hard to neutralize. And Nicaragua has not done this to threaten its neighbors. It is ridiculous, it is absurd, to think a revolutionary country would carry out a military adventure against its neighbors. It is contrary to the thought, the ideas of any revolutionary party of this hemisphere, continuously threatened.

Who can conceive that a country like Nicaragua can harbor the intention of waging a war against a sister country? Against Costa Rica or against Honduras? It is absurd. This would be to serve imperialism, on a silver platter, a golden pretext to attack Nicaragua. It is absurd and inconceivable.

They say Nicaragua is arming, but against whom is Nicaragua arming itself? Who is threatening Nicaragua? None of the neighbor countries is threatening Nicaragua. Nicaragua's traditional threat has always come and continues to come today from the most powerful imperialist country. That is where the threat comes from. Nicaragua made the efforts to prepare itself and organize the people for the people's struggle. Is it that difficult to understand that Nicaragua did not receive arms to fight against its neighbors, nor does it have any interest to fight against them? It is just trying to defend itself from the traditional threat, past and present.

Can we criticize a country for doing that? What are we supposed to do when we are threatened? Should we disarm ourselves, or go down on our knees? No revolutionary country, when threatened, disarms itself or goes down on its knees. [*Applause*]

This is understandable. That is why we can say with absolute certainty that our peoples want peace and they are willing to contribute with efforts for peace in the world and in our region.

It is an honest attitude. What can we gain from war? War for what? We will defend ourselves only if we are attacked or invaded, like the lion's cubs of which we talked yesterday. Spanish lion's cubs to which Daniel referred yesterday, recalling Rubén [Darío].* Not just a thousand cubs, but millions of cubs, and not just Spanish cubs, but Spanish, Indian, and African cubs we are. [*Applause*]

What interest can we have in waging a war with our neighbors? Even in our country we have a military base [U.S. naval base at Guantánamo] against the will of our people. It has been there throughout the twenty-six years of the revolution, and it is being occupied by force.

We have the moral and legal right to demand its delivery to our people. We have made the claim in the moral and legal way. We do not intend to recover it with the use of arms. It is part of our territory being

---

*Rubén Darío was Nicaragua's foremost national poet. He died in 1916.

occupied by a U.S. military base. Never has anyone, a revolutionary cadre, a revolutionary leader, or a fellow citizen, had the idea of recovering that piece of our territory by the use of force.

If some day it will be ours, it will not be by the use of force, but by the advance of the consciousness of justice in the world. Meanwhile, billions are spent there uselessly or are spent to try to humiliate Cuba.

Should we decide to attack the base, it would be the pretext that imperialism would use to label us aggressors, warmongers, and to attack our country. The same attitude is observed by any other revolutionary country or group of responsible leaders. I cannot speak for the Nicaraguans, but I know how the Nicaraguans think, based on our relations of many years. Therefore, revolutions cannot be exported. Nor do our countries have the slightest intention of fighting or attacking their neighboring brothers.

We are willing to cooperate. I was saying a few moments ago that we want and need and have a right to peace. We must demand peace, not as a gift but as a right. We need peace the same as the world needs it. We will be glad if there is peace in the world. It is not possible, however, to have détente and peace in the world if our region and our peoples are attacked. This would be a disturbing factor in all international relations.

I explain this in order to express here all our convictions and the reasons for our principles and the ideas of our party. Talking to the Contadora foreign ministers, I was able to explain to them our opinions on what we have been discussing, as well as our willingness to cooperate.

We sincerely believe that this can be truly achieved. We need to negotiate agreements and this is not easy. There are also complex problems, but right now I can think of two essential things.

One, we have to promote a dialogue and political negotiations between the FMLN-FDR [Farabundo Martí National Liberation Front–Revolutionary Democratic Front] and the Salvadoran government. We must encourage these political negotiations. We must support them.

It is necessary to find negotiated political solutions in El Salvador. This is an essential factor in the solution of Central American problems. We cannot think of any solutions in the area if it means that El Salvador would be excluded. It would be a tremendous mistake to think that the Central American problem, particularly in El Salvador, can be solved through the extermination of all Salvadoran revolutionaries. These revolutionaries have demonstrated their ability to fight, their courage, and their morale in combat for five years, and they are unbeatable.

In addition to talking, one has to watch many things and learn from the experiences of others, events that occur in various places, the development of revolutionary political movements. We can say that the Salvadoran revolutionaries are nowadays the most courageous and experienced in Latin America. [*Applause*] These revolutionaries are among the most experienced in the entire world.

This is only the logical and the natural outcome of the struggle. As obstacles and forces are encountered by a fighting people over a long period of time, the people develop an even greater fighting strategy and gain even more experience.

We might say that it is fundamental to dismiss the notion that if we want to find solutions in the area in good faith we can solve the problem by doing away with all the Salvadoran revolutionaries. We must have agreements to guarantee Nicaragua's integrity and security against direct aggressions or dirty wars. This is essential.

Actions are required to guarantee peace and security for all the Central American countries without exceptions, because all are brother countries and need peace. If there is good faith — and we are willing to work in good faith — it is possible to have peace in the area and friendly relations among Central American and Caribbean countries, and Cuba.

We can even have good, normal relations between our countries — in this case I mean Cuba — and the United States. This is based on revolutionary conviction and realism.

Very different systems exist. It is up to them to change it when they so desire. I have not yet met anyone who has demanded a change in the U.S. social system. Ah, but the United States has this mania of trying to change the social systems of other countries. But each nation's sovereignty has to be respected.

We also declare our willingness to live in peace with all other countries, but in a peace based on respect. I repeat, we will never kneel before any threat.

We consider ourselves capable of living on good terms with all our neighbors, near and far, from the Caribbean and Latin America in terms of respect and peace, regardless of their ideology and economic system.

And I repeat, these situations that can bring changes in some countries are historical factors. We don't renounce anything, we don't renounce any principle, and of course we don't renounce history and the realities of history.

I reiterate here our sincere willingness, which we expressed to three Contadora foreign ministers yesterday, to have peace. It is possible to have peace. This will require the good faith of all, and all will have to make concessions of one type or another. We cannot have peace if some make concessions while others make none. Peace based on the demands of the other party is not peace, but rather shameful surrender. And no revolutionary country either sells out or surrenders. [*Applause and shouts of "Never!"*]

I avail myself of this occasion to state my viewpoints to the Nicaraguan people as we inaugurate this achievement of peace, this sugar mill. The real dream of revolutionaries is to be able to achieve many works like this, factories, hospitals, and schools, and to be able to develop the country's education, public works, public health, production of foodstuffs, and increase the people's cultural levels and their dignity. This mill is a symbol of the most intimate dreams of revolutionaries. [*Applause*]

A few words more, with the noble intention of concluding. Regarding some of my impressions during this trip, I will say that we were curious to see how the Nicaraguan people were, how the cities looked.

I was favorably impressed when I saw the cleanliness throughout the city of Managua, the beauty of the city, the changes, the orderliness throughout the city, and the green areas. There have been noticeable changes since I was last here. I was favorably impressed. It was especially pleasing to observe the Nicaraguan people's high morale, combativeness, and enthusiasm. This explains the great tasks they have carried out during these last years.

If the construction of this sugar mill was a Nicaraguan enterprise, an enterprise that was really a feat, I believe that what the people have done throughout these years has been an even greater feat. They have countered aggression, fought courageously and with dignity during the aggression and the dirty war which has been waged against them.

How were they able to withstand economic problems throughout these years, which also brought problems for the whole world?

How were they able to meet the challenge of the country's institutionalization and the elections while simultaneously facing a war? The elections were held with the traditional liberal rules — we call them the liberal bourgeois norms — in this arena. These are the classic electoral norms, casting a direct ballot.

And they did not harbor the slightest fear. They were conscious of their authority, of their moral strength and, above all, they were conscious of the people's revolutionary quality. [*Applause*]

The challenge was accepted, but the enemy did not accept the challenge; U.S. imperialism did not accept the challenge and tried to obstruct the elections, because it was aware that the people support the FSLN.

Imperialism did everything possible to obstruct the elections; it exerted all kinds of pressure, resorted to all kinds of pretexts, manipulated the situation and the people — this manipulation was quite apparent and evident — to obstruct the elections or postpone them forever.

The Sandinistas had talked about holding the elections in 1985. Later many people asked the Sandinistas to move the elections forward, so they were brought forward.

Once the elections were brought forward and the government convoked them, others demanded that they be postponed. Other demands, many more demands would follow the first ones, with the intention of wearing down the country with a dirty war, the human and economic wearing down of a country with a dirty war. There would be economic pressures and boycotts, and the people would be submitted to an endless electoral process.

That is why I think, why I am firmly convinced, that the FSLN's decision to stick to its pledge and the date of the elections was the intelligent, correct, and appropriate thing to do. The FSLN did not fall into the trap.

Journalists, more than a thousand journalists, came from all over the world. What did they witness? The people's support for the revolution and the people's enthusiasm. It was not merely support, it was enthusiastic support, and it was evident to all the world. We have been able to ascertain at every level a certain truth. The elections were absolutely honest, as they seldom are anywhere else. The elections were not only honest; a great percentage of people voted in them. This percentage is rarely observed anywhere else in Latin America or even in the United States itself.

In addition, the FSLN received a percentage of votes far greater than those ever received by any other political party in Latin America. [*Applause*] This is a real and objective fact. What right does anyone have to challenge these elections when they were held according to the traditional norms?

Yesterday we had the opportunity to participate in the inauguration ceremony. Its simplicity, seriousness, formality, and solemnity were impressive. It included the participation of all sectors, including the executive branch, the [National] Assembly, and state officials. It even included the church's participation. I have seen my picture today in some newspapers; I was beside Monsignor [Pablo Antonio] Vega, president of the bishops' conference.

It was a pleasure, and at various times we exchanged views on different topics in an amiable way. His attitude impressed me favorably, because we were able to talk with complete freedom during that ceremony and exchanged views. He left us with a positive impression.

I also had the opportunity to greet the apostolic nuncio in Managua. We talked for a few minutes, and it was a nice conversation. I reminded him about the role played by a nuncio in Cuba. In the beginning there were some conflicts between the revolution and the church. I will never forget the role played by a nuncio, Monsignor Charles Tachey, because it was positive and constructive and helped us establish normal relations with the Catholic church in Cuba.

I might add that we established normal and respectful relations with the Catholic church and all the churches in our country. This was not a prerogative generously granted to an institution; it was based on the principle of respect for the religious beliefs and customs of any citizen.

We are not talking only about respect; more than once I have asserted my appreciation and admiration for the work carried out by many members of religious organizations, especially by many nuns, in our country, taking care of the sick and the elderly. We really appreciate this extraordinary work. I once said at the National Assembly that the nuns who run asylums are models of communism. I referred to their attitude, spirit, generosity, and charity. [*Applause*]

We are extraordinarily pleased because the relations between the church and state are improving in Nicaragua. No one could be interested in creating a conflict. I think that all would benefit from an improvement in these relations, based on our experience. Appropriate relations, based on absolute respect, should prevail between the state and the religious organizations.

Yesterday we had the opportunity to hear Compañero Daniel Ortega's speech, and I must congratulate him for it. It was serious and responsible. He explained the Sandinista Front's goals in every sector, for a mixed economy and political pluralism; and he even talked about a foreign investment law.

Nicaragua could build this sugar mill with its own resources and the collaboration of others. It builds a mill that is the property of the Nicaraguan people, not of a foreign enterprise.

But if a great oil deposit is discovered on the Pacific or the Atlantic Coast and the country does not have the resources or technology to exploit this resource, it can perfectly well reach an agreement with an organization that has the technology or resources to exploit it. Many countries do this, because this does not violate any national interest if the government places the country's interests above all else, if it cannot be bribed, if it does not sell itself to a company, if it analyzes everything. And this cannot happen any longer in Nicaragua, in line with the outline they have proposed.

Companies have come even to our country to talk about creating an enterprise to drill off our coasts, and if the appropriate circumstances and conditions are present in our country, we will accept the establishment of a mixed enterprise; all this is possible. We still do not have a law for this, but I do not think such a collaboration would go against our principles. We would have this collaboration if it proved very advantageous to us, and we would demand proper controls. We cannot conceive any other way; it must prove advantageous for us and must not go against any principle.

With the proper plans, the country can continue development. I imagine that you will exert yourselves to exploit all your resources and build many works like this one and other industries. I know there is also room within their conception for a mixed economy. This does not contradict principles.

The main problem is the achievement of development, a correct use of national resources, an intelligent use of national resources, and above all the defense of the people's interests.

You can have a capitalist economy. What you undoubtedly will not have, and this is the most essential thing, is a government at the service of the capitalists. That is something quite different. [*Applause*]

It will be a government of the people and for the people and it will defend the people's interests. These actions are not in conflict with revolutionary guidelines. Can it be done, must it be done? It depends, because each revolution is different from the others; each revolution is based on different conditions, forces, and situations. No one can say: This is the prescription for all countries. Each country must write its own prescription.

We know that great problems currently prevail in Third World and Latin American countries, and we do not harbor the slightest doubt or see the slightest contradiction in the realistic, courageous, and wise policy of the Sandinista National Liberation Front. [*Applause*]

The work that lies ahead is, of course, difficult. Every revolution is difficult and complex. Should anyone believe that a revolution is easy, it would be best to advise him from the start to give up the task or goal of making a revolution.

A revolution is much more difficult and complex than any other task. It is much more difficult than a war. I assert: Waging a war is easier, much easier, than making a revolution, driving it forward, developing a country, and building an economy. How many obstacles, how many problems!

This is especially true when you must carry it out in a country that has only a terrible heritage of underdevelopment, debts, and illiteracy. It is extremely difficult, and it involves all kinds of complex problems, regardless of the country's specific situation. You can bear witness to this.

I will tell you something that might prove useful, my Nicaraguan brothers: You should know that the task that lies ahead is difficult and complex. However, it is also a noble, honorable, and worthwhile task. I believe that to be a revolutionary — in a revolutionary epoch — is a great privilege for any human being.

People don't become revolutionaries just because they want to. Could anyone want to be a revolutionary back in the Middle Ages? Could anyone be a revolutionary? No one is a revolutionary because he wants to be, but because a revolution is a need and a possibility at a determined historical moment.

I sometimes ask: Could anyone in our country have been a revolutionary during the sixteenth century and try to achieve social and political changes? Could that have been possible in the seventeenth century, or in the eighteenth century? Maybe during the second half of the nineteenth century, when many of our Latin American peoples were already independent, when our people felt the need and saw the possibility of struggling for their independence. And our people struggled for many years.

Were there no courageous and heroic people in the other centuries, capable of being as courageous and heroic as that generation? Yes, there were, but the historic moment did not exist.

The generation of 1868 had it in our country. The generation of 1953 had this privilege in our country. The people of Nicaragua, and the youth of Nicaragua, had this privilege in the 1970s.

No one should complain; no task is more honorable, noble, or stimulating than the task of being a revolutionary. However, it is also the most difficult, and it requires responsibility, self-sacrifice, discipline, and facing a thousand problems. We always say this to our people: We have advanced far in many fields, but we have difficult tasks ahead, and we have raised this with the people. We have said that we must overcome the basic problems of our productive sector in the next fifteen years. We must increase our exports, consolidate our economy, and not think about new consumer goods. We have discussed this with the people, with the youth, planning for our future.

The Nicaraguan people also have these responsibilities, this task. Difficult problems must never, can never, deter a real revolutionary. Great efforts must be exerted in agricultural and industrial production, despite the lack of raw materials and resources, amidst a dirty war, despite lower prices and undermined production. Therein lies the merit, heroism, and glory of revolutionary peoples who confront and defeat great obstacles. History is full of these examples.

I tell you sincerely: I see in the Nicaraguan people a magnificent, courageous, struggling, intelligent, and hard-working nation, and they will emerge victorious. They will emerge victorious from their struggle against economic obstacles. They will not lack collaboration from abroad. They will not lack friends who make efforts to help them.

However, the essential thing is the people's struggle, the use of natural resources, the savings in raw materials and fuel. This is essential, and I am convinced they will emerge victorious.

I am also convinced they will defeat this dirty war, with or without new budgets. Of course, the open allocation of funds to wage a dirty war, violating all norms of moral and international law, would not contribute to achieving peace in the area; it would not be an act of good faith, of goodwill.

I harbor the hope that peace and stability in the country will be achieved even faster through the efforts of countries in the area, through the efforts of many countries, in the quest for political solutions.

Our most heartfelt hope is that Nicaragua's right to live in peace will be achieved without any more bloodshed, without sacrificing more sons.

I harbor that hope, and, as I said, I see it as a real possibility, provided there prevails common sense, wisdom, good faith, and goodwill.

However, I also know that you will be able to defend your right to dignity, independence, and justice, regardless of the sacrifices involved.

I am completely sure that the people of Nicaragua will know how to honorably and gloriously fulfill this responsibility, which flows from the privilege of living in revolutionary times.

I am fully convinced that you, like the Cuban people, will emerge victorious. I also said not too long ago in Cuba: I harbor the hope that there will be peace for you, peace for the peoples of Central America, peace for the peoples of our hemisphere, and peace for the world.

Thank you. [*Ovation*]

We Will Not Renounce Our Principles

Interview with 'Washington Post' Correspondents

Karen De Young: At least verbally, this administration has been the most implacable enemy, at least in terms of rhetoric, that you have had in a long time. Do you think that [the December 14, 1984,] agreement on migration which has been signed is some indication that there has been a change?

Fidel Castro: It is true that this administration has been one of the most hostile toward our country in the economic field; it even banned travel by U.S. citizens to Cuba except for journalists — those who can come here are somewhat privileged — or those with relatives in Cuba and certain other cases for special reasons.

This government has stepped up the economic measures, the economic blockade, the pressure on different Western countries to obstruct trade with Cuba. It has tenaciously exerted major pressure on all European nations and Japan so they won't buy our nickel, with measures such as the ban on buying steel made with Cuban nickel or equipment made with Cuban nickel. Pressure was exerted on Japan, Britain, Italy, the FRG [Federal Republic of Germany], and all the other allies of the United States to block the renegotiation of Cuba's foreign debt. In effect, they have been very diligent in this direction.

In the political field they have also been very aggressive and in the military field they have been constantly threatening. All this is true, and yet we are grateful — seriously. Why? Because this forced us to undertake two major revolutions: one in the field of defense over the last four years. In the face of the U.S. threat, we have totally changed our concept of defense. We have increased our strength multifold, to the extent that we have really become an invulnerable, unconquerable, and unoccupiable country. We have organized the entire people as never before and

This interview was conducted January 30, 1985, by correspondents Karen De Young, Jim Hoagland, and Leonard Downie. It is excerpted here from the February 24, 1985, Granma Weekly Review, *which published the interview in its entirety.*

developed our ideas in the field of defense to such an extent that any military adventure against Cuba is doomed to fail.

Jim Hoagland: Are you trying to prevent what happened in Grenada from happening here?

Castro: No, if you want I'll explain that later.

What I want to say is that every citizen of this country knows what to do in the event of blockade, in the event of a war of attrition against the country, of bombing, invasion, even in the event of territorial occupation — and on a really solid, technical, and scientific basis. We believe our people have become an invincible people, unless they are wiped off the face of the earth. We said psychological, moral, and political conditions have been created; there is the awareness for a resistance which would be endless and untenable for the enemy. It would be very costly for us and we of course do not want to pass that test; it would really be very costly for the aggressors, a truly unpayable price! We wouldn't wish it on the people of Cuba or on the people of the United States; we would not want that kind of glory or victory. But I say calmly: we are today an incomparably stronger country than at the start of the Reagan administration. We know that and so do U.S. war experts.

Second, the hostile measures, the increase in economic measures against Cuba, and the international economic crisis have obliged us to undertake a genuine revolution in the field of the economy that is yielding very good results and is even more promising for the future. We have become much more efficient in the use of material resources and energy, of productive resources, than ever before; we have been able to work out ideas with the experience of all these years in the field of planning, in the way to draw up plans, priorities for investments, in order to achieve greater efficiency in economic and social development and the structure of production which best suits our future needs.

Since we have already made so many advances in the social field and have a reasonable level of clothing, shoes, household appliances, electricity, water, communication links, transportation, recreation, and food, with an average of 3,000 calories a day and eighty grams of protein — and in our country the statistics coincide with reality, whereas in others the average is meaningless and some consume five times more, and others far less, than the average. Since the state of health and education of the population is excellent, we have told young people that the main effort must be in the field of economic development; if a new textile mill is built, we shouldn't think of greater textile consumption per capita but rather of exporting and thus giving priority to investments for development, making optimum use of material and human resources with a long-term outlook.

With this in mind we have worked on the 1986-90 plan and the plan for 1990-2000, over the next fifteen years, for establishing an ideal production structure while meeting hard-currency obligations — which are not very high and in fact are the lowest in Latin America — to cover our import needs from that sector, develop trade with the socialist countries, which is very beneficial for us, and in the field of social development to give priority only to projects which have a great bearing on the population.

We are really becoming good, efficient administrators. I can give you some figures: in these years of crisis, 1982, 1983, and 1984, in this period the economies of Latin American nations as a whole declined by 9 percent while Cuba's grew by 24; this is for the 1982-84 period. Last year our economy grew by 7 to 8 percent, during 1984. In coming years our growth will be more moderate but much more centered on the solution of fundamental problems. We are also the only country — one of the few in the world, I think, I don't know if there is any other — that can draw up plans on a fifteen- and twenty-year basis without in any way counting on trade or economic relations with the United States.

We have created these conditions with the blockade and without trade with the United States for a long period of time; and we've achieved reliable development in the economic and social fields. What other country in the world has that privilege? In that sense we consider ourselves privileged. We have made the greatest effort in the last few years and in large measure we owe it to the current administration. We must really be grateful. . . .

[In response to additional questions on Cuba's relations with the U.S., Castro recounted his discussions with visiting U.S. congressmen and with Catholic archbishops. In referring to the possibility of discussions and talks with the U.S., Castro mentioned the agreement on migratory relations, the Shultz-Gromyko talks, and the negotiations between Washington and Angola regarding the situation in southern Africa, with the Angolans in close contact with the Cubans.]

Hoagland: Regarding the list of steps that could lead to an improvement, that is, one by one, there's a big omission: Central America.

Castro: Whose omission, yours or mine?

Hoagland: You spoke about Africa; you mentioned the possibilities of the coast guards, the list, but nothing about Central America.

Castro: Yes, you're right. I didn't mention it, and I'll explain to you why. I mentioned southern Africa because we are there, because of the presence of a considerable force in Angola, and because the Angolans are negotiating with the United States. I can convey our attitude regarding those talks by virtue of the fact that we have been cooperating with Angola in its efforts to achieve a solution. We are also informed; we have been in close contact and coordination with them. I was referring to the concrete fact that the United States and Angola are talking and we're involved, although not formally present in the negotiations; however we're participating and cooperating in fact in the efforts to find a peaceful solution. We also spoke about Cuba with regard to the agreement on migratory questions and other topics that can be discussed with the United States.

I didn't mention Nicaragua, because the situation there is not like that of Angola. We do not have a military force in Nicaragua, nor is the United States negotiating with the Nicaraguans in Nicaragua. It is a situation that differs from that of Angola. In all sincerity, it might have seemed incorrect for me to include Nicaragua or Central America in that list of points.

Now, I visited Nicaragua; I spoke there publicly. What one says publicly regarding politics has certain value, especially when one reasons and explains a position. I don't like to say: this is our position, we want to help Contadora, without explaining why we want to help Contadora. I spoke there of our disposition to cooperate in solutions for Central America.

I spoke about this with the legislators because they asked me a lot about my opinions and ideas on the topic.

I also spoke with the foreign ministers of the Contadora group, but I couldn't, in fact, identify Central America as a topic for possible conversations with the United States. While in Central America we have close relations with Nicaragua and with the revolutionary movement in El Salvador, we don't have an army in Central America. And — I repeat — I cannot state that we could discuss the problems of Central America and Nicaragua with the United States; I can't say that. That's why I didn't mention it; it's not that I forgot it in the least.

On the other hand, I think that a point could be reached in which we can cooperate and we are willing to cooperate in finding solutions to the problems in this area. I didn't mention it, because it wasn't correct to mention it in the context of the points I explained.

De Young: Then, do you not think that this would be an area where some exploration would prove fruitful for mutual cooperation between the United States and Cuba?

Castro: Well, all these questions are very delicate because the questions on Central America and Nicaragua must be discussed by the Nicaraguans and must be decided by the Nicaraguans, exclusively. On Central America, there's a group of countries and it's up to them to discuss and resolve their problems. We can't discuss on behalf of any of those countries and we must be very careful about that.

What we can do now is cooperate in the search for solutions given our friendly relations with the Nicaraguans and other forces in Central America. Having cleared that up, we can't discuss on anyone's behalf or take decisions on absolutely anyone's behalf.

The legislators asked me that question and I spoke with them about our willingness to exchange impressions with the United States on any subject on which the United States is interested in exchanging impressions and in knowing our points of view, on any subject; even if they want to talk about religion with us we are willing to speak on religion; we are willing to speak on economic problems, on the problem of the underdevelopment of the Third World. We are willing to speak with them on any subject.

Our countries can exchange impressions and let us hope that will help resolve the problem to some extent.

If such exchanges of impressions are considered useful, if the United States deems that useful, there's no objection on our part to exchanging impressions on subjects that are part of any problem, at any time. And it seems to me that under certain circumstances this can be useful, because I think that it would be good for us to know the points of view of the United States, and I am absolutely certain that it would be good for the United States to know our points of view on many world problems since we have broad information about them and relations with many countries. I think that my talks with the legislators proved that and so did my talks with the bishops.

I said to the bishops that we would talk with no reservations, no bias of any kind, that we were looking to communicate on differing viewpoints. I did say that, in my opinion, I was in a better condition to talk in that spirit since I had attended religious schools from the first grade up to my last senior high school year. I had, moreover, lived the whole experience of religion, of the church, of religious work; but none of them had attended a party school. That's the difference. On that plane, we discussed many topics.

I believe there's a dogmatism, a schematism on political themes; rather than ideas, there are very often beliefs. I've seen that in the world. Some of the positions are weak, some reasoning is very weak, certain criteria don't stand up to analysis. I've seen it; very often I see persons sustaining a belief rather than an idea. They don't have an idea as to this or that being bad, but believe it to be bad, and that belief often lacks foundation. I'm telling you the truth, as I see it.

In the United States itself, very often opinions are beliefs, not ideas, and many of the statements are not sustained on solid foundations. They are not sustained on solid foundations on many subjects concerning the world. I don't wish to offend anybody, but I say that the viewpoints are very simplistic, very simplistic and very schematic. I don't know whether the blame for this lies with the press or TV or schooling, the habit of believing rather than reasoning it out, of not meditating on a subject. This is the way it is, that's the way that is; it is simply said, this is bad, very bad. Cuba is bad, Cuba is ruined, and the revolution is a failure, it's a failure. Once that is said everybody starts repeating it; 500,

10,000, 100,000 people, millions of people then know and say that the revolution is a failure, that the Cuban model is bad while another is good.

There are times when going a little deeper people come up against the amazing fact that the results in those countries do not bear comparison with the results in Cuba, with what we have done over these twenty-six years — they do not stand up to any comparison. If, for instance, we dissect the data, with facts and figures, nothing that the rest of the Latin American countries have done even remotely approximates what we have done over the past twenty-six years, in spite of the blockade, U.S. hostility, threats to our country, and our efforts in the military field to defend ourselves.

And so those who speak about the failure of the Cuban revolution are simply voicing a belief. When they are ready to analyze it and start comparing Cuba's indices in every field with the richest country in Latin America, with the country having the greatest wealth and resources — we're not going to compare them with Jamaica or Haiti, or whatever, Paraguay — with the richest country, and start charting what they have done in these twenty-six years and all the indices we have achieved in every sense, then comes the question: where's the failure? Ours is a reality today. Twenty-five or twenty-six years ago, all we could talk about were ideas, criteria, goals, dreams; but now that twenty-six years have gone by, we can talk about the things we've done and compare them with all the rest. The day that a serious comparison is done of Cuba's all-around indices with those of a given country, even the richest country in Latin America, they'll see that there's no possible comparison.

I'm giving you this example because there's a lot of bias, a lot of set ideas, many truths taken as evident. I used to believe that there were only a few evident truths and that they were already embodied in the Declaration of Independence of the United States; but now I discover there are thousands of supposed evident truths in the United States, nearly all of them are considered evident.

It seems to me that by talking to others and listening to their points of view, and perhaps we too need to hear your points of view, any exchange of impressions would be useful.

De Young: If I may ask you a specific question on Central America. You said when you were in Nicaragua last month that one of the most important things that would have to be done to bring peace to Central America at this time was to encourage a political solution between the government of El Salvador and the FMLN-FDR. Since the U.S. government and Duarte have voiced their opposition to the main conditions set by the FMLN-FDR for a negotiated solution, do you see any room for maneuvers, any movement on the part of either of the two parties?

Castro: I made that statement because I objectively believe that it is posible to find a solution to the Nicaraguan problem in line with the Contadora efforts, within the framework of the Contadora efforts.

It seems to me I have sufficient information on that entire process: the work of Contadora, the U.S. viewpoints, Nicaragua's viewpoints, what worries one, what worries the other, where the main obstacles lie. I am convinced and I told this to the Contadora foreign ministers — the foreign ministers of Mexico, Panama, and Colombia; Venezuela wasn't present — that it was possible to find satisfactory solutions for both parties. I am fully convinced. It's not faith, it's not a belief; it's, in my opinion, a well-founded idea.

Besides, I'm convinced of something else: it's inconceivable for the United States to try to solve the Nicaraguan problem through intervention; it's inconceivable, I just can't picture it.

I can't picture it, first because it's absolutely unnecessary. I'm not even referring to the legal or moral problem for I think, in the first place, that it's unjustifiable from that angle. But viewed in practical terms, the United States has no need to carry out an action of that nature since the problems can be solved through negotiations.

Secondly, there's no justifying the political cost of that action for the United States in its relations with Latin America. Latin America is made up of many small, and some mid-size, and some large countries. Yet Latin America is a family, and this must not be forgotten. Latin America was a lot more incommunicado some fifty or sixty years ago. Even when there was the U.S. intervention in Santo Domingo nearly two decades ago, when it hurriedly dispatched 40,000 soldiers to land there, there was another spirit in Latin America. The Latin American countries were then tightly controlled by the OAS [Organization of American States], they were very much subordinate to U.S. policy, they were not then afflicted by the terrible crisis they are suffering now; their hopes were in the Alliance for Progress, the $20 billion offered by the United States, and other miraculous remedies.

Today's Latin America is entirely different from that one in every sense. I saw the reaction that took place in the whole of Latin America at the time of the Malvinas War, its strong spirit of solidarity with Argentina, in spite of the fact that no one harbored the slightest sympathy for the military government; and yet there was almost unanimous support from all countries for Argentina. That's a fact. I see much broader communication among Latin American countries, very much clearer ideas about the problems and the hopes and interests of its peoples. They were offered the sky as the limit twenty-four years ago, and what have they had in these twenty-four years? Are they now better off than twenty-four years ago? Is there greater well-being now than twenty-four years ago? Is their economy better now than twenty-four years ago? No.

Now, what have they gone through? Argentina endured the military governments, thousands of people missing — no one knows how many, whether it's 10,000, 15,000, there is even talk of 30,000. Even accepting the figure of 15,000, it was a horror tale never before experienced by Argentina. Uruguay used to be the Switzerland of America, it had never experienced before such a similar horror tale. Brazil endured twenty-one years of harsh, repressive military dictatorships. Chile used to be another Switzerland also and has now endured nearly twelve years of bloody, fascist military dictatorship; it has experienced for the first time so much horror.

Those countries are now emerging from that situation but, above all, they are faced with a very serious, very grave, and moreover insoluble economic problem — the worst thing is that these are insoluble situations so far. Twenty-four years ago they were told that everything was going to be solved with some reforms and $20 billion in a given number of years. Now they owe $360 billion, their population has doubled, and their economic and social problems are triple what they were twenty-four years ago. Now they must pay $40 billion each year by way of interest, in the midst of a more complex and difficult economic crisis than they have ever known before. That's the reality. It is the truth and they are desperate.

Any questions?

De Young: Everything you say is true.

Castro: I haven't said everything. I still haven't demonstrated it; [*Laughter*] if you are patient and listen a little I will try to substantiate it.

I have a lot of contacts with Latin Americans, even with traditional conservative politicians. Even the conservatives are disappearing in Latin America! I find the conservatives radicalized, there are stories they no longer want to hear about, because they had governments, such as the one in Chile, that did away with tariff barriers, following the liberal theories of the Chicago School to seek efficiency, competition from within and abroad. The doors were opened to goods from Japan, Taiwan, South Korea, and Singapore; the national economy was ruined; millions of people were left unemployed; the debt rose to $22 billion in Chile, $45 billion in Argentina, $5.5 billion in Uruguay. The conservatives see this problem, what theory? They are radicalized.

Now the military governments are in retreat. They don't want government, they can't retain power. They don't want it even if it is given to them, because the countries have become unmanageable. Now then, these civilian governments coming now don't have to fear a military coup. There may be some madman in Argentina, Uruguay, or Brazil who wants a coup but they are in a minority; the majority of the military men are not mad. Ah, but when the economic situation is fine, the economy advances and there is some internal trouble, nearly all, 90 percent, are mad and want a coup. Now they don't.

These governments come in and come up against the following situation: the standard of living in Argentina has declined by 30-40 percent. In Uruguay it has dropped by 50 percent, they owe $5.5 billion and export $1- or $1.05 billion; the standard of living has dropped by half; textile exports are hard hit by the protectionist measures of the United States; its chief export commodity is meat, its main market was Egypt, and the European Economic Community countries, with subsidized meat, have taken that market from them. This is the same EEC that before imported sugar and now demands a quota of 5 million tons on the world market, sugar which is also produced on a subsidized basis, thus ruining dozens of Third World countries.

They find that the markets are depressed. How can this problem be solved? With what standard of living? It isn't the same to start cutting back on 100 as on 50. Of the money that led to the debt some was invested in the country, or was frittered away, part of it was syphoned off while yet another part ended up in the United States. We would have to see how much of that debt is the result of flight of capital to the United States. That is the problem facing [Argentine Pres. Raúl] Alfonsín, [Uruguayan Pres. Julio] Sanguinetti, and [Brazilian President-elect] Tancredo Neves.

They say: we want to pay the debt but don't want to affect the population; we don't want to implement a recessive policy. They don't want to do it. What can they do, what will happen?

Never in history has there been such a social and economic situation, never in history. But there are worse things, because even a beggar reads magazines and finds luxury cars: Buy this luxury car, buy this, buy that. There are people who are going hungry with consumption habits that have been created in those countries, imported habits. Those countries are in a critical situation. It's not a question of civilian government or the struggle between civilian and military government. The problem is much more far-reaching.

In Peru there was a military government that was replaced by civilians who took more than half the votes cast and won a majority in parliament. Barely four years of civilian rule have passed and now they have the support of only 3.8 percent of the population with tremendous social instability.

Latin America is a powder keg, the situation is explosive. How they are going to emerge from this situation, I think, is a really serious problem and we should give thought to all those problems. With the situation as it is at this time, any military action against any Latin American country is playing with fire next to a powder keg.

There is another basic reason: U.S. intervention in Nicaragua would force them to kill many people, undoubtedly many Nicaraguans, and people from the United States would also die. There would be a heavy loss of life, I am absolutely convinced, and if they think in objective terms they will understand this. Nicaraguans are a brave, patriotic people and the Sandinistas have the support of the majority of the people; neutralizing and disarming every Sandinista one by one is an impossible task for an army of occupation. That is why I say an intervention in Nicaragua is inconceivable.

So, to answer your question.

If a solution is possible in Nicaragua within the Contadora framework, there is, in my opinion, also the fact that Contadora has not taken up the problem of El Salvador. The situation in El Salvador, which has been the center of the problem, has been cast aside and forgotten.

What I said was there can be no conceivable solution to the problems of Central America as long as there is still the idea of exterminating the revolutionaries in El Salvador down to the last one. I base myself on the idea that they can't be exterminated, on the conviction that they can resist indefinitely. They are now the most experienced people in Latin America in this field. And so I say, it might be illusory to concentrate on Nicaragua to come up with a solution, while forgetting the problem of El Salvador and while the view prevails that the revolutionaries there must be exterminated down to the last one. It seems to me unrealistic to seek a solution on such a basis, which is why I say we should further the dialogue between the government and the revolutionaries, encourage and support that dialogue, and seek a negotiated political settlement in El Salvador.

De Young: However, the positions of the two sides seem to be irreconcilable at this moment.

Castro: I don't believe so. I really don't.

De Young: In what area do you believe there's possible grounds for agreement?

Castro: I believe that if the two sides are really seeking peace in the country, that peace can be found.

I cannot and should not try to come up with formulas, because that's a task for the government and the FMLN-FDR.

I'm sure that when the Salvadorans who are now fighting speak of a dialogue they are being serious about it. However, I will say that we must not delude ourselves. If they're told to surrender, they are not going to surrender; if they are told to give up their revolutionary ideals, they're not going to give up their revolutionary ideals. I believe there are many serious problems to be solved in both civilian and military areas before a concrete formula can be worked out. And I believe that this is to the country's and to everybody's convenience; it might even be more to the convenience of the government than to the revolutionaries.

This is the way I see it: whereas the revolutionaries can go on resisting indefinitely, it remains to be seen whether or not the government and the army can do the same, whether or not the contradictions between civilians and military go on indefinitely, whether or not the contradictions between the extreme right wing and the Christian Democratic government can go on indefinitely. It's a situation fraught with potential problems for [Napoleón] Duarte, for the army, for the right wing, for [Roberto] D'Aubuisson. In my opinion, fraught with potential risks for everybody.

When I say that encouragement and support must be given, I think that the revolutionaries have their country's interests at heart, and those of the region and Nicaragua even. I believe that they have them so much at heart as to demonstrate they are amenable to seek negotiated solutions, although I must admit it won't be easy.

I admit that it's a complex problem and that getting all sides to come to an agreement is not easy. In fact, I believe it will be easier to find a solution in Nicaragua than in El Salvador, but I also realize that, if a solution is found in Nicaragua and the war in El Salvador continues, the situation in Central America will continue to be a complex one. That is the fact of the matter.

What's happening now in Nicaragua and El Salvador? I think that at this time the United States hopes to destroy the Nicaraguan revolution from within through a whole series of economic difficulties similar to those of any other Central and Latin American country, plus the damage caused by war, on the one hand, and the actions of the counterrevolutionary bands on the other.

I am convinced that the United States hopes to liquidate the revolution through the effects of the two factors: economic stranglehold and the actions of the bands. And I think that as long as the United States harbors such hopes it will not be speaking seriously about a willingness to find a negotiated political solution which, the way I see it, would be the most convenient for the United States, because if the idea is to destroy the Sandinistas, why save their lives?

I'm convinced that this is the prevailing logic at this moment. I am also convinced that the Sandinistas can face these difficulties, with the resources they have and the assistance they are receiving from abroad, if they make good use of those resources.

Several days ago there was talk about Soviet ships, seven Soviet ships on their way to Nicaragua with weapons. In all truth, there wasn't a single round of ammunition aboard those ships. The report about those seven ships carrying weapons was absolutely false, because there wasn't a single round of ammunition aboard. What was important was that they were carrying cargo: oil, foodstuffs, raw materials, and equipment. Those ships were carrying essential commodities. That is what I believe is of significance: the fact that they were not carrying ammunition but rather cargo that Nicaragua needed very much.

With the resources Nicaragua has — despite the war and the sabotage that has affected fishing, lumber, gold mining, cattle raising, and coffee production — with what it is producing and the assistance it is receiving from various socialist and Western countries, the country can face up to its economic difficulties. What's more, I am convinced that the bands will be defeated whether or not they get a budget, that is, whether or not the U.S. Congress approves the budget for helping the counterrevolution. In fact, it seems to me that if such a budget is passed in open defiance of world public opinion, with the purpose of waging a secret, or so-called secret war against the Nicaraguan government, it will be a blow to the Contadora group's efforts, it will affect U.S. authority and its role in the area and detract from U.S. credibility in the eyes of world public opinion. The United States stands to gain nothing. The theory that the credits must be passed in order to pressure the Nicaraguans into negotiating is false. The Nicaraguans have always been willing to negotiate and to find a solution, whether the budget is passed or not. I believe that their morale will be further strengthened when United States persistence on its dirty war against Nicaragua is exposed to world public opinion and to all the Nicaraguan people. This will give the Nicaraguans added strength and I believe they will receive greater international support. To me, the whole thing seems absurd.

[Arturo] Cruz made a tremendous mistake. He went to ask the U.S. Congress to grant him funds for a war that has already cost the people of Nicaragua, the Sandinistas, 4,000 lives — largely civilian lives, including women and children: a total of 4,000 lives and between 6,000 and 7,000 wounded. When a man travels to a great power such as the United States to propose that it go on providing him with money for a war that may take the lives of another 10,000 persons in his own country, don't even begin to imagine that the Nicaraguan people are going to applaud such an action! They will look on it as an act of treason. I really believe that the United States has nothing to gain from such a stand. For me it is inconceivable that there be any such interference in a problem that can be resolved taking into account the interests of Nicaragua, the United States, and Central America. That's my opinion.

I don't think it's so difficult to find a solution in Nicaragua. I think it'll be more difficult in El Salvador, given that not so much effort has been made in that direction. The problem has been sort of put aside and it's only now that they're beginning to worry about it. It's a complex problem calling for a great deal of work. I came up with no formula, because in my opinion this is no time to come up with a priori formulas, and least of all could I be the one to come up with one. It's simply an idea, a concept, a reality. Work must be done in that direction; any effort that is made in that direction is worthwhile. If Duarte spoke with the

FMLN, that must be given encouragement and work must be done in that direction. In fact, even the pope and the bishop of El Salvador spoke in Caracas and expressed their hope that the dialogue will be resumed after the elections are held.

I think that Duarte is in a tough spot given the opposition from the right wing, from D'Aubuisson. He's under strong attack. I don't know what the army's position will be, but it's obvious that Duarte is now in no condition to resume the dialogue and must therefore wait until the elections. However, I know that when the FMLN expresses this will to negotiate, it is neither a slogan nor a political ploy or tactic. It is being serious. I say that because I know it to be a fact.

Of course, as long as the idea exists of a military victory being possible, of them liquidating the revolutionaries down to the last one as an exemplary punishment, so that never again will there be revolutions in Central America or anywhere else, then neither the United States nor Duarte nor the army will be willing to negotiate. Unfortunately, it'll be necessary to wait until they are persuaded of the contrary. I mean, I do believe that a solution is possible, but before that happens a few premises will have to go, among them the premise that Nicaragua can be destroyed from within, and that the Salvadoran revolutionaries can be exterminated and defeated.

De Young: Are you implying that you also think that the FMLN cannot score a military victory in El Salvador?

Castro: You mean now?

De Young: Or in the future.

Castro: Well, it doesn't seem easy, under present conditions, for there to be a military victory in the near future. The way I see it, neither the military will defeat the guerrillas nor will the guerrillas defeat the military in the near future. It mustn't be forgotten that the Salvadoran army has suffered many defeats. What's more, any other army would be completely demoralized by now. But I say that the Salvadoran army is like a suit on a hanger. You can hit it from every angle, hit it a hundred times and it won't fall off because it's on the hanger — and the hanger is United States might, United States economic resources, United States military resources, the weapons, the helicopters, the planes, the advisers, and the political support. That's what keeps the Salvadoran army going. Without the United States indirect interference in El Salvador, the revolutionaries would defeat the army, for sure.

That army, the recipient of a torrent of supplies, of resources of all kinds, is holding up and can be maintained there. Under present conditions, the revolutionaries cannot defeat the army, but the army is also unable to defeat them. Whose side will time be on, who will be able to resist the longest? If that's the way things stand, I think it would be logical for everybody to seek a way out of this situation other than military victory.

Of course, I'm not speaking for the Salvadoran revolutionaries. I'm simply expressing my opinion, according to what I know and the information I have regarding each side's position.

It'll take some time. It won't depend only on good will. Either these two premises have to be dropped, either the idea of a military victory is dropped or there'll never be serious negotiations in Nicaragua or El Salvador. Unfortunately, that's the way things stand. But words, arguments, and analysis of the events will certainly help to persuade those who must be persuaded. I'm convinced that a negotiated solution would be in the best interests of the United States and of the Central American peoples. I'm thoroughly convinced. If I didn't think it wouldn't be to the convenience of the United States it would scarcely be worth even talking about it.

Hoagland: Let's see if we can establish a contact that would contribute to an exchange of views between the United States and Cuba about these questions, because two years ago a Cuban official said that Cuba had not sent military supplies to the revolutionaries in El Salvador since January 1981. Is that statement still valid?

Castro: A Cuban official said that, since 1981? I don't remember that.

De Young: I remember that Carlos Rafael told me that.

Castro: What did Carlos Rafael tell you?

De Young: That Cuba has sent no arms or military support to El Salvador since early 1981, following the final offensive.

Castro: I don't believe Carlos could have said that in such absolute terms, in that way. What I seem to remember, perhaps what he said at that time, was that the Salvadoran revolutionaries had not received arms or supplies for a long time after that final offensive.* I don't want to go into details about this. We're talking about the political aspects of the problem and I wouldn't want this interview to end with a request for information about concrete facts, supplies, and such things. I don't think I should talk about this, I don't deem it proper to do so. We're talking about the problems in general and these are already the details of whether they received or did not receive any, who sent and who didn't send them, if it's possible or not possible for them to be sent. The most I can tell you is that under present conditions, in practice, it is extremely difficult for the revolutionaries to receive supplies. That's all I can tell you. I'm not judging or analyzing; I'm not denying or affirming anything. I want to point this out as a reality. But that isn't a problem that concerns them, it is not a fundamental problem for them.

We have our own experience, because we waged our war against Batista's army. We started with only a few people. We started with eighty

*Later in the interview, De Young stated that she had recalled that Rodríguez had been speaking of Nicaragua, not El Salvador.

and then there were only ten or twelve of us fighting an army bigger than that of El Salvador. Whereas the Salvadoran army is better advised, equipped with more modern arms and more planes, Batista had 70,000 men ready for action, and in twenty-five months' time we fought the war against Batista and defeated his army. Barring a few exceptions — a couple of times we received an insignificant number of arms — 90 percent of the weapons and 90 percent of the ammunition with which we waged the war was captured from Batista's army. We waged a war without logistics. Because I believe in that possibility, because I lived through that experience; the miracle that makes or can make a revolutionary movement is that of waging a war with the arms captured from the enemy.

It is my conviction that the Salvadorans can go on fighting for five and maybe ten years more without collapse. For the Salvadoran revolutionaries, logistics are logistics. And that's something the Salvadoran army can't do. Three months without logistics and it'll be very difficult, I'd say practically impossible.

I'm not saying that the Salvadorans should receive logistics in order to continue the war. I can even imagine the struggle in the worst conditions and without logistics and still insist on the fact that they can go on fighting indefinitely. Time will tell.

Hoagland: According to your answer, you reserve the right to send supplies to the guerrillas if you deem it the proper thing to do. That's precisely the problem the United States raises with respect to Cuba.

Castro: Are you asking me from a moral standpoint?

Hoagland: I'm asking you from the standpoint of improved relations with the United States.

Castro: Well, an improvement in relations with the United States can never occur on the basis that we renounce moral principles in the face of the United States. When I speak about renouncing principles, I am not talking about renouncing principles in terms of philosophical, juridical, legal, or moral questions, but rather with regard to a willingness to work and struggle to find solutions to the problems. I think that is our position, but it is not a position whereby we are going to renounce our principles, our morale, and our point of view, but rather to work in a direction in which there is no need for either war, weapons, or ammunition. That is our position.

This doesn't mean that we make the solemn pledge that we are going to renounce a certain thing or other and say that we feel very happy about improving relations with the United States on the condition that we promise never to send a bullet to any revolutionary. No. There are other things. I think that any correct path, in terms of international relations, cannot be based on tricks, lies, or any kind of maneuvering. I don't believe in the outcome of lies, tricks, or renouncing principles. I would say that international relations must be based on principles, and I mean a principle of international relations that we can accept: that no government interfere in the internal affairs of another. That is a principle and it is a principle we can accept, evidently, as a correct principle. Now, this implies a principle that is binding on everyone, an international norm: that nobody interfere in internal affairs; that we, although we may be sympathetic to certain ideas and certain intentions, do not interfere, but neither should the United States or others interfere.

Now, in reality, in what Latin American country has the United States not interfered in the internal affairs or intervened in one way or another? Central America is full of stories of interventionism on the part of the United States. Not long ago, 40,000 soldiers intervened in Santo Domingo to prevent the triumph of a popular movement. There were more than enough pretexts: they were subversives; Cuba was behind it all. But long before Cuba existed as a revolutionary country, even before I was born, the United States practiced intervention in Latin American countries.

When I go to talk with the United States, I'll have nothing to talk about, because you have completely interrogated me here.

I think that the topic we are addressing is very important. We can have a principled policy which is to all intents and purposes feasible. I think we must responsibly struggle for a principled policy and norms in Latin America. We can do that. I think that when discussions have bases like these, they are serious and frank. They don't involve anyone renouncing their ideas, changing their banner, or renouncing the spirit of solidarity. And clearly we are not going to renounce any moral or political principle. It would be illusory to think that relations can improve by renouncing principles. I think that relations between countries, between the United States and Cuba, can improve on a basis of principles, and I think that everybody stands to gain. These are the principles of the UN and the Organization of American States; these principles are to be found in all the constitutions.

I think that when we talk about improving relations, it must be on this basis, not that we say that we renounce a principle: "We solemnly pledge not to do a certain thing." If that is to be the price for improved relations with the United States, we cannot pay that price. I say this in all honesty. It's preferable not to talk, not to converse, not to think about it. It will have to wait until they can be persuaded that it cannot be that way.

I think that what happens between the United States and Cuba is important, more so for the United States than for us. I say this frankly. The problems that the United States can have with this hemisphere are serious, because I speak in all frankness when I say that I am going on the objective situation of those countries and the way events have unfolded. I think that the United States must think in the long term and develop concepts and ideas that guide its relations with Latin America in the future, because, really, the idea of intervening every time there is social change is an absurd idea and no one can guarantee that social changes are not going to occur.

So I am telling you the truth, between you and me: I think it is impossible to export a revolution, because revolution is a product of a series of economic, social, historical, and cultural factors that no one can export. An army can carry out a coup, can do anything, but a revolution cannot be exported. A revolution cannot come about if the conditions do not exist. It can be encouraged. I would say that the greatest influence there can be on these problems is in the field of ideas. Ideas have been the driving force behind revolutions everywhere. So, Christianity was a revolution that took hundreds of years to come about but when it did it wrought a moral revolution. The ideas, shall we say of the French Encyclopedists, Voltaire, Rousseau, influenced, made possible or facilitated or propelled the social revolution, but not only because of the content of those ideas, but rather because those ideas adequately corresponded to the conditions existing in France at that time.

All revolutions have thinkers who precede them, but no thinker emerges where the conditions which inspire revolutionary thought do not exist. That was the case with the French Revolution and the U.S. Revolution. During the first century of the colonization of North America, no one could have spoken of revolution; no one could have thought of a revolution for independence, because the factors which determine or inspire revolutionary thought did not exist. The truth is that the ideas emerge once the problems exist. You may have the most revolutionary ideas 300 years before and have no influence, but the reality is that no one has revolutionary ideas before the realities exist. In medieval, feudal France, rampant with all kinds of injustices, thinkers who analyzed that situation emerged and said: "this is bad, this must change," and began to inspire those who brought about that change. But that thinker would not have accomplished anything if the social conditions had not existed.

In the United States, no one spoke of a declaration of independence 100 years before, but when the conditions, the contradictions between the colonies and the crown were ripe, ideas emerged and ideas were also taken from Europe, especially France.

Marxist ideas did not come into being until a developed capitalist society emerged, along with a large working class and growing social conflict. The thinkers then began to develop ideas about new realities. Before then, there only utopians. Campanella wrote and Thomas More wrote. Did they write about socialism? Yes, about a utopian socialism. Marxism couldn't emerge in the society of Rome or Greece! No one was going to speak of socialism. They did speak of democracy, but it was the democracy of a minority in a society where there were slaves and all sorts of injustice.

What I am saying is the following: ideas exert influence, they help revolution, but they help where there are the requisite conditions. Now, who is going to think, for example, that a revolution is going to break out in present-day U.S. society? That doesn't occur to anyone, because economic, social, and cultural conditions are different. Now, if you situate it in a country like Bolivia, it is impossible to govern it. [Bolivian Pres. Hernán] Siles Zuazo is a man full of good intentions and the desire to work for his country. The Bolivian Communist Party is helping Siles Zuazo and cooperating with him to save the democratic process so that the country can advance, but the conditions are so difficult. The social situation, the economic crisis, unemployment are so intense that although the Communist Party is with the government, the workers and the population in general are taking to the streets, occupying the factories, and going on strike. Why? Because they are hungry, because they cannot tolerate the economic situation. There you have an example where the Communist Party supports the government and, nevertheless, there is tremendous social instability as a consequence of the economic and social situation.

I honestly believe that revolution cannot be exported. But, on the other hand, I also believe that it cannot be prevented. It can neither be exported nor prevented. I am completely convinced of this viewpoint. In reality, neither can we export revolution to Latin America nor can the United States block the social changes in our countries. Of course, ideas, subjective factors are elements which exert an influence over events.

I do not think that man makes history; I don't know if it was Carlyle or another philospher or thinker who said that man made history — man makes no history. If George Washington had been born during the first years of the colony, he wouldn't have been the leader of the War of Independence in the United States. Although he would have had the same sentiments of goodwill and nobility, he wouldn't have been able to. If Lincoln were to be alive now, he wouldn't play the role he played. If Lincoln had lived during the struggle for independence, he wouldn't have been the Lincoln we know, the man who fought against slavery and played that role. How can there be a fighter against slavery if there is no slavery or after slavery has disappeared? This could come about when there was slavery, and not only slavery, but also industrial developments in the North and a conflict of interests between the North and the South. Individual persons do not make history. They can interpret events, develop ideas, think, and help. They can help, ideas and subjective factors, but they cannot decide.

As I see the current situation in Latin America, I say that there will inexorably be changes — not because someone wants them or because someone promotes them, but because the situation demands it.

What is the United States going to do? Intervene in all the countries where there are changes? We admit that it could do so in Grenada, in a country of 400 square kilometers and 120,000 inhabitants. Imagine if someday a revolution were to occur in Brazil. Is it going to solve the problem as it did in Grenada? Insofar as changes occur in small countries like Cuba, Nicaragua, or any other Central American country or Caribbean island, it may still physically be able to send troops. Well, it's more difficult in some cases and virtually impossible or useless in others.

But, when there are social changes in South America, can it prescribe intervention?

De Young: What did Grenada mean to you, not necessarily from the point of view of the invasion, but from the point of view of the revolutionary process?

Castro: Which revolutionary process, that of Grenada or of Cuba?

Interpreter: Of Grenada.

De Young: Wasn't it the right time, the appropriate time for a revolution?

Castro: Look, I am going to give you my opinion on Grenada. In a small country, a group of men like Bishop with ideas, tired of Gairy and all that, took power. It was a case in which we were as much surprised as the United States. There was the sudden news that Maurice Bishop and his movement had taken power. We knew Bishop; more correctly, we knew about Bishop. This is an example, it broke out alone. Even in Latin America, in Bolivia, for example, in 1952, there was a revolution. The workers and the peasants disarmed the army.

Bishop was a realist; he was not an extremist. He understood the problems of his country which were very complicated. The country didn't have a currency; it lived off tourism. Under very difficult conditions he began to make social changes. Bishop was not building socialism. He advanced social measures, an agrarian reform. Bishop did not nationalize any hotel; he took no measure which could be called socialist. He began to seek help and resources to push forward education, health, and some economic development programs. In other words, Bishop was inspired by a revolutionary theory; he was inspired by a political theory, but he was not trying to build socialism. He was actually trying to develop his country with the cooperation of everyone, of the European Economic Community, Britain, socialist countries, Cuba. That's what he was doing. He maintained a broad policy. Not long before his death, Bishop had visited the United States, and we were in complete agreement with his policy, a careful, moderate, realistic, and intelligent policy. That's the truth. We helped them; we made an effort because it was a small country. If we were to help India, with its 700 million inhabitants, no matter how much we might give, it would be little. But in a country as small as Grenada, a small effort is important. Do you understand? If we give $100 million of aid to India at a given time, that would signify fourteen cents per inhabitant. If we gave $100 million of aid to Grenada, that signified approximately $1,000 per inhabitant.

A project like the airport in which we provided the equipment, the materials and the labor force, the blueprint, is not important for how dearly it cost us, but rather for its worth, shall we say $60 million. It might also be said that it was a project that had British, French, Canadian, and even U.S. cooperation — a U.S. enterprise did excavation work. It was, moreover, an airport that did not have even one military stone; it was a civilian airport. As they live off tourism, they had a small airport. I don't know, the airport for Grenada was like the canal for Panama, like the railroad to California for the United States; it was vital, a vital project. We could do it; we had engineers, numerous engineers, people who could go there to help them, work, and at the same time teach the Grenadians. So, an airport that cost $60 million in Grenada is like a $6 billion project in Cuba. That's why, with a relatively small effort, we could help the country a great deal.

Well, I'm not going to talk about that; I will simply say that all the theories meant to justify the invasion of Grenada are false, completely false. The idea that it was an arsenal from which to distribute arms is false. The fact that there were a few thousand rifles is because the Grenadians, just like any people in a similar situation, always view the arms they have as too few. They request more from some, then from others, from everyone. When the domestic problem emerged, these people — an extremist group, hard on theory, that conspired against Bishop and killed him — divorced themselves from the people. Then they collected the weapons. The troops found these weapons put away, because they were the arms of the militia that had been gathered up. That's the reason the weapons were there.

Now, that group really committed political suicide and created what I consider an absurd situation by removing Bishop from office and, above all, by killing him. Bishop was a man loved by all the people. None of this justifies the U.S. invasion; in no way does it justify the U.S. invasion. And neither were the students in the remotest danger, because those people even strove to give the students and U.S. representatives every guarantee. All that was a pretext to destroy a political process that was dead.

U.S. politicians and the U.S. press did not maintain a principled position regarding the problem. At first they criticized the invasion. Then, as a result of the campaign, all the propagandizing that was done, the people arriving and kissing the ground, the majority of opinion, the press, and the politicians supported the invasion of Grenada. It was not a very glorious page of history for U.S. politicians and the U.S. press, to tell the truth. We know very well all that happened there and we can only judge by our conscience. I think that what Bishop was doing was correct; his policy was correct.

Now, the U.S. administration was helped by the extremists. The United States used force to wipe out a political process that was already dead.

We did not leave there simply because it was said that an American squadron was on its way. Under those conditions we wouldn't leave there or anywhere, I guarantee you. We are somewhere and we're told that an American squadron is on its way, well, we don't leave there and that's all there is to it. What's more, the instructions that the people received were: be careful, fight if they attack, fight if they actually attack, because the government was indefensible. You cannot defend a country whose goverment has divorced itself from the people. We told people to fight — to tell the truth, we even told them not to fire if there was any move to repatriate or evacuate the students, because the end of the runway they were building was very close to the School of Medicine. We told them that if they saw any movement on the runway, any landing on the runway for the purpose of evacuating the students, not to interfere in that operation, even if it was in the runway area. And people were told to fight if attacked.

I'm going to tell you the truth. If people had been given other instructions, to take positions and fight any landing there, there would have been a high number of U.S. casualties. People didn't even fire against the planes during the first moments. When they were landing, they had instructions to fire if attacked. That's the truth. Then they landed and went to attack the Cuban cooperation personnel. And then there were clearly serious errors on the part of those who were directing people. Despite the warnings that there could be, in our opinion, a U.S. intervention, all the weapons were stored in boxes; no one was armed. So, getting the boxes, finding the arms, all this occurred as the landing was in progress. This created tremendous disorganization there. If the internal situation that necessitated telling people to defend their places of work if attacked had not existed; if those circumstances hadn't existed, rest assured, they wouldn't have been able to land there so easily. They definitely would have had a large number of casualties.

The internal situation that evolved in Grenada was an absurd situation. No group of people could have been in a worse state of mind than they were. Our people were very angry, very indignant about the events, about Bishop's murder. Those were the circumstances.

Now I think that was unnecessary. Even if the United States hadn't invaded that country, that government was spent. There's no arguing the fact that it was spent. We had decided to finish the airport and leave, with perhaps the exception of the doctors. We would have left the doctors. But our cooperation with that government would have ceased. That's because we follow a norm and a principle. Who do you think those who carried out the coup distrusted? Us. I want you to know that even Bishop, during the brief period he was free, and Bishop's friends asked us to help. We adhered to the position: this is an internal affair and we do not meddle in internal affairs. We did not trust those people who took power at all. We were so indignant that we planned to withdraw from there when the airport was finished. And I think that when we withdrew no one else would have helped the government, it wouldn't have been able to keep going. The United States carried out an invasion for the sake of invading a country, as a symbol, as a show of force.

You asked if this was the result of Grenada, and I say it's not. We began to fortify ourselves when Reagan won the elections, apart from the fact that we'd seen the Santa Fe document and noted a series of ideas. We saw that far right, conservative, aggressive thinking was gaining strength in the United States. We analyzed the factors that determined this and they are many: the economic crisis and its effect on the United States, inflation and its concomitant factors, the Santa Fe document, the line that Cuba be given an opportunity to renounce being revolutionary or risk liquidation. We thus began to prepare ourselves. When the events unfolded in Grenada — when was that, in 1982 or 1983? In 1983 — we had already been working intensely for two years on strengthening our defenses and fortifying the country. When the Grenada events took place, we stepped up a great deal more. The only influence that Grenada had is that we are even more decisive, more motivated, and have even greater conviction in our actions. I would say that the Grenada events multiplied our strength, but I will add something: they multiplied the strength of the Sandinistas and everyone fortified themselves after Grenada.

History will some day judge the facts.

De Young: But by late 1983 you began to withdraw personnel from Nicaragua.

Castro: In 1983, no. You say after the invasion of Grenada?

De Young: December 1983.

Castro: No, we actually gained experience from Grenada. In Grenada, there were many fifty-some, sixty-, and sixty-five-year-old men. In Grenada there were a large number of people who were not in physical shape to mount a resistance in the event of an attack. The measure that we took was to choose the cooperation personnel who had the physical conditions to resist any invasion there, in other words, to join the Nicaraguans and take on the kind of struggle that might be waged there. We arranged for only the number of personnel strictly necessary for all the tasks of cooperation we are carrying out in building the sugar mill, in agriculture, in education, and in health. Of course, we've had teachers there and there was a reduction in the number of teachers. We had trained a number of Nicaraguan teachers in Cuba and since the beginning there's been the assumption that our teachers would gradually be replaced by Nicaraguan teachers as they were trained. We helped them train around 1,500 teachers who gradually replaced our teachers.

Also, since such a campaign was being conducted concerning Cuban cooperation personnel, teachers, we analyzed the situation in the area and decided that it was positive for the Nicaraguans to train their own personnel to carry out these functions and to reduce Cuban personnel involved in the kind of activities that they can carry out. We are now aiding them with university professors, in other kinds of education, but elementary education in the countryside is being handled by the Nicaraguans. As part of the prevailing political situation, the situation of tension, the presence of Cuban cooperation personnel was being used a great deal in the campaign against Nicaragua. So it was really more convenient for political reasons that they themselves undertake the work of elementary education in the countryside.

We do have the essential personnel there for many other fields of cooperation. The war itself impedes economic work, does it not? You can't have teachers in an extensive war zone, because the teachers were always unarmed and Cuban teachers isolated in the mountains were running certain risks. This is the policy we are following: to have the indispensable cooperation personnel, not one more than necessary, but neither one less than necessary. There is considerable cooperation personnel there; I'm not going to say the number because that's up to the Nicaraguans to say, not us. If they want to say how many there are in the various fields let them do so. Around 500 construction workers were building the sugar mill. Now that the sugar mill has been completed they are leaving. There is a group of workers helping to start up operations in the sugar mill. They have the cooperation personnel that they have required from us, not one more nor one less. Among the cooperation personnel, there is, for example, a sector which is very difficult to replace: the doctors. There are several hundred doctors. We have cooperation personnel in the economic sphere, as well as the military sphere, the number of which I am also not going to give. If there is an agreement regarding the withdrawal of the cooperation personnel from this field and the Sandinistas subscribe to it, we will immediately comply with the agreement and withdraw. If they request that we withdraw half of the military cooperation personnel, we'll withdraw them. If they request that we withdraw all of them, we'll withdraw all of them. In other words, if the agreement is as such, if it includes the withdrawal of cooperation personnel, we do not need verification of any kind, nor are we worried. We'll comply with the agreements that they subscribe to.

Now, if the Sandinistas do not subscribe to an agreement, under no concept would we unilaterally withdraw cooperation personnel from there. We withdraw the cooperation personnel that they request, that they agree to. If the agreement is that all the cooperation personnel are withdrawn, we'll withdraw all the cooperation personnel, but the Sandinistas must actually determine this. This is not an issue that we can decide unilaterally simply because it suits us to withdraw the cooperation personnel. That we cannot do.

Hoagland: I want to be sure that I really understand what you meant with regard to the verification.

Castro: I think that the verification would benefit the Nicaraguans more than anyone else, because, in reality, for three years there have been bases, training camps, supplies from Honduras and Costa Rica to wage the dirty war in Nicaragua and this has always been denied. If the verification is effective, practical, and logical, and not humiliating, it would benefit the Nicaraguans more than anyone, in my opinion. I have no doubt that it would benefit them the most and, therefore, verification is not an impediment to an agreement.

Hoagland: I wanted to confirm that.

Castro: I was saying that we do not need verification. The surest thing in the world is that if the Sandinistas make an agreement, we will comply with it. If the agreement is to withdraw half of the military advisers, we'll withdraw them. If it's to withdraw all of them, we'll do so. If it's to withdraw all the cooperation personnel, we'll do that too. We don't need any verification because we're not going to resort to tricks and lies, nor are we going to disguise a soldier as a doctor. That's foolish. A country that has self-respect, does not partake in such things. Moreover, my opinion is that the ideal would be to withdraw all foreign military cooperation personnel from Central America and to end all arms supplies to Central America. That's my exclusively personal opinion, but I'm not proposing anything. We will comply with the agreement which the Sandinistas reach. That's our position and, moreover, we are in favor of seeking political solutions in the area.

I believe that our thinking is very clear from what I've told you. We don't have any kind of contradiction, because our opinion of the Central American, Latin American situation for us, in reality, is very clear. What we think is not contradictory; it is consistent. We fortunately have our line, our position void of contradictions, with nothing to hide. The area's entire situation and what we must do is clear to us.

De Young: Can I ask you a question about Angola?

Do you see any chance, if there is an agreement between South Africa and Angola facilitated by the United States leading to the withdrawal of Cuban forces from Angola, of this perhaps reducing tension between the

United States and Cuba, which would in turn reduce tension in other areas?

Castro: I think that wherever solutions are obtained this helps diminish tension everywhere. I think an isolated agreement in one place not only helps relations between the countries of the area but exerts a positive influence on the whole international scene. Well, were there to be an agreement there, an agreement acceptable to the Angolans — the Angolans are the ones who must decide — with real guarantees for Angolan security, that is possible. We feel those guarantees should include: implementation of [United Nations] Resolution 435, the independence of Namibia, a halt to aid for UNITA — that is, the South African FDN [Nicaraguan Democratic Force] — with verification, of course, by means of an international agreement signed by the various sides at the Security Council. In a period of time it would be possible to withdraw — the Angolans have said three years — the Southern Troops Grouping, which constitutes the bulk of the [Cuban] forces stationed there, leaving others in the central and northern parts of the country whose withdrawal would be discussed and agreed upon by Cubans and Angolans, depending on the prevailing climate of security. That is the idea.

The South Africans have been organizing subversive groups and using them in Angola for eight years now. Angola is a very big country with extensive communications, large bridges, and those groups can do a lot of damage. The Angolans would need time to replace our troops with their forces; they can't do it all of a sudden.

They are working in good faith to find a solution. The countries of southern Africa, of Black Africa, have a very firm position on this. They oppose linking Resolution 435 to the withdrawal of Cuban troops.

I will tell you the truth, the Front Line states of Black Africa in general are not happy with the idea of the withdrawal of Cuban troops; they feel very threatened by South Africa. That is a fact and you can go and speak to them; the countries of Black Africa are the ones best able to explain their positions. We know that all the independent countries of southern Africa are not happy with the withdrawal idea, because the Cuban forces are the only outside forces that have helped them against South Africa. They feel that when those forces leave they might be at the mercy of South Africa, because South Africa has been very aggressive, and they are very distrustful.

There is something else: even though the South African forces pull back to their border, they can be at the Angolan border in twenty-four hours, while we are 10,000 kilometers away. These are the realities and they totally distrust South Africa. Neither Angola nor the other countries of Black Africa are happy at the prospect.

I don't want to speak for them, you can talk to them; you can ask Nyerere for his views, Zambia and Zimbabwe for their views, the Congo and

Mozambique. They of course want an overall solution, with peace for Mozambique and Angola, with guarantees; but they are very distrustful of South Africa, because it has been very aggressive and has created counterrevolutionary bands in Angola and Mozambique.

In Mozambique there was peace, there was no civil war, there were no problems. The South Africans organized former Portuguese colonialists, soldiers who served with Rhodesia's Ian Smith, and Blacks who had been with the Portuguese. They organized and trained them and they supplied weapons, planes, and helicopters. The war in Mozambique was created by South Africa.

South Africa also sponsors subversion in the small nation of Lesotho.

None of these countries feels protected against South African activity, not one of them. They also have strong feelings of rejection for apartheid.

All African states, all nations of Black Africa, states ruled by both leftist and rightist movements, are united by their hatred of apartheid, their revulsion of apartheid. They are not resigned to it; there is not one that isn't against apartheid. We have supported those who have fought apartheid, and fought the aggressors.

Hoagland: I understand that right now the Cuban troops in the south are stationed along a static defense line, for protection in the event of South African attack.

Castro: Of course, they are in a strategic line, because the South Africans have certain advantages near the border, near their air and logistical bases; that is the area they move in. Our forces defend a strategic line further back to cope with any large-scale South African attack. Their positions and defense and counterattack mission are determined by rigorous military and technical considerations.

Hoagland: Do they participate in the fighting against UNITA?

Castro: No, they do not participate directly in the fighting against UNITA. That is a task for the Angolan units, although we give them troop combat advice and support with technical means if required. We have trained many of their command cadres, selected from among the best fighters.

Hoagland: In the event of withdrawal, would it always be to the center and north?

Castro: No, those forces would be brought back to Cuba.

Hoagland: But after the withdrawal of the troops from the south would there still be 10,000 Cuban soldiers north of the thirteenth parallel?

Castro: Yes, about 10,000, because the problem is that figures have been given on the number of troops in the south, but not on those in the center or north, only approximate ones. They are reserves in the event of a complicated situation arising. If an agreement is reached, we will strictly fulfill our obligations. There are 20,000 in the Southern Troops Grouping, and they are the bulk of the Cuban forces.

Angola has many strategic points. It is a very large country, nearly a million and a half square kilometers. It is fourteen times the size of Cuba, with thousands of kilometers of roads, large rivers, bridges, many vital strategic points, hydroelectric power plants, etc.

Our forces occupy a number of strategic communications links and airports.

Cabinda is a very important spot for Angola. Everybody wanted to take Cabinda, and it is vital for Angola's economy. In 1975, Zaire attacked Cabinda to take over the oil. Gulf Oil is working there and I think they are satisfied. They have worked and turned out their oil, they have their business and nobody has obstructed them, and it has been well defended. We are not trying to defend the interests of Gulf Oil, we are defending the interests of Angola and that oil benefits both Angola and Gulf. We defend the interests of Angola and indirectly those of Gulf. Those forces are not covered by the negotiations taking place.

The positions occupied by the forces in the south can't be vacated in a few weeks, because the Angolan army must take over, and it needs time and cadres, new units and means, because it must also fight the UNITA mercenary bands. They need some time, as we see it, not less than three years to be able to take on this task; that is reasonable, perfectly reasonable. If they did otherwise, they would face some very serious problems. They need more time to replace the other troops, since it is a huge country with a series of strategic spots: airports, bridges, industries, and hydroelectric plants. We are currently defending many of those points.

They have a strong army, which is gaining in experience, cadres, and fighting spirit. They have increased their forces and, in time, in the future they will be able to defend their country against foreign attack while also opposing subversion and fighting UNITA.

UNITA exists because of foreign aid. UNITA struck a deal with South Africa. For Black Africa this is treason, a deal with the South African racists is treason. We are the ones who benefit most from a settlement. I tell you frankly, we benefit most; we have been there for nine years, more than 200,000 Cubans have been to Angola. This is a real effort and we have no economic interest in Angola at all. But if a solution acceptable to Angola does not materialize, we will firmly continue with our support to that country as long as is necessary.

It has often been reported, perhaps even by the *Washington Post*, that the Angolans pay for the Cuban troops stationed there. I want to say that no life of any Cuban has its price. It cannot be paid for with $1 trillion or $100 billion. Our military cooperation has never been paid for in any country of the world where we have given it, never! Neither in Angola nor anywhere else. Some countries with the means have paid for civilian cooperation: doctors, engineers. In the great majority of countries, that cooperation is also free.

Often the United States does not understand how we can do this, all that it costs, if Cuba doesn't have the hard currency. That doesn't cost us hard currency. We pay salary here in Cuba for all those rendering internationalist cooperation; civilians, military, officers, all have their salary paid here. Many are from the reserves, workers from the reserves who are in military units. Their salary is paid in Cuba. The country where they go provides housing and food and we pay their salary. We have thousands of people working in those conditions now, without involving hard-currency expenditure. Nor does their return mean unemployment, because we are paying them here. Nor does it mean a cut in spending because they would do other work in Cuba. It doesn't create unemployment or any other problems.

We can do this for a basic reason which is not economic: we have the people to do it with. That is the secret, and that is what the revolution has created. That is what I was telling you about. I talked about the 2,000 teachers, when we had 2,000 teachers in Nicaragua, it is because we could do it; but we could send 30,000 or 100,000 because they have been educated with that idea. These are motivations and moral values that the revolution has sown in them all. In this, we have an overwhelming advantage over all nations of Latin America and the Third World. I don't think any other country with a relatively small population has such top-quality human potential.

Sometimes the country we are helping is very poor and we also pay part of the expenses of our personnel. But the general rule is: housing and food are provided by the country and we pay the salaries. We send eight doctors to one apartment; it proves easier for the host nation to have eight doctors in small lodgings. If they seek a doctor in Europe, they must provide a home for the family, pay his vacations, and spend about $40,000 or $50,000 a year. Meanwhile, eight of our doctors live in one apartment, they are provided for, and are not paid for their work. Those are the bases of our cooperation in all countries.

A few countries with the means to do so pay for civilian cooperation, a few countries, for the doctors, teachers, engineers, construction workers. There are two or three countries, which I won't go into. About 90 percent of the countries are very poor and we don't charge for our help.

We also have 22,000 scholarship students in Cuba from more than eighty countries; many doctors, engineers, and technicians from these countries have been trained in Cuba. We are sincerely concerned about the situation in Third World nations. It is not simply diplomatic and political activity, it is a reality which we feel and have experienced and which we raise at all international forums: at the UN, before the socialist countries, in the Movement of Nonaligned Countries, everywhere. We have become very aware of the social, sanitary, educational, and other problems. It is not a case of seeking relations; although of course there has been a quest for relations because, in response to the efforts to isolate us, we tried to extend our relations. I truly say we are deeply concerned about the tragedy of the Third World. I personally involved myself in these problems of cooperation, doctors, teachers, cooperation in agriculture, etc.

I think a major effort of international cooperation and large-scale investment is required in Africa if we are to come up with a strategic solution to its food problems and prevent a natural holocaust there. And I will tell you the truth: rather than spend money on space weapons and star wars, I think the world and even God — for those who are believers — would be much more grateful if the money were used to prevent the disaster which is threatening Africa and hundreds of millions of people, since the desert is moving south or north at increasing speed. Television programs broadcast images of widespread famine all over the world and people find out what is happening.

In social terms, the situation in Africa is different from that of Latin America: tens of millions, hundreds of millions of people live in hamlets as they did hundreds or thousands of years ago. They live there with their rudimentary farming. They are very stoic and resigned. They are killed by disease, hunger, and drought, but there is no explosion; it is not like in Latin America. In Latin America, there are many millions of blue- and white-collar workers, intermediate sectors, intellectuals, educated people. What I am trying to say is that the class structure in Latin America is different from that of Africa. You can't say Africa is exploding in social terms; you can say Africa is dying. Latin America is exploding; it has a different social structure.

Hoagland: Regarding Angola, why do you think the United States is playing a positive role?

Castro: Well, I say it would be positive if results were to be obtained. I would even venture to say it is positive that they try to seek political solutions to regional problems. If they are truly seeking a solution I think several factors are involved: there is antipathy for South Africa all over the world; there is a lot of antipathy for apartheid even in the United States.

In the United States, there is a current opposed to apartheid and cooparation with South Africa. I think the United States is interested in its relations with Black Africa, and it really doesn't want to appear as being linked to the policy of apartheid. I think the United States has an obsessive desire to get Cuban troops out of Angola, perhaps because of their special mentality. It seems that the only country in the world that can have troops everywhere is the United States, and the fact that a small country such as Cuba has some troops in a few places would seem to violate a tradition, established norms. It would seem to be truly inconceivable. I really don't know why they have magnified it so much, but it could be summed up as appearing to them as irreverence and disrespect. We really didn't send those forces there to offend or irritate the United States in all truth; we would rather send doctors and teachers than soldiers. We only hope that one day none of these countries will require military cooperation.

I think it is forgotten that we have had links with the MPLA since they started their war of independence, for almost twenty years. When the MPLA was on the brink of winning independence, those other groups were created. UNITA was really set up by the Portuguese as a counter organization to the MPLA, and UNITA joined forces with South Africa to crush the MPLA. We didn't send troops initially; at the request of the Angolan patriots, we sent instructors and weapons for the MPLA. They were in the south, in various places, a few dozen instructors.

When the invasion, the frontal South African attack took place, allied to UNITA, in their advance they attacked the military training school and the Cubans with their students resisted the South African advance. The first Cubans were killed there. Afterwards, the aggressors continued their advance toward Luanda, and Zaire attacked from the north. As the South Africans rapidly advanced from the south, we sent the first unit by air, a battalion of special troops, which occupied positions south of Luanda, along various strategic routes. In those days, bridges had to be blown up over the Queve River as they approached Luanda. That unit helped hold back the South Africans. A complex situation had been created and it had to be solved; we weren't going to leave that unit there alone. That was what decided the dispatch of other units.

That was how events unfurled. We had never thought of sending troops, but neither had we thought of the likelihood of such a situation, a blatant South African attack in which Cubans would be killed and the lives of other instructors jeopardized, along with Angolan independence itself. We had to send the units, and then the others. Then we sent all that were necessary to get them out.

They were about 1,000 kilometers inside Angola and we put the pressure on. When they realized that the battle was for real, they started to pull back toward the Namibian border and at the end held talks with our officers on the border. Then there was a period of calm, a certain period of calm and then they started up again. They started their raids on Angola, on the pretext of the struggle against SWAPO.

We know the South Africans very well, their psychology; we don't underestimate them at all. They have spent a lot of money on weapons in the last ten years. But neither do we overestimate them. We are aware of their problems, their limitations, their psychology, and their way of doing things.

I think the South Africans right now are obstructing U.S. efforts in the area. The greatest problems faced by the United States are not with Cuba or Angola; they are with South Africa. That is the truth as we see it.

Hoagland: Can I ask you about a couple of details which normally you would not discuss? But since there are things of which I think you can be proud, in the context in which we have been talking, allow me to ask them.

How many Cuban lives have been lost in Angola since 1975?

Castro: We have had our casualties but have not given out any information. We didn't feel it was convenient to do so. Our policy has been not to give casualty information; that has been the policy right from the start. The enemy must not have that information. We will know how to honor in a fitting manner those killed in revolutionary struggles, here and elsewhere.

Hoagland: The situation in Ethiopia seems to have stabilized very rapidly, allowing for a significant withdrawal of your troops. Is that so?

Castro: I think the situation in Ethiopia is different. Ethiopia was always independent. It had many more cadres than Angola and many more skilled personnel, a population of 35 million people, a strong army, a soldier that is strong and has great endurance, who can walk 100 kilometers over twenty-four hours, fight all day. They are champions in long-distance running, they have tremendous resistance, they have a tradition of organization and struggle, and they currently have a large, really large army.

Angola is a country which became independent after four centuries of colonial rule, without a tradition of government and organization. They have had to create everything in a few years, in a large country but with a small population. South Africa is a stronger and more powerful enemy, with industrial development and modern weapons. The situations are different.

The role of our forces in Angola is important given the conditions there. They have subversion from within and a threat at the border. Our forces play an important role and are greatly needed for a period of time, even after an agreement is reached. They can't do without our forces all of a sudden.

In Ethiopia our forces are smaller, have always been smaller, more modest, but well-armed units with good firepower. Aid was given to Ethiopia at a difficult time; it was needed because they had been attacked by twelve mechanized brigades, tanks, and artillery, while at the same time there were problems in the north with the separatists. It was a difficult moment for them when they needed to consolidate their forces.

Somalia clearly calculated that those difficult moments were the time to attack. We did all we could to avert that war, because we had relations with Somalia; we even visited Somalia, Ethiopia, and Aden. We met in Aden: Mengistu, [Somalian President] Siad Barre, the president of South Yemen, and myself, and we spent many hours talking well into one night. Siad Barre was intransigent: he was reclaiming the Ogaden. We said to him: well, I trust you won't think of going to war — because Siad Barre claimed to be a socialist and revolutionary. A revolution had triumphed in Ethiopia; actually the revolution in Ethiopia was much more real and profound than in Somalia, because there were even slaves in Ethiopia and a terrible social situation. It was a genuine revolution.

Mengistu is a person with great qualities, in my opinion exceptional, one of the most responsible, capable, and courageous leaders in the Third World.

Well, at that meeting, Siad Barre promised he would never attack Ethiopia, and the war started a few months later. I think he made a mistake in military terms; for political reasons he started bit by bit, one brigade here and another there, little by little rather than all of a sudden. If he had thrown all his forces into battle, the situation would have been more difficult. He advanced in various directions with a certain dispersal of forces; but in the end he created a difficult situation. At the time, the Ethiopian government was new; it was being organized. That was when we gave the aid. We actually acted as attorneys for the Ethiopians; we talked to a lot of people about Ethiopia and their just struggle; we sent weapons, a few thousand weapons, instructors; but there was a critical situation. I think our aid at that time was very important and they greatly appreciate it.

Since then, the Ethiopian army has developed considerably; our presence there is more or less symbolic alongside the Ethiopians; it is not the same as in Angola. By agreement with the Ethiopians, our personnel there was reduced to certain limits and it all depends on them. I think they appreciate our aid and view it as an element of solidarity; and in Ethiopia as well we can't decide unilaterally that we will pull out the troops. We can't do that anywhere.

If you cooperate with a country you can't just decide: look, I'm leaving because it suits me, because I know it would please some people, or it might please the United States. We can't work in that way. In themselves, those units stationed there are a force with combat effectiveness and capability; but vis-à-vis Ethiopia and its military power, it is symbolic.

The Ethiopians are the ones who must decide, they know our views. As long as they feel the presence is necessary, we will maintain it; when they feel it is not necessary we will withdraw.

Hoagland: Mr. President, if you have any patience left for one more question, I think I still have strength enough to ask one.

Castro: Ask your question and let's see if I still have enough strength left to answer it.

Hoagland: People who live in Cuba claim that they have seen a man who resembles Robert Vesco. Is Robert Vesco in Cuba?

Castro: I don't know if he's in Cuba, but he may be or he may pass through here sometime.

Let me tell you something. Once we got a request for medical service in this country. The person you mentioned was in need of medical assistance and we provided it. Under similar circumstances, we would provide such service to anybody else.

I don't know that person. I have no relations whatever or business with him. The reasons why he came here for the first time and was given medical assistance were humanitarian reasons. And of course I know about people who have talked with him, because he has information and knowledge about many things in this world and they say he has a lot of money. We are not in the least interested and we have no economic ties or business with him. He was given medical assistance and any time he or anybody else needs it under similar circumstances we will provide it. Now, as far as business or economic ties of any kind are concerned, there are none. It is possible that his expertise, his know-how of, say, industrial technology could be useful to us. He is said to have a wealth of economic and commercial information, but what he has here is simply the possibility to receive such services as the one I mentioned. He's not forbidden, to put it bluntly, to come here. And neither are we under any obligation. He is simply treated as a human being. That's the kind of relations that exist. Frankly, I could say that I don't know who you are talking about, that I don't know him. But I'm not in the habit of doing that.

You've asked me more than the State Department, the Pentagon, and all the United States intelligence agencies would have asked me. You wanted me to tell you how many had died in Angola, if we had sent arms to El Salvador, and if Vesco is here or is not. I don't think these things have anything to do with the interview we're doing, but since you're talking with me and I'm not afraid to answer any question, I have answered you and I don't think we are violating anything, any moral or international principle, by doing this. We consider it our prerogative, our right. As far as Vesco's money and business are concerned, we're not in the least interested in a single cent and even if he showed up here with $1 billion we'd simply say we were not interested. Understand? I like to make that very clear to you all. I don't know whether I'm doing the right or the wrong thing, but I'm not doing it for my sake but rather for the sake of this person.

De Young: Was that the result of Figueres's efforts?

Castro: Look, I don't want to implicate more people in this, you understand. All I'm saying is yes, he was here, he is allowed to come here, he asked for medical assistance and I'm glad he did because this demonstrates the prestige of our medicine.

If you also want to ask us if we're in the drug business, I can assure categorically, we're not in the least involved in the drug business and that this country has never been in the drug business. It has never made a single cent out of the drug business. What's more, I can say, so that you'll be better informed — and it isn't that we're aspiring to sainthood, nothing could be further from our mind, although given the improvement in our relations with the U.S. church and the Cuban church we might be canonized one of these days. [*Laughter*] Well, a dossier could be drawn up, were someone to be canonized because he saved many lives, helped the poor, helped the children, and all that. We could draw up a tremendous dossier including statistical data on how many children's lives have been saved in these twenty-six years of revolution as a result of the revolution's measures and medical program. I can tell you that the figure runs close to 300,000, for children under one, between one and five years, and up to fifteen years of age, we can give you all the figures. And how many poor people, how many unemployed, how many without an education, how many hungry and undernourished people we have liberated from poverty, hunger, and ignorance, and how many millions of children and adolescents we have educated.

If a rational review of the social work of the revolution were to be done, without labeling us as such evil, demonic, cynical people, I believe it would show that the revolution has done as much for the poor, the sick, the hungry, and the suffering as have all the saints put together. But, really, we're not looking for canonization.

I can tell you one thing, though. This country has been made many offers. We've been in it for twenty-six years. You want me to tell you about one of these offers? There was a Mafia group in Miami that controlled gambling in Florida and whose influence extended as far as New York, and we were offered several million dollars for a single service: finding out the winning number in the lottery one week ahead of time. We were told there was no need for any trick. All we had to do, they said, was to pick out the winning number one week ahead of time and let them know what that number was. [*Laughter*] Many people in Miami and the rest of the United States were laying the numbers based on the Cuban lottery. They trusted the Cuban lottery, and the organization offered us I don't know how many million dollars and even though then we were poorer than we are now the answer was no. This country has been made proposals running to hundreds of millions on a steady income basis, yet the answer has always been no.

Of all the Caribbean countries, Cuba is the one that has the largest number of drug traffickers in jail; hundreds of them. We have all the figures on how much cocaine and marijuana was seized, how many planes and ships, dozens of them, how many U.S. citizens, how many Colombians. We've really become the police of the Caribbean and we often wonder why, since the United States doesn't pay us for this service. We've been following this policy for twenty-five years. It's become a tradition. For your information, I assure you that we've had plenty of offers. You know how brazen those underworld characters are. We would have practically solved our foreign exchange problems, but we're not interested in that kind of money. I mean it. I don't know whether it has to do with morals or the fact that I studied the catechism or studied all about Christian morality in Christian schools, but to me it is a question of Christian morality and Marxist-Leninist morality, and that's what we go by. We don't care what others say or what they're saying every day. We're not worried. I'm more worried when the *Washington Post* publishes groundless editorials.

De Young: I have a very brief question. Why weren't you at the [CMEA] economic meeting held in Moscow?

Castro: Well, as I've already explained, lately I have left Cuba only on a few occasions, and this has to do with the amount of work I have here and, above all, our efforts to bolster the country's defense. I've made a point of traveling as little as possible in these times of tension. That's the truth of the matter. And, as I said before, we've been very busy here because we've also been working in the area of the economy, drawing up and revising our plans, applying new ideas. I don't mean changing our basic ideas but rather introducing a series of measures to optimize our efforts.

To a point, until now our plan was very often the sum pressure of all agencies defending their various sectors, and we had to work on that. All the sectoral ideas and the subjectivism have to be done away with, and we all have to work with the idea of the economy as a whole.

The plan would be drawn up by the [Central] Planning Board and, when it was finished, discussed with the agencies. Now it's to be drawn up with the direct participation of the Council of Ministers' Executive Committee from the outset, that is, with the participation of all those in charge of each branch and each agency of the economy and services. The Planning Board functions as a specialized agency in drawing up the plan along with the central government and participates, helps, and cooperates in the joint effort, but not like in the past when, as an agency, it had practically sole responsibility in drawing up the plan. There were several criteria, theoretical criteria, presuppositions, and in the end the plan was discussed with the agencies, but they did not participate in the actual drafting. Now, all those that have all the information in all areas, on all production centers, participate. I think this is an important, in fact, essential, and more realistic change, with broader participation by all: enterprises, factories, and the organs of People's Power.

The People's Power organs are vested with many powers. They are in charge of practically everything: health, trade, and education services, almost everything. The central government is in charge of national industry: electricity, transportation, finance, foreign trade, basic industry, the sugar industry, and others of a national nature. The rest is practically all under the jurisdiction of People's Power, and People's Power participates in economic activity and investments.

There was also a growing trend for requesting resources to meet everyone's needs. It had become almost a habit, and nobody ever asked how much production or exports had grown. All they talked about was what they needed: so many teachers, so much of this and that; everybody talked about needs, and for many years they really got what they asked for, all the budget resources they asked for. The result was anything but optimal effort, and this is what we've been working on.

Investments are being made on a priority basis. There were times when a factory was being built to turn out export products for the hard-currency area and somewhere else another project was under way — maybe a recreation center — and the two were competing for sand, stone, construction materials, and manpower. Things have changed. We now say this one waits, while we give absolute priority to this center that will produce for export or for trade with the socialist countries, because we stand to benefit from such trade. We have established prices that are not world market prices, but rather stable, guaranteed, profitable prices. It is not like in sugar, whose price sometimes rises to twenty cents only to drop later to fifteen, then to ten, and later to five. We have stable prices with the socialist countries, guaranteed prices, protected against inflation, because if the prices of the commodities they send us increase, the price of our exports to them increases proportionately.

De Young: You have really given a lot to this economic project, to what we might even call an economic revolution, and you've asked people to give up their coffee break and stop building their recreation centers.

Castro: Fine, I'll answer your question. Start taking notes.

De Young: Wait. I haven't got to the question.

Could it be that you're demanding too much of the people, that it's like in 1971 when you personally had to tell the people that things had to change, that it was necessary to work harder and perhaps why they were unable to achieve their objectives? Could a similar situation be arising now?

Castro: It's a good question and I'm going to answer it, but since she keeps interrupting me before I can finish an idea — what I say doesn't matter to her; I hadn't even finished my train of thought.

We've said, well, we have to meet our export commitments with the socialist countries. What was happening with these countries? Well, if there was a drought, for instance, or a plague, and we couldn't meet our production goals for sugar, then what did we do? We took part of the sugar away from the USSR and sent it to the world market. In other words, we didn't meet all our commitments, and yet we expected them to meet all their commitments to us. That's really how it was. We said, this cannot and must not happen again, when our most advantageous trade is with the socialist countries. We've said that this cannot be the way to get hard-currency exchange: we've stated that as a principle, too.

In light of that, we have given priority to production and the development of production and industry for the hard-currency area, in order to meet our debt payments, which aren't much, are not all that high, and secondly to acquire adequate amounts of raw materials and products we cannot acquire from the socialist countries, goods which complement production. Sometimes we receive fifteen kinds of raw materials from the USSR, the German Democratic Republic, and Czechoslovakia for a factory, but we need three more kinds that we have to get from the other area. It's a small amount but it's important, because from that market we acquire some medicines, some foodstuffs, and raw materials that complement the products and raw materials we get from the socialist countries. Thus, although it is only 15, 16, or 17 percent of our total imports, it's important. If we make long-range programs to structure production and exports, investments destined for production for the socialist countries is often for both. With nickel, for example, one part goes to the socialist countries and another part goes to the world market, but we're making the investment with the socialist countries. We're building a nuclear power plant with the socialist countries, but when it's finished it will mean an annual savings of $500 million in fuel.

Then there are investments in major social services, such as cardiovascular treatment, cardiovascular surgery for children and adults. Well, this is a significant service and brings peace of mind to many people, it solves many problems. It's more important than a recreation center, for example.

And then come the social problems, including housing and schools. This is grounded on another principle: in the first years of the revolution we devoted a great deal of investment to schools, hospitals, all kinds of social works, infrastructure, highways, roads, bridges, dams. We've gone a long way in the social sphere, that is, we don't have to make huge investments in that area now. Of course, there are still some things that need to be done, some art schools, for instance — we haven't completed that program yet — and various types of cultural and sports programs. For example, we've set aside areas in Havana and several other places for swimming complexes, pools that would be used for recreation in the summer and for training youngsters and adolescents the rest of the year. It's there, waiting for us. We've wanted to start on it, but it's got to wait. These are things we'd like to do, and I myself advocate some of these works. I too have my subjectivity, and I ask: how is the network of hospitals? In such and such a place, here and there, a specialized hospital, a children's hospital, is needed. It's not that there isn't service there, but the facilities are old and we want to build a new hospital. That can wait a year, or two or three years; it doesn't affect health services because we're incorporating into the community many doctors in schools, factories, who will be working directly with the population.

In other words, we're going to continue working in the social area, but in a qualitative way. More doctors, better organized services, better teachers with better skills; in short, there's a lot that can be achieved in terms of quality. In sports, we can better utilize the facilities we have.

For example, 17,800 teachers have graduated with degrees in physical education and sports in the last few years, 3,000 in higher education. I've said, let's see where all these teachers are and what they are doing, and let's utilize that teaching staff well, because when we started we didn't have any of that. We have tens of thousands of students in sports schools, that is, schools that meet all the educational requirements and also have all the sports facilities for those with greater aptitude, and we're going to make better use of them.

Now, with regard to your question, I am going to tell you two things. The knowledge that we now have, speaking in terms of 1982, 1983, 1984, and 1985, and the experience we have in the economic arena is incomparably greater than what we had in the 1960s. Fifteen years have gone by and everyone has a great deal more experience. During that period we had many ideas, well-intentioned ideas, but they were not very realistic; we wanted to skip stages. Later we proceeded to rectify many concepts, many ideas that were the result of an impatience to advance more. Moreover, it was a period when we paid a longshoreman who loaded ten tons the same that we paid one who loaded three. It was a period during which we virtually discarded budgets. The total amount of money and raw materials that were needed was calculated but in that period we had no unit economic calculation. This was intended to limit bureaucracy, on the one hand; it was an egalitarianism that was unrealistic regarding wages, almost a communist formula. We said: the construction of socialism is a period and a socialist formula of retribution in keeping with the work and work capacity must be realistically applied. During that period we were virtually implementing a communist formula of distribution. Now, of course, we distribute many things in a communist way: education, health, many services. But we apply a socialist formula of wage distribution throughout the economic sphere and in services. This is a very important point.

I'm going to give you an idea of what we've achieved. In 1970, the year of the ten-million-ton harvest, the sugar industry was still not mechanized except for some of the lifting and hauling. We then employed 350,000 workers in cutting the sugarcane. Now we employ less than 80,000; we are employing less than 25 percent of those we employed in 1970. In 1970, we had to mobilize industrial workers, students, soldiers, everyone, to also cut cane. It was very costly.

We have achieved a really fabulous increase in productivity. We no longer have to mobilize workers from the city or students, and the figure declines every year. We've made a great deal of progress in many areas which now permits us to undertake realistic things. A learning process has to be of some value.

Now, regarding what I've put forward to the people about recreation. I myself have been pushing a plan for camping and it is really magnificent. We take advantage of rivers and sites along the coast. It is an economical undertaking which provides for half a million people in the summer. Of course, we plan to go on expanding this program in the future, but we have said: let's wait and see how this project goes.

We are going to be building hotels for tourism, because at times we were going ahead with the camping plan while a hotel that signifies $3-4 million income a year was going up slowly. Despite everything, the demand for tourism is greater than capacity and it is growing. I don't know if it's because people see a healthier tourism here, not based on gambling and drugs.

In other words, it does not really signify a sacrifice for the people, because we have achieved very satisfactory levels in all the basic services, even recreation and sports. That is, they can wait for these things; the swimming pools can wait; the recreation plan can wait. But we will accomplish everything. As I put it to people, let's do less now so that we can do more later. We've said the same to the youth. We have said: you must be the bearers of these ideas because they have to do with the world in which you will live and the economy you will have in 2000 and after 2000, those of you who are now fifteen, sixteen, and seventeen years old. This has to be your banner, it falls on you more than us. We have made a well-reasoned and well-founded call to all the workers, to the population as a whole and we have conveyed to everyone what is the key to success. And the students, the young people, and the workers have discussed it.

We have said there is a great crisis in the world. There is no clear path for the Third World, or the industrialized world for that matter. However, we have economic, material, and human resources at hand. We have a clear path and we are going to do things adequately and optimally. We are not going to use resources irresponsibly. We are going to devote ourselves to solving the problems which are basic to development, so that every year we won't have to worry about how much foreign exchange is or is not coming in, if the price of sugar increases or drops. We have put this forward on a solid footing and everyone has understood this perfectly well.

Ours Is a More Just Society

Interview on MacNeil/Lehrer NewsHour

Robert MacNeil: Mr. President, every time that you begin to talk about improving relations with the United States, Washington says, "Show us deeds, not words." What actions or deeds are you prepared to make to improve relations with the United States?

Fidel Castro: You said every time I speak of improving relations; actually there are not many times. Now then, I have read a few statements in which it is said that they want deeds and not words. I believe that is a style of speaking. I would say a style of a great power. I understand that it is not easy for the United States to change its style. We are a small country; we cannot speak in those terms. But we are also a country with a lot of dignity and no one can suppose that we would beg the United States for an improvement of relations. We have never done so, and we shall never do it.

My intention is not for them to believe what we say but rather, that they simply analyze our ideas and go deeper into them and make objective analyses of events. It is not a matter of faith, of confidence; it is a matter of objectivity.

MacNeil: Let's go through an objective analysis. The State Department and the White House always say that there are three obstacles to improving relations between Cuba and the United States. They are your allegiance to the Soviet Union, what they call subversion in this hemisphere, and the large number of your troops in Africa. Sometimes they also mention human rights in Cuba. The White House mentioned human rights in Cuba this week again. Can we discuss in detail each of these,

This interview was conducted in Havana on February 9, 1985, by Robert Mac-Neil and was televised February 11-15 on the MacNeil/Lehrer NewsHour; it appears here in full according to the written transcript provided by that program. It is from the MacNeil/Lehrer NewsHour, © 1985 Educational Broadcasting Corporation and WETA and is reprinted by permission. Castro's remarks appear here as they were simultaneously translated by a Cuban interpreter, with minor editing for clarity and consistency.

starting with relations with the Soviet Union?

Is there a formula by which you could keep your ties to the Soviet Union and improve relations with the United States?

Castro: If the United States believed that there are three obstacles, actually these are quite few; I thought there were much more. Now then, if we analyze these three types of obstacles, the first — that is the relations that we have with the Soviet Union, with the socialist countries, and with any other country — these are matters of our sovereignty and cannot be questioned, or at least we are not ready to discuss that. And this is always — this is something that I always say very frankly.

If, in order to improve our relations with the United States, we must give up our convictions and our principles, then relations will not improve on those lines. If we have to question our sovereignty, then they will not improve either. Relations between Cuba and the Soviet Union are based on the strictest respect for the independence and sovereignty of our country. We have friendly relations, very close relations, and these relations cannot be affected in order to improve relations with the United States.

I believe that the United States would not respect a country that would do such a thing. The countries that do those things simply are not respected, and actually we are not going to change either our flag or our ideas. Our relations with the Soviet Union, our friendship, will be maintained untouched. I say this being fully frank and fully sincere. And it is necessary that this be understood.

MacNeil: The director of Cuban affairs in the State Department, Kenneth Scoog, said in a speech in December that what Cuba could not do and still retain Moscow's favor is to alter its fundamental commitment to unswerving support for Soviet policy. And so my question is: Isn't that unswerving support for Soviet policy the price of the Soviet aid that keeps the Cuban economy going?

Castro: Well, we coincide in many things with the Soviet Union because we have political principles in common. It is a socialist country; we are a socialist country. We do have many things in common with the Soviet Union and in many international problems we have a common stance that is based on political ideas and principles. It is a friendly country, and we will not reject its friendship or feel ashamed of it because, actually, we are not going to fight with our friends in order to become friends of our adversaries. That we shall never do. And the Soviets have never imposed any conditions on us, on their assistance. They have never attempted to tell us what we should do, what we must do, with which countries we are to trade and with which countries we should have relations. So I simply can't understand where these theories come from. But if our relations with the Soviets are an obstacle and if someone thinks that we are going to sell out or that we are going to give up our banners or our flags, or that we are going to change our ideas, that is an error. Cuba is a country that cannot be bought. And countries that are bought are simply not respected.

MacNeil: I think what the United States government is saying is that your economic dependence on Moscow makes you automatically a part of the Soviet camp in having to agree to policies like the Soviet intervention in Afghanistan. Would you, Fidel Castro, who values the independence and integrity of a small country, would you alone have approved the Soviet intervention in Afghanistan if you had been free to make your own choice? Did you privately and personally approve of the Soviet intervention in Afghanistan?

Castro: When the question or issue was put forth at the UN, we said clearly that in that conflict, in that attack — that tremendous attack against the Soviet Union led by the United States — we were not going to be on the side of the United States. Simply that. And we were then on the side of the Soviet Union. That is, we did not deal or delve on the topic; that is what we said. This is our position because of this.

MacNeil: But isn't that the point? That your friendship and dependence on the Soviet Union makes you part of the camp and therefore take positions which Washington regards as anti-American positions?

Castro: You establish this dependency as something that is actual in fact and deed. But in today's world, in the economic area, no one is absolutely independent, not even the United States or Japan or Western Europe. They depend on oil, raw materials, and they need markets, they need trade from many other countries. That is, no country is totally independent economically.

MacNeil: Is it not true that your role in return for all the aid you get from the Soviet Union is to be a thorn in America's side?

Castro: If that were true, we would not be talking about improving relations with the United States. If our role is to be a thorn, then these relations would not be convenient for us. Actually they do not bring us great benefits, either. That is, we are based on a conviction, and it is the necessity to struggle in our area, in Central America, throughout the world. It is actually a duty we have to lower tensions and to achieve relations of peace in the world. And I say this sincerely, although I am a revolutionary. I was a revolutionary, I am a revolutionary, and I shall always be a revolutionary. And I will not change a single of my principles for a thousand relations with a thousand countries like the United States.

MacNeil: Will the Soviet Union continue to provide you with the aid and support it does, do you believe, if you have good relations with the United States?

Castro: Look, our relations with the Soviet Union, with the socialist countries, are solid things based on principles and have absolutely nothing to do with our economic and political relations with the United

States. I will say one thing though. The Soviet Union and the Soviet people feel great appreciation and great respect for Cuba. But they respect Cuba because they admire the courage of Cuba, as other peoples do. Cuba's staunchness and Cuba's capability to resist for over twenty-six years the aggressions, the economic blockade, and the brutality of the United States.

MacNeil: Would the Soviet Union like it if you had better relations with the United States, if the blockade perhaps were lifted, and, if the economic burden on the Soviet Union were shared or lessened?

Castro: If the United States will pay us for our sugar at the price the Soviets pay, or if they buy the nickel and maintain the type of relations and trade that we have with the socialist countries. But I believe that the idea that we have any need to trade with the United States should be totally eradicated. Everything we have done during these twenty-six years, we have done without trade with the United States. And our future has been conceived without trade with the United States. Actually, we have not asked the Soviet Union — generally we don't ask their opinion on our economic or political relations in the international arena. But I know the Soviet Union very well and I know the policy of the Soviet Union, and the Soviet Union would never be against Cuba's developing its economic relations with the other capitalist countries, including the United States.

MacNeil: So, to move on to the second point that Washington says is an obstacle to better relations — what White House spokesman Larry Speakes called this week: your subversion in the hemisphere. Let me quote you again Mr. Scoog of the State Department: "It is Cuba's striving, with Soviet support, to introduce Marxist-Leninist regimes throughout the hemisphere, which still lies at the heart of our differences." Would you comment on that?

Castro: Well, I could also accuse the pope of practicing subversion in Latin America in preaching Christianity and Catholicism. He has visited many countries even recently. He has met with natives and said that the land and the land properties had to be given to the natives. And he declared that schools were necessary for the children, jobs for the workers and for the families, medicine and doctors for the ill, and also foodstuffs or housing. That is more or less what we preach. And besides, that is what we have done in our country. So we will continue being Marxist and we'll continue being socialist, and we will always say that our social system is more just.

But we have also said, because we are convinced about it — we have said the following, which is my answer to that. On the one hand Cuba cannot export revolution because revolutions cannot be exported, and the socioeconomic factors, the cultural-historical factors that determine revolutions, cannot be exported. The external, the huge external debt of

Latin America cannot be exported. The formula applied by the International Monetary Fund cannot be exported by Cuba. The unequal trade cannot be exported by Cuba. Underdevelopment and poverty cannot be exported by Cuba, and that is why Cuba cannot export revolution. It is absurd, ridiculous to say that revolutions can be exported. But in the same way the United States cannot avoid them either.

The United States accuses us perhaps of wanting to promote change. Well then, we would like to see changes occur, but changes will come whether the United States likes it or not, whether Cuba likes it or not. I could answer by saying that the United States wants to maintain an unjust social order that has meant for the peoples of this hemisphere poverty, hunger, underdevelopment, diseases, ignorance, and the United States wants to maintain that. And we could also say that the United States wants to avoid change. If we are accused of wanting to promote change, we can also accuse the United States of wanting to avoid change and of wanting to maintain an unjust social regime. But actually we can neither export it, nor can the United States avoid it.

MacNeil: In supporting militarily the Sandinista regime in Nicaragua, is Cuba not helping to sustain and introduce a Marxist-Leninist regime?

Castro: In Nicaragua, by offering military cooperation? Well, we are helping an independent country, we are helping a just revolution to defend itself. That's simply what we are doing. In the same way that, for example, the United States has also sent weapons to other people in this hemisphere. It sent weapons to Somoza. It sent weapons to Trujillo when Trujillo was there. It sent weapons to Pinochet. It sent weapons to all the repressive governments of Latin America, governments that murdered, tortured tens of thousands of people, governments which disappeared tens of thousands of people. They had no moral obstacle to giving any economic, financial, or military assistance to these governments. So, on what moral grounds can there be questions about our right to help Nicaragua, and Nicaragua's right to receive that aid? I ask the following: Can the United States help the counterrevolutionary bands, supply weapons to them, explosives, to fight inside Nicaragua — something that has meant the lives of thousands and thousands of people — and on the other hand question Cuba's right to give aid — economic, technical aid, and even some cooperation in the military field? Can they question Nicaragua's right to receive it?

MacNeil: So you would not stop giving such aid as a condition of improved relations with the United Staes?

Castro: We shall not make any unilateral decision in our relations and cooperation with Nicaragua. What we have said is that in Central America a politically negotiated solution is possible. What we say is that we support the effort of Contadora to seek peaceful solutions in Central

America, that we support it staunchly, sincerely, and that we believe that political solutions exist and peace solutions exist that are convenient for the Nicaraguans, for Central America, and for the United States too, and that we are ready to struggle for that. And also that the agreements that are reached shall be complied with by us in a determined way. Any agreement reached between Nicaragua and the Contadora framework shall be complied with by us to the very letter.

MacNeil: How hopeful are you now that some political settlement can be reached in Central America?

Castro: I am absolutely convinced. I have a lot of information about the work of Contadora. I have heard all the discussions of the burning issues there, the positions of the United States, Nicaragua's positions. And I am convinced, fully convinced, that it is possible to find formulas that would be acceptable to all parties. I have that conviction. I am convinced about that.

Now then, for this to happen the United States really must want to cooperate in finding a political solution. I believe that as long as the United States is convinced that it can destroy the Sandinista revolution from within by combining the effect of the economic measures against Nicaragua with the economic difficulty inside Nicaragua and the actions of the counterrevolutionary bands — as long as they're convinced that they can destroy the revolution from within, the United States will not be seriously ready to seek a political solution to the problems of Central America. Because if it believes that it will destroy the revolution, why negotiate? Why reach agreements? Now, when the United States becomes frustrated that it cannot achieve that goal, that the Nicaraguan revolution cannot be destroyed from within, because of the questions I mentioned, the problems I mentioned — I believe the Nicaraguans can face the economic problems with what they produce and with the aid they are receiving, the economic aid they are receiving. If they handle it correctly, efficiently, they can face the economic problems. I'm convinced of that. I am also convinced that they can defeat the bands and that the bands will never be able to defeat —

MacNeil: Excuse me. By the "bands" you mean what are called in the United States the *contras*?

Castro: Yes, the counterrevolutionary bands that will be defeated. They will be defeated. So then a situation will confront the United States: that is, the United States will have no other alternative but to negotiate seriously to seek a solution or to invade Nicaragua. And since, in my view, a U.S. invasion in Nicaragua is inconceivable, since it would mean such a serious mistake, a terrible mistake, that I simply do not think that the United States would really get to the point of making that mistake. I cannot assure you that the United States might not do it, but I say that it is inconceivable that under the present circumstances in

Latin America, under the present circumstances of crisis, with the present feeling on the part of the Latin American peoples — in these times we're living in, an aggression and invasion against a Latin American country would be catastrophic in political terms; it would mean a high political cost, and not only a political cost but also in terms of U.S. lives —

MacNeil: Let me turn to Africa. The third of those obstacles that Washington sees to improving relations with you are your troops in Angola. You talked recently about circumstances arising which would cause you to bring them home. What would happen — what would have to happen to start bringing the Cuban troops out of Angola?

Castro: What is needed there? Well, discussions have taken place with the participation of the United States. The United States has had dialogue, talks with Angola's leadership. The Angolans keep us informed about these negotiations or talks that have been held with our support and with our full cooperation. That is, they have carried out these negotiations in close contact with Cuba.

MacNeil: Could you withdraw any of your troops before there is agreement?

Castro: No. The Angolans would not agree with that, and from our point of view it would be a mistake. And the Angolan proposal — that is, if those circumstances come up and Angola commits itself — and Cuba of course would support the proposal — to withdraw in a period of three years what is called the Southern Troops Grouping, which is made up of approximately 20,000 men. And even the figure was given. This is the bulk of our troops, actually, but there are still troops in the center and the north of Angola, including Cabinda. The Angolans have not included these troops in the negotiations, these present negotiations, and their position is that withdrawing those troops would have to be discussed between Angola and Cuba whenever it is considered that the Angolans can dispense with these troops.

MacNeil: Do you think that this projected settlement of the Angola situation — does that erase Cuban troops in Angola as an issue between you and the United States?

Castro: Before, there were no troops in Angola and relations were very bad with the United States. The day when there are no troops in Angola or in some other place or when there are no advisers in Central America, maybe the United States might invent something else.

MacNeil: Just to sum up our conversation about improving relations with the United States. Why is this the right time to raise this, and realistically speaking, how hopeful are you that it can happen?

Castro: Whether this is the right — best moment? I believe that if the United States is objective, if it is realistic I would say that it is the best moment for the United States, not for us. Actually, we can go on for five, ten, fifteen, twenty more years. The only obligation on our part, really, is toward peace. If there's peace here and in other areas, we will feel more pleased; if relations are normalized, even more pleased, because it would then be a progressive progress. Peace is convenient for all, but from the political point of view I am convinced — and I'm saying this completely frankly — I think that the United States benefits more than us. We can sit here and wait calmly and see what happens in the coming years.

[*MacNeil: White House spokesman Larry Speakes said that one of the obstacles the Reagan administration sees to improved relations with Castro is what Speakes called violations of human rights in Cuba. I asked Castro about that.*]

Castro: What are the violations of human rights in Cuba? Tell me. Which ones? Invent one. Do we have disappeared people here? Look, if the United States —

MacNeil: Well, let me give you an example of what he said. For instance, human rights organizations, like Amnesty International, estimate that you have up to 1,000 political prisoners still in your jails here. Do you have political prisoners still in jail in Cuba?

Castro: Yes, we have them. We have a few hundred political prisoners. Is that a violation of human rights?

MacNeil: In democracies it is considered a violation of human rights to imprison somebody for his political beliefs.

Castro: I will give you an example. In Spain there are many Basque nationalists in prison. They're not political prisoners? What are they? Because you also have to analyze what is a political prisoner and what is not a political prisoner. Now then, those who committed crimes during Batista's time, did we have the right to put them on trial or not? Okay. Those who invaded Cuba through Playa Girón. Did we have the right to try them or not? Those who became CIA agents, those who placed bombs, those who brought about the deaths of peasants, workers, teachers. Do we have the right to bring them to trial or not? Those who, in agreement with a foreign power like the United States and backed by the United States and inspired by the United States, conspired in our country and who struggle and fight against our people in this revolution — because this revolution is not of a minority; this is a revolution of the overwhelming majority of people. What are these people? What are they? Political prisoners? Those who have infiltrated through our coasts, those who have been trained by the CIA to kill, to place bombs: Do we have the right to bring them to trial or not? Are they political prisoners? They're something more than political prisoners. They're traitors to the homeland.

MacNeil: Is there anybody in jail simply because of his political beliefs — because he dissents from you politically?

Castro: No one is in prison because of either their political or religious beliefs.

MacNeil: After Jesse Jackson came here last summer you released twenty-six political prisoners. Are you going to release more of the kind you were describing a moment ago?

Castro: Of course we would not be willing to release them. It's a bit under 200, actually, in that situation. These are people who are potentially dangerous. We are not going to release them and send them to the United States for them to organize plans against Cuba, or for them to go to Nicaragua or Honduras or Central America as mercenaries, or to go to any country to prepare attacks so that when I visit these countries they organize a true human hunt, as they have done on other occasions. That's the psychology instilled in them by the CIA and the U.S. authorities.

MacNeil: The other human rights question that is raised by the United States is that you don't have a free press. Your revolution is now twenty-six years old, it's very stable. In your recent speeches you've told of how successful it is. Why wouldn't you feel confident about allowing the press to have a full expression of ideas and discussion and opposition?

Castro: Well, you are right. We do not have a press system like that of the United States. In the United States there is private property over the mass media. The mass media belong to private enterprises. They are the ones who say the last word. Here there is no private property over the mass media. There is social property. And it has been, is, and will be at the service of the revolution. Here we do not have any multiparty system either, nor do we need it. The political level of our people, the information level of our people, is much greater. In surveys that have been made in the United States an astonishing high number of people do not know where Nicaragua is, where the countries of Latin America are. They don't know what countries are in Africa, what countries are in Asia. There is an incredible, astonishing ignorance. That does not happen here. Your system might be wonderful, but at least the results of ours are undoubtedly better.

MacNeil: May I raise a point? Your system, which you say works very well, it does presuppose that the leadership of the country, you, are always right, that you are infallible. Is that not so?

Castro: No, it does not presuppose that, because we are not as dogmatic as the church, although we have been dogmatic, and we have never preached a personality cult. You will not see a statue of me anywhere, nor a school with my name, nor a street, nor a little town, nor any type of personality cult because we have not taught our people to believe, but to think, to reason out. We have a people who think, not a people who believe, but rather who reason out, who think. And they might either agree or disagree with me. In general the overwhelming majority have agreed. Why? Because we have always been honest; we have always told them the truth. The people know that the government has never told them a lie. And I ask you to go to the world, tour the world, and go to the United States and ask if they can say what I can say, that I have never told a lie to the people. And these are the reasons why there is confidence. Not because I have become a statue or an idol but rather simply because of the fact that they trust me. And I have very, very few prerogatives in this country. I do not appoint ministers or vice-ministers or directors of ministries or ambassadors. I don't appoint anybody, and that's the way it is. We have a system, a system for the selection of cadre based on their capacity, etc. I have less power, 100 times less power than the president of the United States, who can even declare war and nuclear war.

MacNeil: But doesn't the system mean that the revolution is always right?

Castro: You, when you had your independence war you did not even free the slaves and yet you said you were a democratic country. For 150 years, you did not even allow the Black man to be part of a baseball team or a basketball team, to enter a club, to go to a white children's school. And you said it was a democracy. None of those things exists here — neither racial discrimination nor discrimination due to sex. It is the most fair, egalitarian society there has ever been in this hemisphere. So we consider it to be superior to yours. But you believe that yours is the best without any discussion whatsoever. Although there might be multimillionaires and people barefoot begging in the streets, without any homes, people unemployed. And you believe it's perfect, because you *believe* things.

I don't think that type of society is perfect, really, I think that ours is better. We have defended it better. It is a more just society and we believe in it. Now, we make mistakes, but whenever we make a mistake we have the courage to explain it. We have the courage to admit it, to recognize it, acknowledge it, to criticize it. I believe that very few — that there are probably few people like the leaders of a revolution who are able to acknowledge their mistakes. And I first of all acknowledge it before myself because first of all I am more critical with myself than with anybody else. But I'm critical before my people, critical before the world, the U.S., everybody. Far from — but don't worry. If this analysis had not been correct, the revolution would not be in power. The revolution would not be in power.

MacNeil: How do you measure that? How do you, as the leader of this country, know that for sure when you don't have the vehicles for public expression and open discussion of issues that the democracies have, for example? How do you know that the people feel that way?

Castro: We have a party with almost half a million members. They're everywhere, in every factory. We know more than the United States about the things that happen there.

MacNeil: But isn't the dynamic of a one-party state that the instruction and information goes downwards, and if people disagree with it, they don't dare say so? And so dissent which may exist doesn't come back up the system.

Castro: Actually, we know what there is, and we know the way our people think much better than what the president of the United States knows about the way the U.S. people think. You should have no doubt about that whatsoever. We have many ways of knowing this. Facts prove it. Let's suppose that people might not agree with the revolution. How could we have millions of people organized to defend the country? Could we have a nonpeople? Tell the South Africans, your South African friends, to give the weapons to the Blacks in South Africa. Tell your friend Pinochet to give the weapons to the people of Chile. Tell your friends in Paraguay to give the weapons to the masses, to the people. Tell many of the friends that you have in the world — you speak of democracy. The first and most important form of democracy is for the citizens to feel part of power and part of the state. And how do we prove this? We have an armed people, men and women, millions of people. If they were not in agreement they could solve things rapidly. We would not be able to stay in power for twenty-four minutes. Do you want more proof of that?

MacNeil: I have seen it reported that increasingly Cuban troops are refusing to go for service in Angola, that the families of troops who have been there are getting more and more unhappy over the Angolan experience. Is it true that you're feeling public pressure to end this?

Castro: For revolutionaries to fulfill an internationalist mission is something that is considered a great honor, and that should not make anyone feel strange when people have motivation and when people have ideals. Of course that implies sacrifices. It implies sacrifices from families as they separate from their relatives for a certain period of time. In some cases it means risks undoubtedly. It means sacrifices. But our people can carry on these missions because they are prepared to do so.

MacNeil: How many have been killed in Angola?

Castro: That question has already been asked by a journalist, and I told them I was not going to answer the question because our rule has been that we would not publish the number, that the enemy should not have that information. And we are maintaining it as a secret. Some day all of that might be published. The family knows when there is a loss. They are informed about it immediately —

MacNeil: But isn't it a matter of public interest and the concern of the Cuban public as a whole, the cost in lives of your activity in Angola?

Castro: No. They know well that this is a policy that is followed and that it is a correct one. Because we base ourselves on the people's confidence and support of the revolution's policy.

MacNeil: Tell me an example of a mistake you feel you made and admitted.

Castro: In politics we have committed few mistakes, fortunately. We have been quite wise. In the decisions we have made in the economic field we made mistakes, and these were mistakes that resulted from our ignorance, because in general revolutionaries have ideas, very noble ideas: to have education, to have health for all, to have work, to have jobs, to have development. That is, very noble ideas, but very general.

MacNeil: You said in your speech to the National Assembly, we do not become capitalists. Do you begin to lean a little to capitalism?

Castro: No. To the contrary, to the contrary. Every day — mentally, spiritually, philosophically — I'm more convinced about the advantages of the socialist system over capitalism, more convinced about the fact that capitalism has no future. Well, I say no future on the long-term basis. I am not saying that capitalism will disappear in ten years. But the present capitalist system is no longer the capitalist system of the past century.

MacNeil: Aren't you allowing creeping private enterprise in permitting free markets where vegetables and food and things can be sold by the people who — to open new supermarkets where goods, consumer goods, otherwise scarce are priced at full market prices and not at supported prices? Is this not creeping private enterprise?

Castro: When you asked about mistakes, I said that in politics we had — but you did not allow me to continue, because you asked me other things. But that item was not dealt with. In the development of the economy, where at the beginning we did not have any experience, and where we even had an attitude of certain disregard for the experiences of other socialist countries — actually we were a bit self-sufficient. Actually, this is something that has happened to many revolutionaries. At times they believe that they know more than the rest. In the economic field we made mistakes, which we call idealistic mistakes. In essence these were wanting to jump over historical stages in trying to get to a more egalitarian society, even more egalitarian. We had almost gotten to the point of distributing — of depending on the needs of the people, not according to their work, the amount and quality of their work. When we came to the point of understanding that this had negative effects, that our society was not yet a society with the necessary communist culture and consciousness, we rectified this. But it's not that we are leaning to capitalism. The more I analyze today's world, Third World, even the problems of the industrialized countries — unemployment has not been cut. In Europe unemployment is growing yearly. And you can plan and they can plan how many unemployed they can have in 1990 and the year 2000. The deeper I think and the deeper I meditate, the less capitalist I feel.

MacNeil: Can we move to defense? In the last year or so you have greatly increased, as you've said, your military capacity. You said on January 2 that you've increased the number of weapons, the number of weapons by three times. You have roughly a quarter of a million men on active duty, the 190,000 reserves, a million people as militia, 190,000 — my question is: Why does Cuba need this very large armed force?

Castro: Of course I will correct you. Armed forces and reserves are more than half a million: militia, territorial troops, over one million. We have tripled the number of weapons, but we have multiplied many times our resistance capability by changing the conception. In the past the conception was the army and the reserves were the ones to defend the country. The conception today is that all of the people today defend the country, in every corner, in every city, in the countryside, in the mountains. And they're actually organized. The idea is that every citizen in this country is armed.

MacNeil: Is this a lesson from Grenada?

Castro: Well, no. After Grenada we intensified it. Not only us. The Nicaraguans also. The Grenada events did not weaken us; they actually made us feel stronger and multiplied our determination and our will and our readiness to become stronger and fight.

You ask why so many weapons? The United States, our adversary, being such a powerful country, the country that harasses us, the country that blockades us, the country that threatens to invade us — they don't understand why we make these efforts? The country that is investing in war — $313 billion, one third of their budget, taking that away from sick people, from aged. We at least don't do that. And they don't understand why we, being neighbors of the United States and feeling threatened by the deeds and words of the United States, why we make an effort to defend ourselves? Actually do we have to explain that?

MacNeil: You had an invasion scare last fall, last autumn. You had exercises, you had people, including children, digging air raid trenches. Are you relaxed now? Are you now not fearing an American invasion?

Castro: Look, we were relaxed, we are relaxed, and we will always be relaxed. For twenty-six years we have been relaxed. That's one thing. Another: The measures we have taken to defend ourselves — we are not going to wait for a government of the United States to decide to attack the country for us to then start preparing ourselves. We have prepared ourselves. We are preparing ourselves, and we will continue preparing ourselves. Always. So, hypothetically, if the United States were to become, let's say, not a socialist country, let's say a Marxist-Leninist country and more communist than the USSR and China, we here next to the United States would not disregard our defenses. It is a philosophical principle. If one day—

MacNeil: So one of your motives — excuse me for interrupting. So one of your motives for seeking or suggesting improved relations with the United States is not so that you can relax your military investment?

Castro: No, I don't think so. I think that we would continue doing what we're doing, preparing the defense of the country, preparing the people. I believe that the only advantage for us, as for any other country, is simply peace. The day when the nations prove that respect for the independence of other countries exists and that there is real peace, when the others give up their weapons and the United States gives up its weapons, we will give up our weapons. In any case, we could box, we could play baseball, track and field, Greco-Roman wrestling, what have you.

MacNeil: Let me ask you to turn your mind back. You said many times and in some of your speeches recently that your revolution, by your definitions, has many successes — in medical care, in literacy, in infant mortality. By those definitions your revolution is a success. In what way does it disappoint you?

Castro: Do you ask if I feel any frustration? No. I have no frustration. I feel no frustration whatsoever. I can tell you this directly. We have done more than what we dreamed of doing. Many of the things we're doing now — we had some general ideas but not as precise and complete as we have now. I can tell you that reality has surpassed our dreams in what we have done. And we're not speaking about the future. It is not the same as it was at the beginning when we spoke of our good intentions; but rather we now speak with a revolution that is twenty-six years old. And it has certain advantages. I'm not speaking of things that we are intending to do but rather of things that have been done.

MacNeil: Finally, let me ask you a couple of personal questions, if I may. Do you want to go on being the president of Cuba until you die?

Castro: It depends on how many years I live. If I'm told that I can be useful now, I would say yes. I think I can be. If I could not do my job because of the experience I have now, I would also tell you that. I think that I am useful. I don't think that I am indispensable. Nothing is opposed to my philosophy more than that. I believe we have done a lasting work that goes beyond us, beyond all of us. And if it were not so, why have we worked so much? If it were not so, we would have failed. But our work is not a work of stones. It is not of material but of consciousness, of moral values, and that is lasting. Either being president or not being president I am fully hopeful that the others will be better, and the sooner a new generation that is better than us comes, a more capable one, to replace us, the better. If we live three, four, five years, maybe ten, I don't know. But the day when I do not really feel that I could fulfill my duty and do my work because of my physical capabilities or mental capabilities, I will be the first to say it. If I live many years, you can be sure that I will not die as the president of this country. For sure the first one who would not want that is me. If I want my mind to keep being clear and illuminated, in order to come to that very minute, to that very minute when I can notice that I have already done my work and that others can do it. So if I tell you now that I'll resign — I'm a soldier of the revolution, and I think I can still struggle, but I have no personal affection for honors and power or force, or the force in power. You have a president that is older; maybe at that age I won't have the physical or mental capabilities to do my work.

[*MacNeil: I asked specifically what aid Cuba was giving to the guerrilla groups in El Salvador.*]

Castro: I said that I do not want to make any declarations or any commitments about that. I'm not saying yes, I'm not saying no. In practice, in reality, it is almost impossible, almost impossible for military supplies to reach the revolutionaries in El Salvador. That's what I said. Because it is practically impossible to have military supplies reach them. The revolutionaries in El Salvador have the capabilities to resist indefinitely, even if they were not receiving any military supplies, even if they were not receiving any supplies, not even a single bullet. They are in a position to resist indefinitely. They are also in a position to receive supplies; that is, the way we did in our struggle — with the weapons that belonged to the army of El Salvador. And I believe, I am absolutely convinced that the revolutionaries in El Salvador can resist indefinitely without receiving any type of supplies, without a supply of weapons from abroad. And that is not the essential issue.

[*MacNeil: I also asked the Cuban leader, looking at the hemisphere as a whole, which countries he considered ripe for revolution right now.*]

Castro: I would say that from the point of view of social conditions and objective conditions not only Central America, but actually and more importantly, South America. In that area from the objective point of view, a situation has been created that is a prerevolutionary situation. I am absolutely convinced of that. I do not want to say that this hemisphere will unavoidably explode, but I am absolutely convinced of the fact that the problems are very serious, that the social problems have tripled, that the population has doubled, and that they face situations in which you find no way out.

During Kennedy, when Kennedy put forth the Alliance for Progress, he thought, he was already worried about trying to avoid revolutionary situations. He believed that by investing $20 billion over a certain number of years and with certain social reforms the problems of Latin America could be solved. Twenty-four years have elapsed since then. The population has doubled. The social problems have tripled. The debt is $360 billion. And in interest alone they must pay $40 billion per year — double the amount Kennedy thought was going to solve the problem in a certain number of years. To this we must add the flight of capital, the repatriation of property, and other problems. The prices are depressed and, in my opinion, it is the most critical and serious situation that history has ever encountered — the history of this hemisphere. I firmly believe this.

And if a solution is not found to the problem of the debt, I am convinced that the Latin American societies will explode, because there is a situation of despair among the workers, among the middle strata, and even in the oligarchy. But in this case the problem is general, a general problem. And it may explode not in one country; it may explode in many countries. I believe that the debt — that they cannot pay for the debt. It is not that they don't want to pay for it. No, they can't pay for it. But I'm not only referring to the debt. The interest, the $40 billion in interest, they cannot pay it. Even if they wanted to, they cannot pay it. And the effort or imposition to force them to pay it will actually bring about a social convulsion, a revolutionary explosion. I even believe that it will be necessary, at least to have a ten to twenty years of grace that would include interest.

MacNeil: Let me understand you. You're saying that to prevent an explosion in Latin America the international banking community needs to give them twenty years of grace on interest? Is that what you mean?

Castro: Right. I am absolutely convinced that if under the present circumstances they are obliged to pay not the debt — because they could postpone the debt for ten, fifteen, years and it could be upwards to twenty-five years — they cannot pay the interest on the debt. And if they continue demanding the payment of this interest, an explosion will take place. As long as it's a question of social changes in small countries, in Grenada and Central America and Cuba, mention can still be made of the madness of solving them through invasion. If one day a change takes place in South America — in Brazil, in Peru, in Chile — and I forgot to mention it, which is really one of the countries of the Southern Cone, where, in my opinion, there is a prerevolutionary situation. The United States knows now, at least they understand it, that if the situation of Chile continues, in the not-too-distant future they might face a Nicaragua or even something worse than Nicaragua in the Southern Cone. And that is the situation that we see. How will they solve it? Will they send a battalion of the 82nd Airborne and send it by air? Everybody understands that that cannot be and if those risks exist I believe it will be convenient for the United States to change its conceptions about this hemisphere and stop being the sworn enemy of social changes and learn to coexist with them. That's my reasoning.

[*MacNeil: Castro said that after the abortive Bay of Pigs invasion in April 1961, when Cuban exiles backed by the CIA tried to overthrow him, Cuba continued to fear an American invasion. The fears persisted even after President Kennedy and Soviet leader Nikita Khrushchev discussed the situation in Vienna.*]

Castro: The Soviets had that concern and we naturally had the same concern.

MacNeil: This is after the Bay of Pigs?

Castro: Yes, after the Bay of Pigs. They asked us what measures we thought could offer Cuba some guarantees. So then we said that the only guarantee, the greatest guarantee that could be obtained, the greatest guarantee or the most sure one was the fact that an aggression against Cuba would mean an aggression against the Soviet Union. That was the thesis that we put forth. The concrete idea of the missiles was theirs. I explained it and we accepted it. But without any hesitation because we were being harassed. An invasion had just taken place. The pirate attacks were continuing, constantly. Constant mention was being made of an invasion against Cuba. For us the missiles had their inconvenience; I confess that the inconveniences that we least liked were the political inconveniences of having the missiles here. But from the point of view of security for the country, it implied at least what is called a nuclear umbrella, because we were facing the dual risk of a conventional war, a specific risk — that is, an aggression against our country — and a universal risk, that is, the case of a general nuclear war. That was our point of view.

And our opinion, after twenty-six years, is that that decision we made was correct. It was very well based, and it was totally legitimate. That cannot be questioned. Now, for example, you are deploying missiles in Holland and Belgium, in countries that are much smaller than Cuba. In the Federal Republic of Germany, Italy, and even at that time there were missiles in Turkey. But in light of international law, our decision and that of the Soviets was totally unobjectionable. The United States assumed a position of force in the face of that situation. But the decision cannot be questioned either from the moral point of view or from the legal point of view, because I think that perhaps the Soviets might not be very pleased about the U.S. adventures of installing missiles, intermediate missiles, near the borders of the Soviet Union. Examine — study that. Think about that.

MacNeil: When the crisis was at its very height, did you personally think — did you believe that nuclear war was a possibility on one of those days?

Castro: Yes. Yes, I believed it was a possibility.

MacNeil: What did you feel about your role in having brought it to that point?

Castro: It was not me. It was the United States that led us to that point. It was the United States that initiated the blockade, that organized the invasion, the sabotage, the pirate attacks, the mercenary regiment, and those that spoke of an invasion against Cuba. It was the United States; it was not us. And I believe that we answered correctly. I have no doubt whatsoever. What were we to do? Yield? The United States can feel sure that we will never yield. Under conditions such as those we will fight.

MacNeil: After Khrushchev decided to withdraw the missiles, which you protested, what did he say to you, Nikita Khrushchev? Did he say to you, "We've made a big mistake, we shouldn't have done this"? What did he say?

Castro: Look, we would not have opposed seeking a solution, no. We would have agreed to sit down and discuss it. We would not have preferred war, for the sake of war under any circumstances. We disagreed because the decision was made without consulting us. That is the crux of the problem. You ask if Nikita apologized. We of course made the protest. This is historical and not really anything new. Actually this affected the relations for a certain period of time. I also explained that afterwards we understood that we had no reason for having that problem for such a long period of time. Nikita put forth these two ideas: a war was avoided and Cuba was not invaded. Those are the points he put forth, the basic points. At that time — time had to advance — when twenty years elapsed or fifteen years, after that came international détente because we, to a certain degree, rendered a particular service. When the war came very close then the leaders of the two big powers became more aware of the danger. They worked; they were able to achieve détente. But at that time we were not in agreement. We were not pleased. Now then, after fifteen years elapsed it was proven that they were right, that a war, a nuclear war, was avoided and that Cuba was not invaded. At least during these years we had to accept that they were right. It's not the way we would have done it. But actually the objective thing, the argument was right, the fundamental argument.

The Political and Social Situation
of Latin America Is a Powder Keg

Interview with Spanish News Agency

Ricardo Utrilla: To turn to Latin America, what do you think at present of the possibility of a direct U.S. intervention in Nicaragua and what would be Cuba's attitude in that event?

Fidel Castro: Unfortunately, the possibility of a U.S. intervention in Nicaragua exists.

Now, as we have said in our conversations with the Americans and the legislators, it seems inconceivable to us that the United States should commit such an error. I'll tell you why. Setting aside the fact that it constitutes a violation of the norms of international law, which beyond everything it would clearly be, I don't think that these norms would be a persuasive element for someone with an imperialist mentality who considers invading any small country his right.

But, firstly, I have said that from a practical standpoint it's senseless to invade a country to solve problems which can be solved perfectly well through political and peaceful means, through negotiation, because I think that possible solutions for Central America do exist, solutions which satisfy the interests of Nicaragua, of the Central American countries, and of the United States itself.

Secondly, because Nicaragua is a country of the Latin American family. I think that the experience of the Malvinas is sufficiently recent, the terrible reaction that the Malvinas War wrought in Latin America and how, despite the fact that the Argentine government was an indefensible, completely isolated, and discredited government, the Latin American nations unhesitatingly supported Argentina, that is, they supported the Argentine people. They supported the Argentine nation in its war against the British and there was a deep sense of solidarity.

These are new times; we are no longer living in the 1920s or in the be-

---

This interview was conducted February 13, 1985, by correspondents Ricardo Utrilla and Marisol Marín, from the Spanish news agency EFE. It is excerpted here from the March 3, 1985, Granma Weekly Review.

ginning of this century when the United States would intervene in Santo Domingo, in Haiti, in Cuba, in Central America, or in Nicaragua without any great protest. In those days they would intervene, not out of fear of communism — this is new, a new variety of pretext — or fear of revolutions.

When there was no Cuban revolution, no Russian revolution, in those times the pretexts were different: sometimes a $5 million debt that wasn't paid would cause a U.S. military intervention in Haiti, or in Santo Domingo, or in Nicaragua. There would be intervention over debts, no respect of any kind, and often in the countries of Central America and the Caribbean.

Now, there are the mass media, greater education and awareness on the part of our peoples of their rights, their independence, and their prerogatives. At that time there was no United Nations, nor was there the Organization of American States, which the United States later took charge of creating, discrediting, and destroying, all in one go.

An intervention in Nicaragua would cause a commotion in Latin America and, moreover, I would say a special, exceptionally critical situation in the economic and social order. Graphically speaking, we say that to intervene in Nicaragua is to play with fire beside a powder keg, because, in my opinion, the political and social situation of Latin America can be described as a powder keg. It would really be a great folly on the part of the United States.

Thirdly, in order to intervene in Nicaragua they would have to commit genocide and kill tens of thousands of men, women, and children in Nicaragua. Perhaps they would have to kill hundreds of thousands of people in full view of international opinion, in full view of the mass media, television, film. No matter how many measures they might take, they wouldn't be able to hide the magnitude of the genocide they would have to commit there with the use of their warships, bombers, tanks, and troops to kill Nicaraguans, that is, to kill Latin Americans, members of the same family.

And lastly, it would involve an elevated cost of U.S. lives and becoming bogged down in a fight against the Nicaraguan people that would be interminable. The Nicaraguans are a militant, patriotic, brave people. Solving the problem of disarming every Nicaraguan patriot is not going to be so easy. Moreover, there was the experience in Sandino's times when a handful of men resisted a U.S. invasion for many years.

There really doesn't exist the technology to counteract and conquer popular resistance. This has been shown everywhere. Look at the example of Vietnam, the problem of the Sahara, the Sahara you Spaniards handed over to the king of Morocco, perhaps thinking in Ceuta and Melilla, as if the king would never begin to reclaim them also someday.

Among Spain's errors, in my opinion — and I say this in all honesty

— among the moral deeds about which Spain cannot be proud, is having handed over the Western Sahara to Morocco. After being there hundreds of years, in the end the Spanish shamefully withdrew from that desert inhabited by the Saharans, who are as Saharan as we are Cuban and, moreover, speak Spanish. It was handed over to the king of Morocco who wanted to control the phosphate mines and the marine riches that comprise the basic resources of that heroic people.

There are 200,000 Moroccan soldiers there and they are impotent in their drive to seize that desert country void of forests, jungles, or great mountains. They are impotent and helped by the United States, with advice from the United States, with sophisticated devices, radar that can detect a man's every movement. Nevertheless, they are impotent and, in the long run, condemned to defeat.

The Saharans are no longer isolated; they are recognized by the majority of OAU [Organization of African Unity] member states and that is a good example.

For five years the Salvadorans have been fighting against an army advised by the United States, an army with many planes and helicopters, conducting many reconnaissance missions, and outfitted with a great deal of sophisticated equipment. They have demonstrated their capacity to adapt to U.S. strategy and technology and also to the abundant military and economic resources which the United States gives to the Salvadoran army.

There are many examples in the world and they are not new. The case of Cuba itself — if you review the history of Cuba, it was a handful of men who waged war for ten years against 300,000 Spanish soldiers and only in the central and eastern parts of the island. We were the Vietnam of the last century.

It's been shown that there is no technology capable of smashing movements of popular resistance, of people motivated by patriotic and revolutionary ideas. It is going to be useless. The political and human price they will have to pay is so high that, as I've told the Americans, a U.S. invasion of Nicaragua seems inconceivable to me.

In the face of United States military might, its numerous aircraft carriers, its complete air and sea domination of the area, the Nicaraguans would be virtually unable to receive any help. All that would be necessary would be for the United States to set up a rigorous air and sea blockade with the military resources it has and no one else has. Cuba simply does not have the means to break such a blockade. In other words, in terms of practicality, it's impossible for us to give them any kind of support in the military terrain under such circumstances.

Our own armed forces are of a defensive nature. Our forces are strong on the defense of the country. Our forces are strong and based on the people, on millions of organized people, all the people organized everywhere, on every square meter of land, in the cities and towns, in the countryside, in the mountains, and on the plains. In other words, they are very strong for fighting a similar kind of war, a popular war against an invasion.

Our air and sea means are limited and made up of means which are completely defensive in character. We know how to employ them in conjunction with land forces that are indeed powerful in the event of an invasion of the country, but we do not have air and sea means to counter a U.S. blockade. If they blockade us, we ourselves do not have the military means to counter such a blockade.

We have plans, programs, ways to resist and know what to do under such circumstances. We have developed all the plans for a blockade, for blockade with a war of attrition, for blockade with an invasion of the country and even occupation of the country. We have studied everything.

The Nicaraguans follow the same philosophy we do. They do not have offensive armed forces, nor would it make any sense for them to use theirs against any neighboring country. It would be to hand the United States on a silver platter a pretext to intervene in the country, to invade the country, to smash the country.

We revolutionaries have demonstrated that we are calm and rational, because we ourselves have U.S. troops and an illegal U.S. naval base on our territory. They have been there since the end of the wars about which I spoke earlier. A puppet government that they put there rented it for 100 years. No, not for 100 years. They rented it and didn't stipulate any limit. In this case the 100-year maximum is recognized by international law.

Utrilla: I think Cuba would be unable to do anything in material terms.

Castro: It is materially impossible. The United States knows this, everybody knows it, and everybody with military experience knows we have no option, that we can't, just as in the case of a blockade against Cuba, break the blockade; we could resist the blockade and resist aggression. The Nicaraguans are guided by the same principle. We are small countries in this area, where the United States has overwhelming superiority in conventional air and naval weapons, not to mention nuclear weapons.

I think this reflects the extent of our peoples' merit. This does not crush us, it does not discourage us, it does not intimidate us; we are ready to struggle. In such conditions we know that an attack on Cuba, for example, would ultimately be a defeat for the United States but one which would be very costly for us. It's the type of glory and victory we would not want, although we know what the result would be. They would need millions of soldiers to keep up an occupation of Cuba and they don't have them, nor would they ever be able to accomplish this unless they exterminated the entire country.

They can drop a few nuclear bombs and wipe us off the face of the earth, but that is not a defeat. History could never consider it a defeat when a people had resisted to the end and kept the flag flying high to the last. A defeat is when you surrender and lower your flag. Exterminating us would be a Pyrrhic victory, if they could, and they can't with impunity, they just can't.

Our country can be exterminated but not defeated. That is our philosophy and the philosophy of the Nicaraguans and the Salvadorans. They won't surrender even if they send $10 billion in arms and economic help to the Salvadoran army.

Utrilla: Then what is the solution in Central America from the U.S. point of view? To permit the continued advance of the Sandinista revolution?

Castro: From the U.S. point of view, they in fact want to destroy the Sandinista revolution. They also tried to destroy the Cuban revolution, the independence of North Vietnam, and the revolution in South Vietnam, just as the French sought to keep their rule over Indochina and Algeria. France is one of the most advanced and powerful countries in Europe in the military field. Algeria is a country which was 85 percent illiterate, almost entirely desert, which has many desert areas, and the Algerian people resisted and won their independence. That is, there have been many wars to block the sovereignty of countries, the independence of countries, to block revolutionary processes, and in the end nothing was achieved.

Now the theory that Nicaragua is a risk for the United States, a threat to the United States, is a legend, a myth. In relation to a small country with a population of three million, among the poorest in Latin America, with a huge debt of billions of dollars, destroyed by the Somoza regime and earthquakes, it is an outright lie that it can threaten the security of the United States, a downright lie.

Utrilla: But as an example to be followed by countries in similar straits and —

Castro: Well, that's something else. They want to destroy the example, which is something else.

Utrilla: That happened with Cuba.

Castro: If the problem can be solved only by having a country renounce its sovereignty and ideas then there'll be no solution.

Utrilla: The thing is that the United States feels that the only way to express the ideas of a people is through Western-style democracy with free elections, where political parties can function, where there is a preparatory electoral campaign, that is, the whole works.

Castro: But that's just what the Nicaraguans did. That is what they have done in the framework of the strictest rules of liberal, bourgeois, Western elections, however you want to call them. They did just that; they accepted. They were asked to move up the date for the elections and they did, with direct balloting and the participation of all parties that wanted to. They even economically helped opposition parties that were organized.

But what has happened regarding the elections in Nicaragua? The United States knew the Right would lose the elections and the Sandinistas would be clear winners, and right from the start they moved to sabotage them, with all kinds of excuses. They then demanded that the elections be delayed. The Sandinistas were faced with the problems of internal war, economic problems, and the elections. At the same time, they submitted themselves to this trial by fire and passed.

They also knew they would win the elections. They were convinced that they had the support of the people, just as the United States was convinced that its parties, its pupils in Nicaragua, would lose the elections. It was the U.S. government that encouraged [Arturo] Cruz to pull out and sabotage the elections. They also tried to have the Liberals, to have [Virgilio] Godoy, withdraw as well. We know this and we know the strategy which the U.S. followed: first tell Cruz to pull out, then pressure Godoy to do likewise and leave the Sandinistas on their own, to discredit and contest the elections.

The United States didn't dare accept the election challenge. Even though it talks so much about elections and its parties and candidates were allowed to run, they didn't dare accept. It wasn't the Nicaraguans who rejected elections of a traditional bourgeois-democratic nature which, as you know, are a farce in many countries.

Even the most expert publicity agencies in the United States are often contracted, along with image-building experts. Election campaigns are organized that cost hundreds of millions of dollars. They are sold just as Coca-Cola or Chesterfield, furniture or perfume, and other products of the consumer society are sold. This can very often be seen in Latin America.

The Sandinistas accepted the challenge of elections. It was the United States that turned down the challenge, trying to sabotage the elections so they could be called into question. But more than 1,000 observers and journalists there saw that the people turned out to the polls and did so enthusiastically.

More turned out to vote in Nicaragua than did in the last election in the United States. In the U.S. elections, the turnout was just over 50 percent, while in Nicaragua it was more than 70, between 70 and 80 percent. What's more, Daniel [Ortega] got more votes than Reagan, a higher percentage of the votes cast. He got more than 60, about 66 or 67 percent. If you add the votes of other parties who claim to be more leftist than the Sandinistas, those who voted for the revolutionary process constituted more than 70 percent of the people. I repeat, between 70 and 80 percent, which is more than in the United States.

What right is there to challenge the elections in Nicaragua? They accepted the challenge; it was the United States that did not accept the challenge of elections.

Now, what I am saying is that there is a solution. I believe and am absolutely convinced that a negotiated political solution is possible in Nicaragua, based on information from all the talks that have taken place, the views of all sides. I am absolutely convinced that a solution exists, which is what Contadora is trying to accomplish, in finding a solution in Central America. Who has opposed the solution and the formula proposed by Contadora? Not Nicaragua, the United States.

The United States constantly claimed to support Contadora until the time came for the test, the moment of truth. The Contadora delegates drew up an act that lays down difficult conditions and limitations for Nicaragua in many respects, but they accepted it. It was a brave decision. They accepted the Contadora act, but the United States did not.

Why hasn't the Contadora act been signed? Simply because the United States has rejected it, is trying to modify it, and mobilized its allied countries in the area to contest the Contadora act. Those are the facts that are known to all.

What do I think? The United States still hopes to destroy the Nicaraguan revolution from within. Why? In the first place because of Nicaragua's economic problems, which are caused by three factors: one, the problems facing all nations of Latin America and the Caribbean. The Dominican Republic has them, as you see, Panama and Uruguay have them, Peru has them, all countries have them, and they are problems arising from the international economic crisis and the low prices of their export commodities, to which the debt is an added problem.

Two, problems resulting from economic measures taken by the United States against Nicaragua. It has been deprived of its sugar quota — as was Cuba. It has been left with but a small portion of its quota, apart from other measures against the Nicaraguan economy, since the United States was Nicaragua's major market.

Three, the action of the counterrevolutionary bands, thousands of men organized, trained, and supplied by the CIA, who are completely given over to, whose main strategy is to affect the economy, affect the coffee harvest, destroy economic installations and transportation. That is, the main order given to the counterrevolutionary bands is to strike at the Nicaraguan economy. Of course, this has had its effect. It has affected coffee production by 30 to 35 percent, fish, timber, and staple legumes.

The United States thinks the Nicaraguans won't be able to hold out and that the combination of economic problems and armed counterrevolutionary bands will destroy the Sandinista revolution from within. I don't think the United States is considering a direct invasion for the moment, that's my personal opinion. That danger will reappear when they realize that the Nicaraguan revolution won't be destroyed from within, because, while production in Nicaragua may not be at 100 percent capacity, it is at 70 or 75 percent, and they are receiving help from abroad, from various Western countries, among them Spain, along with the help from the socialist countries.

As I said previously, those seven ships which the Pentagon talked about, claiming that they were taking weapons to Nicaragua, did not contain a single bullet. They actually contained essential merchandise: oil, food such as wheat and rice, construction material, chemical products, fertilizer that the Nicaraguans need and that — if well administered — will enable them, together with what they produce, to endure the economic crisis. And the bands on the other hand will never be able to defeat the Sandinista army.

Utrilla: Has Cuba given the Nicaraguans military aid, apart from the instructors?

Castro: In what sense?

Utrilla: With material or —

Castro: We have helped the Nicaraguans where we can, though of course not with troops. There are no troops there, not a single Cuban military unit. Nor do they need it. All we have are advisers, instructors, teachers, that kind of personnel.

Utrilla: How many?

Castro: I won't say the number because I don't have the right to say how many there are. I do say there is military cooperation, in the area I mentioned, because they have had to build a new army. They had no officers who had gone through academies. They had no instructors for their military schools. They had no professional cadres, because the officers who had gone to academies served Somoza. They had to build a new army, training hundreds of thousands of citizens in defense, so they needed teachers, instructors, and advisers, and we have provided them at the indispensable level.

Utrilla: So you wouldn't say sufficient, just indispensable.

Castro: Well, I think it is sufficient, but I shouldn't mention figures. Some time ago I gave approximate figures, but I don't plan to do so again. They are not really figures we should be talking about or publishing. We don't object if the Nicaraguans want to do so, but it doesn't seem right to me that we should be giving out information about the number of Cubans there.

There isn't just military cooperation. Our main form of cooperation is not military, it is civilian.

Recently, we opened a modern sugar mill, one of the most important factories in Central America, built in a brief period of time. We supplied about 65 percent of the equipment manufactured in Cuba, plus equipment we had purchased from the socialist countries, 80 percent and more of the components, the blueprint, the equipment, and also technicians, engineers, and construction workers who worked there along with Nicaraguan workers. When it was opened, we donated it to Nicaragua.

All our economic cooperation in Nicaragua has been in the form of a donation, except for the mill. When the mill came up, they asked for credit for its construction. At the time, their production was on the increase: the output of coffee and other items was growing. Then came the action of the bands, U.S. intervention, the hostility of the United States, and key lines of production began to be affected.

We took stock of the situation and said: well, they have economic problems, the best thing would be to cancel the debt. It seemed to be the most correct thing and in line with what we have been saying. Thus, Cuba decided to renounce the credit and cancel the debt on the construction of the mill. We have also helped them in the construction of roads, bridges, and other projects.

Utrilla: Then the debt for the mill was canceled?

Castro: Totally. Now we are in debt to them, because we still have to send a few hundred tons of components. Since the debt has been canceled, we have gone from creditors to debtors, because we must send those items. It has been canceled completely.

Utrilla: And the Salvadoran guerrillas, are you helping them in any way?

Castro: Let me continue with Nicaragua.

We have also given them important aid in the educational field, and public health is now one of our most important sectors of cooperation with Nicaragua. We have hundreds of doctors and health personnel working there. They are especially needed because war has its wounded; they need surgeons; there are surgeons of ours there along with other types of doctors. They in part care for the war wounded, but mostly the Cuban doctors and health personnel care for the Nicaraguan people.

We cooperate in the field of agriculture and in sports. Our cooperation with Nicaragua is basically civilian. I said economic, but I meant to include education and health services, etc. We also train cadres. We have trained about 1,500 teachers; we have a training program for Nicaraguan teachers.

The bulk of our cooperation is civilian, but there is military cooperation. This is known and we have said so. This seems very fair to us. Nobody has any right to contest it, least of all the United States which, in violation of international norms, is organizing, training, supplying, and directing mercenary bands against the people and government of Nicaragua. Can our right to give them relatively modest cooperation for defense be challenged?

However, the Nicaraguans bear the brunt of this struggle and effort, as shown by the fact that thousands of Nicaraguans have died as a result of the bands' attacks, the majority of them civilians: women, children. They attack a bus full of civilians, a truck, villages, and many more civilians than soldiers have been killed by the bands, about 4,000 people in all. The United States knows this, and this is only on the Sandinista side, because we must also take into account the Nicaraguans who have been led to their death on the side of the counterrevolutionary forces. About 8,000 or 9,000 people must have died in this dirty war organized by the United States.

My opinion, of course, is that although a solution exists, the United States won't seriously negotiate or support Contadora and its efforts, as long as it hopes to destroy the Sandinista revolution from within. It is a tragedy but a fact. They hope to destroy the revolution, which is why there are no serious negotiations. If the United States seriously wants to negotiate, there will undoubtedly be peaceful solutions in Central America which satisfy Nicaragua, the Central American peoples, and the United States.

Marisol Marín: Do you think the Sandinistas and the Salvadoran guerrillas pursue or hope to create in their respective countries a Cuban political and economic model?

Castro: Nothing could be further from the truth. I know the views of the Sandinistas and of the Salvadorans, though logically we have more contact with the former because it is an established government, while the Salvadorans are in their country and many of their top leaders have been in the country a long time, but we are also familiar with their views.

Nicaragua is a country with a much lower level of development than Cuba at the time of the triumph of the revolution. Cuba had attained a certain level of industrial development. It had a larger working class, more agricultural workers — there were hundreds of thousands of agricultural workers, hundreds of thousands of industrial workers, a much more developed working class.

Nicaragua is a much more industrially and economically backward country than Cuba when the revolution triumphed. In Nicaragua there is a lot of craft industry still, and many people who earn a living from petty trading. It doesn't have the same level of development as Cuba when our revolution triumphed; conditions are different.

They know full well that their struggle is basically a struggle for independence, national liberation, and social progress; for implementing agrarian reform, educating the entire population, providing everyone with health care. Economic development is the top priority for the Nicaraguan government, not the construction of socialism.

Marín: Do you mean it is not a top priority or not their objective?

Castro: Actually, it's not their objective, it's not a short- or even medium-term objective. If you want you can add that it isn't their current objective. When I say current objective, I am thinking of a relatively long period of time, as they see it.

I think the Nicaraguan plan — and I have no disagreements with it, neither theoretical nor practical, and I say that sincerely — is perfect, given the conditions in their country and in Central America. It is perfect.

I can go on a bit more regarding this question.

This doesn't mean that the Nicaraguans aren't revolutionary; they are revolutionary. It would be a mistake to think that they are mere reformists, mere patriots or democrats who don't want to transform their country in a social sense.

I think the Nicaraguans are revolutionary and I don't think they would renounce, just as no revolutionary would renounce, the objective of transforming their society and even building socialism when socialism is possible and it could become a possibility one day. I don't think they would renounce having their revolution one day go as far as any other social revolution.

It seems to me, for example, that Felipe [González, prime minister of Spain] hasn't renounced the objectives of socialism in Spain, although Spain is a capitalist country and will continue to be one with a large number of both national and transnational firms.

Felipe talks about socialism and I suppose the Spanish Socialist Workers Party plans to build socialism. At least that's what they said when the party was formed. But, I ask, does Felipe plan to build socialism right away? There is a completely capitalist society in Spain, I don't think even the most ignorant expert on economic, social, and historical issues would dispute this, and it would be in a better objective position for socialist construction than Nicaragua.

Well, I don't think the Sandinistas will renounce their objective, on a long-term basis, of building socialism; but in the medium term they have no plans to establish a socialist regime in Nicaragua. Their organization is called the Sandinista National Liberation Front and not the Socialist Party.

That is why I told you, since you asked about priorities, that their priorities are a series of reforms in the structure. I think that agrarian reform is most important; of course, they also nationalized the holdings of the Somoza family, they did not nationalize the bourgeoisie's property because in Nicaragua there was virtually no bourgeoisie, only an embryonic bourgeoisie. Somoza was the one who owned many firms in

Nicaragua, and they confiscated his holdings because they had been obtained through theft and, of course, they were not given to the transnationals or to private enterprise.

I don't think the Sandinistas can be criticized because they confiscated Somoza's property and didn't hand it over to U.S. or private firms. There is the oil refinery owned by a U.S. transnational. People from the United States and other countries, national and foreign firms have property, and there are no plans to nationalize them.

I said there were a series of structural changes and a program of economic and social development. That's what the Nicaraguans face and it must be understood. This is not a fairy tale or an invention, a disguise to fool anybody. Their method is real and we fully agree with it in theoretical and practical terms, because we feel it corresponds to the Nicaraguan reality.

Of course, if Cuba gives them financial and technical help for the construction of a sugar mill, they won't end up handing it over to a private company. But in many countries, among them Mexico, oil is state-owned, the petrochemical industry is state-owned, the iron and steel industry is state-owned. In Nicaragua the state controls foreign trade and financial resources. This has been done by various capitalist countries, although I understand that there are private banks in Nicaragua. But financial control is not held by the private banks; it is held by the state. Control of foreign trade is not held by private institutions; foreign trade is in the hands of the state. There are those kinds of measures.

They must develop the country, that is their program; developing the country, I imagine, by means of a program of agricultural, industrial, and energy development. Economic development of the country is the fundamental task, in which I think private enterprise will also have a role to play as much as possible.

They even planned to draft a law on foreign investment. There were sectors where they did not have the technology or financial resources so I suppose it will be necessary to use foreign resources and companies in those cases. Even in our case, if necessary, there may be situations in which foreign technology and investments are needed.

Development is the main objective of the country, since it is very difficult to have socialism without development. Of course, it will be development that does not benefit capitalism and will not be carried out with the supervision of landlords and capitalists. It will be development under the leadership of a revolutionary government that serves the people and not the landlords, oligarchs, or foreign companies, which is what we find all over the hemisphere.

I think this is very clear and I know very well that this is the program, the program of a mixed economy and political pluralism, yes of political pluralism with no fear.

Now they plan to draft a constitution. I can't say what kind of constitution it will be, they are working on it, but I think the constitution will reflect their program.

Marín: What about the Salvadorans?

Castro: I think the case of the Salvadorans is exactly the same. Of course, El Salvador may have a little more industrial development than Nicaragua, but I haven't heard the Salvadorans talk of socialism. What they want is to rid themselves of a genocidal regime and a system — everyone knows this — which has lasted a long time, in which an oligarchy, a small group of thirty or forty families, owns the country. I think the Salvadorans have more or less the same plans as the Nicaraguans; in fact, I think other nations of Latin America once they reach liberation will not strive for socialism right away or in the medium term.

I think the two basic problems for Latin America are, first, independence — independence is the first thing Latin America must obtain because it really isn't independent — and, second, development, together with structural changes, not only economic but also social development.

There are Latin American countries where the transnationals have made big investments and they have attained certain levels of production, but there has been no social development. Illiteracy still runs at 30 percent and, together with semiliteracy, makes for a figure as high as 80 percent, and sanitary conditions are terrible. Infant mortality is high, life expectancy low, the social problems are endless.

These are the two most urgent problems in Latin America. Of course, neither the oligarchs nor the military who have been at the service of foreign interests, the oligarchy or the United States, will fight for independence. The people are the ones who must fight for it.

I even think, although nobody can be a prophet, that other Latin American countries will, to a greater or lesser degree, adopt the Nicaraguan program. This program is real, that is, it is not an invention, a pretext, or lie; it is no trick. They take it seriously and I think the challenge they have set themselves is admirable. Ah! Because they trust in the people, and, if they work well, they will always have the support of the people.

The secret of remaining in power is not to be found in constitutional mechanisms or electoral systems. In our system, which is different from that of Nicaragua, if the revolution did not have the support of the people, power would be lost, because how are elections undertaken? The people themselves put forward the candidates at the grass roots, and those delegates from the circumscriptions are the ones who elect the municipal, provincial, and national bodies.

Remaining or not remaining in power does not depend on electoral mechanisms. It is a matter of holding onto the support of the people, and if you have that you can retain power with any mechanism. Without their support, you lose power, no matter what mechanism you have. That's a fact.

So they accepted. It is admirable, the first thing they accepted was the type of classical, traditional elections, like those in the United States and other Latin American countries, the rare times there have been elections, because the history of Guatemala, El Salvador, and Nicaragua is not one of electoral processes. From the time of [William] Walker, the U.S. pirate who intervened in Central America in the mid-nineteenth century, until now, it is not a history of elections, except for the case of Costa Rica. Don't look for it in Honduras, Nicaragua, Guatemala, or El Salvador.

Horrible things happened for 100 years and the United States never spoke of democracy there. The United States started talking about democracy when revolution broke out in Central America. Before it didn't say a word.

Marín: When you say that other Latin American countries are following or seem to be following the Nicaraguan plan, which countries are you referring to?

Castro: I am referring to future social changes in Latin America that will inevitably come. I am not referring to any country in particular, but rather to any country where it is truly the people who take power and not the oligarchs, the representatives of big capital, or the traditional army, although, in some cases, in two cases, the army has played a progressive role: Peru and Panama.

We can't generalize when we talk about the armies and, moreover, we still don't know what the armed forces' role will be in these changes. The role of the military in some places will be very reactionary, while in others it may be very progressive. There are two countries where the army has played a progressive role and they are Peru and Panama.

It was the National Guard in Panama, with [Gen. Omar] Torrijos, that led the struggle for demands related to the canal, and [Gen. Juan] Velasco Alvarado's military government [in Peru] implemented important progressive social and economic initiatives, including a fairly thoroughgoing agrarian reform.

Utrilla: Before going on to other broader topics related to Latin America, commander, I'd like to press my previous question a bit: what kind of aid is Cuba providing the Salvadoran guerrillas?

Castro: I already replied to this when the question was put to me before. I do not wish to affirm or deny our aid. For the time being, they have and will have our political solidarity, our support in all spheres, including the international one. In terms of aid in the form of arms, as I recently said, it is almost impossible for arms to reach the Salvadorans. A discussion of the topic is almost metaphysical.

Utrilla: Almost, commander, it is almost impossible.

Castro: It is almost impossible; I can't say that it is completely impossible. I can say that it is practically impossible and also that the issue is almost metaphysical — I say almost because we're discussing a theoretical problem.

I will say that helping the Salvadorans cannot be at all questioned from a moral viewpoint, and, moreover, from the viewpoint of the strictest justice, because the Salvadorans began to fight against a regime that has practiced systematic genocide, that has murdered 50,000 people in the country. The Salvadorans are fighting for their survival. I think that their cause is just and the right to help a country, a movement, a people who are fighting for survival and against genocide is not questionable.

On what moral principle can the United States talk about not supporting El Salvador, contest aid to El Salvador, if they organize, supply, and arm thousands of men to carry out a counterrevolution in Nicaragua?

In other words, helping the Salvadorans is not questionable in moral terms, in terms of principles. It's in terms of practicalities that I say there may be theoretical, moral, legal, if you will, discussion, but to do so in practice is very difficult.

I also said that this was not a basic issue. When we waged our struggle here in Cuba against an army like Batista's, which had 70,000 armed men, we did so without foreign aid, with the weapons and ammunition we captured from Batista's troops.

The main supplier of the Salvadoran revolutionaries today, I can assure you, is the Pentagon, because a part of the weapons and the ammunition the Pentagon sends to El Salvador ends up in the hands of the revolutionaries. And that is a guaranteed supply. History has shown that it is perfectly possible. When I speak of the Salvadorans' capacity to resist indefinitely, I am talking about their capacity to fight under the worst conditions, conditions in which they do not receive even a single rifle or a single bullet from abroad.

They have adapted perfectly well to the difficult conditions of struggle in their country. They have been able to respond to all the tactics and strategies of the U.S.-advised Salvadoran army, and, moreover, they can survive indefinitely, without any foreign aid. I think that this is actually the important thing, not whether someone sends aid or not, but whether it is vital or not to receive it.

I've gone as far as to say that it is virtually impossible. I won't be totally negative about the possibilities, of course, but I think that what's basic in this regard is that they can resist and fight without foreign aid. I think that this is the point, the key issue, the one that matters. That is, can the Salvadorans continue the struggle without foreign aid? And I say: yes, they can continue the struggle indefinitely and resist without foreign aid.

Utrilla: In summary, then, as in the case of Cuba, there is no possible military solution for the United States in Nicaragua and El Salvador.

Castro: Oh, no! There is no military solution in this matter. That is a conclusion I can categorically state. On the other hand, there are political solutions that would be to the benefit of Nicaragua, the peoples of Central America, and the peoples of the Caribbean and, of course, the United States. That's the position I maintain.

So you've drawn correct conclusions.

Marín: Speaking now about Latin America, do you think that the process of democratization, of the recuperation of democracies in Latin America, can benefit Cuba in the sense of gradual reestablishment of relations with countries with which until now you have not had relations or where they were broken? I am concretely referring to Brazil and Uruguay.

Castro: I think that that holds the least importance for us, that is, the issue of relations with countries which have begun a new stage is of least importance. The issues of Cuba's prestige or the moral problem of completely defeating the isolation is not essential. We do not subordinate the issue of relations with Cuba to our interest, rather we subordinate that issue to the interests of each one of those countries. I think that each one of those countries should do what it considers most appropriate to its interests, if it's in their interests to reestablish relations soon or if they prefer to wait.

We are not exerting any pressure in this regard, and we are letting them decide what they consider most suitable and do it at the most appropriate time. But we truly do not attribute any basic importance, to tell the truth, to the relations in and of themselves. There are more important things than this, from my point of view, such as the consolidation of these democratic processes, and I feel that everyone should help and cooperate in this and not present difficulties.

I think that these democratic processes take on a strategic importance at this time and have a deep significance.

The U.S. administration may say that democracy is advancing, but what is advancing is the crisis of the U.S. system of domination in Latin America. This process signifies that military dictatorships are on the decline; that resorting to repression and force to maintain the system has failed; and that the murders, the sophisticated torture, the missing — things the United States taught the repressive forces, the army and the police in Latin America — that all these atrocious methods no longer serve to maintain the system. The crisis is so profound that the military has understood that these countries have become unmanageable.

Utrilla: Is the present case of Guatemala typical?

Castro: We can't say that it is typical. Guatemala's situation is different. It has serious economic, political, and social problems, yet it is different. It has conditions unlike those of the Southern Cone, they're not

the same. Those countries have greater industrial and social development, greater development, shall we say, of the intellectual sectors and
of the masses' political awareness and culture. The circumstances are
different. Central America is poorer, more accustomed to the system of
oligarchical families, military caudillos, interminable military dictatorships. It has had a political experience different from that of Argentina,
Chile, Brazil, and Uruguay.

In other words, the military understand that the situation in those
countries is unmanageable. They are withdrawing from government and
transferring it to civilians after having totally failed in the leadership of
the state and also after having ruined the countries to greater or lesser degrees. In Chile, Argentina, and Uruguay they ruined the countries to an
extraordinary degree; in Brazil, they handed the country over to the
transnationals so that they could go there and produce with cheap labor
in the midst of tremendous poverty.

But I detect a certain difference between the policy followed by the
Brazilian military and that followed by the Chileans, Argentines, and
Uruguayans, who opened the doors wide to competition and wiped out
national industry. The policy of the Brazilian military was different, but
they all know that their countries have become unmanageable and they
are handing over the power to civilians. That is, the crisis is so profound
that they no longer consider themselves capable of ruling.

Marín: Although they are also going to be unmanageable for the civilians.

Castro: They've been handed a tragic legacy: in Argentina, a foreign
debt of $45 billion; in Uruguay, $5.5 billion; in Brazil, Tancredo
[Neves] inherits a $104 billion debt; that of Chile, where there will in-
evitably be changes, is now $22 billion. During the period of the Popular
Unity government, the debt was $4 billion, the price of copper was not
so low, and the situation was becoming very difficult.

Of course, Allende's situation was compounded by being refused foreign credits. The United States adopted economic measures against his
government. But now the civilians are receiving a tragic legacy. In
Argentina, as in Uruguay and Brazil, there is huge, unmanageable inflation and extremely serious cumulative social problems.

A few days ago a journalist handed me an Argentine one-million-peso
bill and said, "Do you know how much this was worth a few years ago?"
I said, "Not exactly." He said, "Two hundred and fifty thousand dollars.
Do you know how much it is worth now? Seventy-nine cents."

Perhaps the great success of these military governments is that they
turned all the citizens into millionaires. Inflation makes the economy unmanageable. Living standards have considerably declined in all those
countries. I estimate that in Argentina the standard of living has dropped
by 65 percent in comparison with before the military's ascent to power;

by 50 percent in Uruguay; and in Brazil, I don't know exactly, but it could be between 65 and 70, at least 70 percent, although I do not know precisely.

Utrilla: More than in Argentina.

Castro: No, possibly not, 70 percent or 65 in Argentina. In Brazil perhaps it has dropped by 70 percent, which is a conservative estimate; it could have dropped even more although I do not know the exact figure.

These civilian governments come into power and are forced to take severe restrictive measures when the population's living standard is no longer base 100, but rather 65, 50, 70.

Now this huge debt will have to be paid back under the conditions set by the International Monetary Fund. The restrictions began in Mexico at base 100. The populations of the Southern Cone will not tolerate further restrictions; no more can be squeezed out of them.

We have very illustrative examples, such as the Dominican Republic. The IMF formula was imposed and they had to fill the streets with the army and police to kill scores of people and wound hundreds more when the first measures were taken. They changed the peso parity. It was equivalent to one dollar and they changed it to three pesos per dollar for the acquisition of a series of imported products, medications, and some others, but they didn't apply it to fuel and certain foodstuffs. Now comes the second phase, for they've already put the dollar at three pesos for all merchandise.

The Dominican people are a people who were under a constitutional regime, an elected government, with a relatively calm situation, and a virtual people's insurrection took place. When they applied the second phase of the measure, they had to send the army and the police to take over the streets of the cities in order to prevent protests. There is tremendous discontent.

Despite the fact that Panama's levels are not low, the attempt to implement some tax measures and to postpone a salary increase for some professionals, doctors, and teachers, also provoked a social upheaval. Of course, it was utilized by right-wing parties that mobilized hundreds of thousands of people. The government even had to rescind the measures, because the Panamanian National Guard has a patriotic stance and is not given to taking to the street to fire on the people.

These are examples of two nearby countries. Now the debt that these countries and all other Latin American countries have is unpayable. Our position is that it's unpayable. This is my firm conviction.

Something very important is that it's not a question of renegotiating the debt, rescheduling it and providing terms of ten, twelve, and fourteen years with three-, four-, and five-year grace periods to pay the principal. The debt can be renegotiated and nothing at all will be solved.

They can't pay the interest, that's the key point, they cannot pay the interest.

Now, at present the Latin American countries have to pay $40 billion every year in interest — $40 billion every year! — which is compounded by the flight of capital and the repatriation of the earnings of foreign enterprises. According to estimates, in recent years the net drain of capital from Latin America alone reached $55 billion. Now, the debt reaches the terrifying figure of $360 billion and the interest due on this will reach $400 billion in ten years.

Twenty-four years ago, Kennedy promoted the Alliance for Progress as an antidote to prevent social convulsions, and undoubtedly the measures were imaginative. He proposed reforms and economic aid totalling $20 billion over several years to solve the problems of development and social problems.

The population is now twice as large as twenty-four years ago and the social problems have multiplied. The foreign debt is eighteen times greater than what Kennedy proposed as aid and the interest payments are $40 billion a year, $400 billion in ten years. So it's not a matter of whether the countries want to pay the debt or the interest rates. It's that they have no alternative; they cannot pay them.

If these democratic processes try to pay the debt — not the debt, but simply the interest rates — they will be ruined politically. And the danger will not be the return of the military, for the military do not want the government even if it were given to them. The danger is a complete political destablization and social explosion. That's what I say is going to occur if there's an attempt to impose the IMF's formulas and collect those interest payments.

So I suggest the following: that Latin America needs a grace period of approximately ten to twenty years as a minimum in terms of its foreign debt obligations, including the interest.

Utrilla: A complete freeze on the debt.

Castro: A grace period of approximately ten to twenty years, no less, on the principal and the interest according to the country and the circumstances. This is what I maintain and what I am completely convinced of. And this is not to solve the problems; it's only a start in order to have some relief, a breather, for after all it won't overcome the problem.

As I explained in the beginning, the problems of unequal exchange and protectionist measures will have to be solved for the development of trade. In other words, it would only be a breather for a new international economic order, just a respite.

This is not easy because the governments of the industrialized countries have their difficulties. Each one reacts thinking about its own domestic problems: I have so many unemployed; I am undergoing industrial modernization, say the French and the Spanish. The Germans see their unemployment climbing to 2.6 million, a record postwar figure, while the British have 3 million. Unemployment is on the rise in many countries.

The United States adopted the most selfish of all policies. It imposed a financial monetary system supported by its great economic might and based on high interest rates, which extracted hundreds of billions from the world economy, including the economies of the Third World countries.

Everyone was depositing their money in the United States, because if they kept it in the currency of their country, it dropped in value. There would be a devaluation and for all those who had money, let's say someone with a million pesos, to use a currency with a certain value, like with the Mexican devaluation, its worth dropped by 25 percent in a few weeks. The same in Argentina, Brazil, everywhere.

With free exchange and inflation, no one was motivated to deposit money that was not secure anywhere and it was taken abroad, attracted by high U.S. interest rates. For the time being the United States has solved its economic problems with this policy of high interest rates and the extraction of money from other countries. But neither can the United States withstand this situation much longer.

Another problem that has affected the world economy is that country's $200 billion budget deficit. The history of the Vietnam War, which was waged without taxes, is being repeated. Now we have an arms race that is being conducted without taxes and a $123 billion trade deficit which is untenable for the U.S. economy. Thus, these are objective realities that must be taken into account.

I also think that one of the bases for the hope that common sense will prevail, if this is seen with due clarity, is that the United States will understand that it is also to its benefit to halt the arms race and seek international détente. Neither can the U.S. economy withstand this policy much longer. It can withstand it only a maximum of six months, a year; the most optimistic estimate would be a year and a half or two years.

In 1984, 24 percent of the net savings of the United States was deposited from abroad. The international economic crisis has not been solved; everything's limited to optimistic words. The U.S. government said that the United States was the driving force behind other countries for economic recovery. It has in fact driven them not to recovery but rather to a worsening of their difficulties.

Regarding the debt of the Third World, we propose the following: since the creditors are primarily private banks, the solution will be for the industrialized countries to take over the debts owed to the private banks, if bankruptcy of the financial system is to be prevented.

The United States has a public debt of $1.65 trillion and this would only increase it slightly. The aggregate Third World debt is less than what is spent every year in military expenditures and will have to be canceled in the long run.

If the world can have the luxury of spending at present a trillion dollars in military expenditures, I wonder why, just once, the debt of Third World countries cannot be canceled.

My opinion is that no other alternative exists. To try to collect this debt, at least in Latin America, would be socially explosive. Although the situation in Africa is very serious, it is different. There, a large part of the population lives in villages as they lived centuries ago. There, the people suffer hunger and drought and die, but the continent will not inevitably explode.

There is a different social composition in Latin America including workers, peasants, middle strata, intellectuals, great urban masses. The social conditions for such an explosion exist in Latin America.

What do the recently elected civilian governments propose? The Argentine government has clearly said that it is unwilling to accept recessive measures or allow the consequences of this debt to fall on the people, that they cannot halt development. The president-elect of Brazil and other political leaders have spoken in a similar vein. But if the countries have to extract $40 billion every year, how is development possible? They would have to adopt terrifying measures on top of living standards which have declined considerably.

It has been said that the debt problem is political, not just technically financial. That's correct, it is political and it's already begun to be revolutionary.

The positions are clear: I don't want to do this, that, and the other. But the formula has not been mentioned. The United States has tried to divide the Latin American countries in the debt renegotiations, negotiating with each government separately. How many times have the main debtor countries met and made the solemn promise that they will not found a debtors' club, when in reality they ought to start saying the opposite and join forces and form a club, a front, a committee, whatever is necessary, and meet with the creditor countries. The creditors are already closely united in the Paris Club and the International Monetary Fund.

What does it mean to say that the problem is political? Simply that the seriousness of the situation and all the foreseeable consequences must be discussed on a political level.

I think that there might be a breather if the Latin American countries are freed from paying the debt. But there would still not be a solution to the problems of underdevelopment, nor would a new international economic order have been established. It would simply be a start.

Utrilla: It seems you view that outbreak as such a terrible thing that it would not work in a positive way for revolutionary Cuba. But if there is an outbreak, a revolutionary outbreak, isn't this in a sense what Cuba would want for Latin America?

Castro: Well, nobody knows how it will be if events keep moving in that direction. Nobody can predict what will happen, of what type or nature it will be. What I am simply saying is that now the threat is not that the military will return to power; the danger is that Latin American societies will explode.

I will give you another example: Bolivia, where there is a president whom I really esteem, with every desire to salvage the democratic process, a Communist Party even which is not involved in subversion or disorganizing the country but is rather an ally of the government, which participated in the coalition that won the elections, which has taken on the policy of the government. And yet the real situation now is that no government party controls sectors of the labor movement which refuse to make new sacrifices. Inflation increases, strikes come one after the other, the social situation is untenable, and the Communists are not the ones stirring up protest, it is the unions, the workers, peasants, the people in general who can no longer take the sacrifices. You see there the presence of objective factors, not subjective ones.

Who will they blame for subverting order? It is the people who are no longer resigned, who no longer accept limitations on their standard of living. Ah! Because the debt must be paid, the interest rates and the demands of the Fund must be met.

Less than four years ago, a civilian government came to power in Peru in elections where they won more than half the votes cast and obtained a majority in parliament. Now that party which won the elections has the support of only 3.8 percent of the voters. Indications are that APRA [American People's Revolutionary Alliance] will win the elections with a majority, but then how will it handle the debt and other social problems the next day? In Peru there is an evident social upheaval in the making, which nobody really understands but which is surely a reflection of crisis and instability.

Those are two countries; I already mentioned the Dominican Republic and Panama, now Bolivia and Peru. The problems of the region are clear. In my opinion, according to how people see it, there will be social revolutions, for better or for worse, there will be social revolutions if this problem is not solved. The other solution can provide a respite and a potentially less traumatic process.

Utrilla: But from what we have heard of your opinion, perhaps Cuba, the Cuban regime, you personally, would look more favorably on a democratic process which would lead to a revolutionary process of a traditional nature rather than an almost cataclysmic explosion whose results are unpredictable.

Castro: I am simply trying to present things as objectively as possible, as I see them.

This issue came up recently when I was asked about the famous question of exporting revolution, and I said that it is impossible to export the conditions which give rise to revolution, because if we are to talk of subversive elements, my view is that the measures of the IMF, the foreign debt, the $40 billion in interest rates every year, the international economic crisis, the drop in the prices of the main export commodities of Latin American nations, protectionism, high interest rates, are all very subversive factors.

I would say the pope's trip was subversive, because the pope visited some Indian communities, neighborhoods of poor people, and spoke of the need to give land to the peasants and the need for schools for the children; hospitals, doctors, and medicine for the sick; work for the family breadwinner; three meals a day. All those things are subversive in the conditions of the underdeveloped nations of the hemisphere.

If the pope had come to Cuba, he would have had to talk about something else. He would not have had to call for schools for the children, since 99 percent go to school, or hospitals, doctors, and medicine for the sick, or work for breadwinners, or milk for children, or three meals a day. He has revealed a situation which exists in Venezuela in spite of its oil income, in Ecuador and Peru, in the cities and countryside of the nations he visited, all over.

But how can all this be solved? He has said this is a duty and need of society, but how is it to be done? There is the debt, underdevelopment, accumulated social problems, interest rates, huge inequality in the distribution of wealth; a whole number of factors have perhaps unwillingly been laying the groundwork for social revolution.

Utrilla: Well, in Marxist terms, those are the objective conditions for revolution.

Castro: Yes, yes, the enormous economic and social problems that have accumulated and the crisis which has developed are the objective conditions for revolution.

Utrilla: Talking about the famous business of exporting revolution, of which Cuba has so often been accused, it is somewhat off the mark but isn't Cuba tempted, in view of the fact that the objective conditions exist, of the dried grass that has piled up, to light the flame, to set off the spark?

Castro: There is no need for the flame. There can be spontaneous combustion, and then not all the water in the world will be enough to put it out.

Utrilla: If the flames go up, it'll really burn —

Castro: I think these are the factors that determine social change. I am not interested in preserving the existing social order; I think it must change. Nor am I interested in preserving the system of U.S. rule over our peoples. My view is that this order can't continue and that system of rule can't be preserved. It will change, and I think the change will start in the light of this situation.

I simply analyze the problem and say with absolute conviction what will happen if this situation continues. I think the explosive situation can ease if the debt is canceled in one way or another, by agreement between the parties or by a decision of the debtors. However, there is already an insoluble crisis of the system, and I have seen and talked to people, noting that conservatives are dying out in this hemisphere.

If you talk to conservatives, they are hardly conservatives any longer, and they are frustrated and desperate. Workers are desperate and so are the middle sectors, and this is very important, because those sectors are very important in such crisis situations. Even certain upper-class sectors are desperate.

I think the order or the system can no longer hold together. I think the question is to be realistic and see if these conditions continue, until there are really explosive social convulsions, because those objective factors exist. The subjective ones are not so evident, not so clear, that is, the organization of the forces that will bring about change. But the same happened at the time of Latin American independence: all the factors existed and then came a new element, Napoleon's occupation of Spain, which gave rise to patriotic juntas that were initially established as an act of loyalty to Spain and ended in the independence of this hemisphere.

I analyze this and I am not advocating one method or another, I am analyzing and thinking about how I see events, and what will happen. Perhaps it would be better for change to take place in the most orderly manner, less wrenching and less bloody. I would say it would be preferable.

I think, I don't go around setting off social explosions, but I think of what happened in other parts and in another era. The situation in France in 1789 was very similar. French society exploded and it was a large and bloody convulsion.

Utrilla: But some social outbursts are reactionary rather than progressive.

Castro: I don't think so. That time has passed. It would only be isolated cases.

Utrilla: No longer in Latin America.

Castro: In many places the military took power and implemented fascism and torture, disappearances; they ruined the nations they ruled. What is the alternative? In Brazil the opening came as a result of the people's struggle, the mobilization of many millions of people on the issue of direct voting, the intelligent action of political parties that united and, although they lost in parliament, won in the electoral college which had been set up exclusively to elect official candidates. Now you can see the political change which has taken place in Brazil. It was not violent but it was profound; that is, the opening is serious and solid.

Now the people are on the scene. In my opinion, there is no risk of a military coup in Argentina, Uruguay, or Brazil. There are always some military with those inclinations, 8 or 10 percent, madmen who talk of coups, but the majority realize it would be crazy. Ah! But when there is social turmoil and the economy is afloat, 90 percent may be inclined to a quick coup to administer the country.

But that is not the case now; those societies are in crisis and the military can't run them. Resorting to repression has already been tried and it didn't solve the problem. They were worn down while the situation got worse. Resorting to force remains in isolated countries, such as the Dominican Republic, where they shoot at the people. But in other key countries, they already resorted to everything and it is impossible to have more disappeared, being tortured or murdered, than those that have already been disappeared or been tortured and murdered.

Utrilla: Yes, that is the case in Argentina.

Castro: So, there were social convulsions and they were halted for some time with brute force in Uruguay and Chile, the Switzerlands of the Americas. They already resorted to the military. Pinochet doesn't have much time left either. The situation is the most critical in Chilean history. Everybody opposes him, people aren't afraid anymore.

As I point out, even the United States doesn't want Pinochet, because it fears a Nicaragua in the Southern Cone. That is the country which I feel is closest to a much more profound social revolution if rebellion breaks out. The United States realizes this and is trying to ease out Pinochet, convince him to leave, or drive him out some way but has not been able to because Pinochet is very stubborn, sassy, answers back, and holds on to power. It's a volcano.

Utrilla: If you have no objection, commander, let's go on to Cuba.

Castro: Fine, but first let me see if I've left something out, some idea — I talked about Chile, that it is not among the processes of democratic opening, that one of these processes may come about, perhaps a popular revolution, if Pinochet's presence spins out. This is the way things look to me. The general situation is important from another angle, because the United States has to take it into consideration. In this context, is it going to bring about genocide in Nicaragua, an invasion of Nicaragua?

I'm simply formulating my ideas. I believe that in this world we must be objective and realistic and be able to foresee what's coming. I believe that there are many who are thinking about these problems. Of course, the industrialized countries and the United States will try to prevent such a thing from happening, but how are they going to do it? Well, it'd be practically a miracle — a miracle in common sense because as a rule such miracles have never existed — Neither the colonial nor the neocolonial powers have ever been capable of foreseeing and forestalling events.

Kennedy showed concern after the triumph of the Cuban revolution. Prior to the Cuban revolution, nobody could speak about land reform, tax reform, or a social program for Latin America, because anybody who mentioned such things was accused of being a Communist. With the advent of the Cuban revolution, they began to worry for the first time.

The peoples of this hemisphere owe a great deal to the Cuban revolution. The United States began to show some concern. I even think that after the Cuban revolution the Latin American countries have become more independent and the object of greater attention. The U.S. government said: well, let's introduce some reforms, let's do something before more revolutions break out in this hemisphere, and it came up with the thesis of the Alliance for Progress, some twenty-four years ago.

How much time has passed? How many new problems do we have now? And what's the solution now? Will they have the wisdom to handle this problem, to say let's be flexible? It's difficult, yet possible. I wonder what the industrialized countries can do. They could absorb the debt with their own banks and give some breathing space.

I believe that would open a new stage. I think this is an irreversible process, and perhaps rational analysis and a realistic approach to the situation might lead to an orderly, not necessarily violent solution.

All I do is analyze, how we see the situation. I even said to the Americans when they spoke of the advantages of normal relations with Cuba, that they would be political, and greater for them than for Cuba. We can sit here quietly in the front row, so to speak, waiting to see what's going to happen, watching events unfold.

I said that politically it was to the advantage of the United States, because that country could at least show its capacity to adapt to changes and realities. I was thinking that when problems like Grenada's are not on some small island, or in Nicaragua, or in small countries of our area, when a profound social crisis breaks out in Chile, Peru, Brazil, or Argentina, the United States would be powerless to do anything, because such problems cannot be solved by landing a battalion of paratroopers with some pretext or fairy tale.

Failing to understand these problems can be very costly. And, I say, you cannot intervene there and apply the remedy of intervention. When it's a case of Nicaragua or Grenada, you can still speak of intervention and of sending troops and battleships. But when the problem arises in South America, things will be very different.

Why did Central America explode, then? Simply because they were unable to foresee what was coming. Why didn't they then start talking about elections and struggling for political change? Why didn't they start worrying about the underdevelopment, poverty, and oppression of ten and fifteen years ago? Why weren't they aware of this before? Ah, well, they weren't and now they want to intervene.

What's going to happen in South America could also be foreseen and they could say: this is the general picture as we see it and it is on this basis that we must draw our conclusions. Nothing would make us happier than to see the big powers act sanely, prudently, astutely, wisely. And I don't think I'm doing anybody any harm by talking about these problems.

Utrilla: I've been thinking that given the way you explain the situation — and it seems to me that you do so in clear, correct terms — it would almost be contrary to Cuba's interests if, for example, the United States was to recognize that your analysis was correct and try to block the revolutionary process in Latin America. I'd say that you're giving advice to one you know to be deaf.

Castro: I think this is tied up with the international situation, because the problem is not strictly Latin American. It involves the whole world. The economic crisis is real and affecting the industrialized countries and, in much larger measure, the Third World countries.

We, of the Nonaligned nations, have said at the UN and everywhere else that the Third World problems are desperately in need of a solution. The Europeans know what is happening in Africa with the drought and millions of people dying. In the past, people died in Africa and nobody heard about it.

Utrilla: But there are no revolutionary focal points —

Castro: I was saying that in the past people died of starvation in Africa and nobody heard about it. Now everybody sees it on TV. Of course, there have been revolutionary changes in several African countries. What happened in Upper Volta, in Ethiopia, in Ghana? The economic and social situation led to revolutionary changes, yet one cannot speak of an explosive situation on a general scale.

Africa's level of economic, social, and cultural development is lower than that of Latin America. The working class, the peasantry, and the cultural elite are less developed than in Latin America. Africa does not have a large and extended middle strata. Neither does it have a relatively high number of doctors, economists, teachers, lawyers, engineers, or architects, or millions of university students like Latin America. Africa is in a different stage of development. Its people are paying the consequences of underdevelopment, economic crisis, and natural disasters. There may be changes, but they have neither the magnitude nor the world repercussions of those in Latin America.

I believe that in the framework of the international situation, we must also take into account the danger of war, the arms race. If the problems we're talking about are to be solved, a number of strange concepts and ideas must be given up. I'd say that ideas such as military superiority, star wars, astronomical military expenditures, and a frenzied arms buildup are incompatible with any solution to the world's serious economic and social problems.

I believe that the idea is to seek peace, international détente, coexistence, and even cooperation among countries. In other words, averting war is as necessary as bringing about social change.

All these problems are closely related and I believe that the solution calls for a change of ideas in many countries, in the industrialized capitalist countries.

The United States in particular must take a realistic stand toward these events. It has done so with China. Twenty years ago they talked about the yellow peril, the red peril. Every peril in every color came from that country.

Now they are investing in that country, trading with China, and making all sorts of investments there. They even prefer a more or less orderly China, where there is social justice, to a feudal, hungry China. Just imagine what would happen if the situation of the old China with hundreds of millions of hungry people was added to that of Africa now.

And yet the Chinese revolution has created different conditions. And now the United States is delighted with its relations with China. They have learned a lesson there. Why don't they learn it here? I'd say that what I have said about Latin America forms part of a broader analysis of the world's problems, of war and peace, the arms race and development. I even think that the only way to tackle the problems of underdevelopment is through the cooperation of the whole world community: the socialist countries and the capitalist countries.

Peace alone can't solve the problem of underdevelopment. Its solution is to be sought within an outlook of world peace, the kind of peace that does not consist solely of stopping the manufacture or reducing the number of nuclear arms, or calling off a star wars program, but is rather one that reflects a real willingness to raise millions of human beings out of poverty by using the resources that are now so absurdly given over to military expenditures.

An objective analysis of the situation might help the industrial powers — including the United States, if it's capable of being realistic — to find new formulas and new concepts which, in my opinion, are possible and applicable.

As far as our area is concerned, the principle of noninvolvement in other countries' internal affairs could be applied, and this is something we're ready to respect 100 percent: no involvement, even though we may sympathize with the revolutionary movements. No involvement either on the part of the United States or Cuba. Let every country take on full responsibility for whatever political and economic system it decides to follow, and let no one try to promote a new social system from outside or prop up an unjust social order.

Utrilla: Don't oppose revolution because it's inevitable.

Castro: In Chile, the United States and the CIA spent millions, brought people out onto the streets, conspired, put Pinochet in power, and there they have him. Did they solve anything by doing this? Is the United States by any chance completely disassociated from the coup d'état in Brazil in 1964? Doesn't everybody know that it instigated the coup against [João] Goulart? The United States is not divorced from these coups and these military formulas, nor from the training in methods of torture and repression in Vietnam. Its advisers and its training schools were the teachers and the universities that graduated Latin America's great thugs and torturers.

Now the United States is testing and improving two great systems of interference in our countries. In El Salvador, it is trying to develop the technique to crush a revolutionary movement that applies tactics of irregular warfare, while in Nicaragua it is applying techniques designed to defeat a revolution using irregular warfare.

Thus, in El Salvador it's trying to defeat the revolutionary guerrillas, while in Nicaragua it's applying a different science, that of how to defeat a revolutionary government through the actions of mercenary guerrillas. It's trying out both techniques. It's already practiced enough the science of direct or indirect intervention in Central America, Brazil, Chile, Argentina, and Uruguay. Has it solved anything? Why doesn't it give the Latin American people's political and social processes a chance to develop freely?

I'm not trying to give advice. I'm only analyzing and reasoning things out. The United States could show a certain capacity to foresee events. But if it doesn't have that capacity, I know what's going to happen. I have no doubt about that.

As I said before, if you talk with Latin Americans, you'll find that there are hardly any conservatives left. It's possible that on occasion you won't notice a great difference between what a conservative tells you and what I say, when it comes to saying that such and such a principle, free competition, the lifting of barriers, or such and such a formula to have industry compete with foreign industry in the production of goods for internal consumption, had ruined the country. They're horrified! They don't even want to hear talk about such economic theories.

Free exchange has also been very costly to Latin American economies. I know cases of people who asked for a loan in national currency, exchanged the national currency for dollars, deposited the dollars in the United States where they gained interest, and within a few months were able to pay back the debt with only 50 percent of the dollars. Many people have lost their faith in the classic, traditional mechanisms.

I've noticed something new in Latin American women, doctors, and intellectuals who have been in Cuba recently for various events. There's a strong inner force that wasn't noticeable before. Last year I met with hundreds of Latin American film directors, producers, actors, and actresses. They have to compete with the U.S. circuits. They produce excellent films and yet they can't even cover production costs because the U.S. transnationals control everything. You can't imagine how irritated people of the most diverse social sectors and strata are.

We have before us a continent at the boiling point; the future belongs to the peoples of this continent. Europe is spent. I say this in all seriousness. It's spent. Europe is politically and intellectually spent, as I see it. The consumer society has its price. Our continent has enormously varying content and values and also many things in common, to the extent that there's a strong movement of Latin American and Caribbean film producers, writers, and intellectuals on this continent, when there isn't in Europe or elsewhere. . . .

[*Later in the interview Castro was asked several questions about Cuba's relations with the U.S. government.*]

Castro: I was saying that the United States is in the habit of using certain phrases, words, and an imperial language; it has an imperial way of talking. Who has told the United States that we are impatient or begging for relations? I am convinced, absolutely convinced that they would benefit more than we would. We put this forward because it seems a correct policy, a duty, a principle, you might say, but some draw mistaken conclusions: that Cuba has economic problems, a foreign exchange shortage, a difficult year, and they come up with the strangest things. They fail to realize that we are calmer than ever because we are stronger than ever in the military and political fields. Furthermore, we are becoming more efficient in the economic field, and in economic development we have a clearer understanding than ever of the path we're on. Our revolution has really matured, along with our cadres and leaders. In the three fields we are better than ever: military, political, and economic.

Marín: Nevertheless, the other day I read a document that appeared in *Granma* about political and ideological work in defense, and it seemed to me that the sense of that document was to prepare for détente, but to prepare for détente in the field of ideas, that is, given the predictable cultural influence of the United States, which would be greater than it is now.

Castro: That would be to give us too much credit, make us out to be too capable and sharp, turning out documents from one day to the next. That document had been in preparation for some time and is in no way related to what we are doing here now. Imagine, it was discussed a few weeks ago and approved, and publication came about recently, in almost a mechanical fashion. Marisol, you can just see how things are.

It has nothing to do with any such goals. I think the best thing we can provide are the explanations that I have given in the speech to the students, in the speech on energy, in the National Assembly, the explanation we provided at the time of the agreement with the United States, in the publication of the interview with the press. We quickly pass on all ideas to the masses, without wasting time. My style is not that of the document — I speak to the people and explain an idea in detail. The people have confidence because they know they are not being lied to in any way, they have confidence because we are level-headed, more so than ever, and we are telling the truth. All those speeches have been discussed in detail so people know what we are thinking and the sense behind what we are doing. They also know there is no urgency, there is no need for relations with the United States. We are one of the few countries in the world at this moment that can say what we will do in 1990, 1995, and 2000, even how many teachers and doctors of what skills we will have, of what level; how much of everything we will have without counting on the United States for anything. It is marvelous! It is really marvelous not to have to count on the United States!

Utrilla: But you count on the Soviet Union.

Castro: Yes, but it is better to count on the Soviet Union, because these problems can be discussed and we can raise things which can be done with them, since they are not governed by national egoism. The United States will always be governed by unequal prices which have been imposed by the world economic system on the underdeveloped countries' products. The debt is with the private banks, the government has often no relationship to the debt. If you discuss an economic problem with a socialist country the government can make decisions; it can grant a grace period, reduce interest rates, it can even delay a debt for ten or twenty years, without interest. Well, that's virtually what we are advocating for the Latin Americans. These issues are raised and discussed and solved with the governments; there is no need to discuss it with 500 bankers. When we canceled the Nicaraguan debt for the sugar mill construction, the decision was made by the Cuban state and not by a private bank; a bank couldn't do that. The Cuban state assumed the debt, it knows the resources it has and it can decide.

It's easier to discuss economic problems with the socialist countries, along with future plans, agreements and prices, because it is a system which is not based on the ruthless egoism of capitalism. And things have gone very well for us, because we raise our problems in a principled and well-founded manner. Our relations are based on revolutionary doctrine and ideas; the capitalists can't base themselves on any doctrine. "I win or lose money on this deal; I sell high and buy low." But we really have many possibilities of discussing and reaching satisfactory agreements with the socialist countries. We analyze the issue, some countries have more resources, they can do more, give more credits, supply greater quantities of a given product. We consider specific situations. We trade with Vietnam at world market prices; relations with Vietnam and Mongolia are different from those with the more developed nations. Our trade relations with China are certainly not the same as those with the European socialist countries; our trade with China is based on world market prices, they pay for our products at world market levels, which of course are now very low.

The USSR is the most developed socialist country, the one with the most resources: then come countries like the GDR [German Democratic Republic] and Czechoslovakia. With all of them we have good relations and varying degrees of trade, depending on their needs and possibilities, credits which are larger or smaller, depending on their possibilities. And things are going very well, and there have never been political strings attached, absolutely not. Even in certain periods when relations were difficult, there was never any form of pressure in economic relations.

Fuel supplied by the USSR has increased year by year, as have the supplies of other products. Even when there were political problems, such as in the wake of the October Crisis [of 1962], this was never reflected in the economic relations between the USSR and Cuba. Sometimes we have been critical, even publicly, and this has never led to any form of economic pressure against our country.

I would also say that there was a period of certain immaturity on our part, a bit of extremism and arrogance on our part. It must be said that there was a period when we felt we knew more than the other countries, that we were more revolutionary than other socialist countries; we underestimated the value of experience. But we really matured afterwards. They were very patient with us during that whole period. Of course, we have the advantage that now we are more mature and handle things differently. We can discuss anything. We don't discuss in public; nobody does that. The United States doesn't do that, but they would want us to engage in public discussions with the socialist countries. When they have differences with Mitterrand these aren't discussed in the press and if there are differences with the FRG [Federal Republic of Germany], Thatcher, or Japan, they have closed-door meetings to discuss them. I think Felipe may also have some differences with the U.S. government, but they aren't made public; they discuss many problems of different kinds. All countries do that with their friends, and we also learned how to discuss with friendly nations. If we have different views on something and are going to discuss something, we don't go to the newspapers to run criticisms of the Nicaraguans, the Angolans, the Ethiopians, the Yemenis, the Vietnamese, or the Koreans. Sometimes one country has one position and the other has another, but we don't go public with these attacks. That's what our enemies want.

We have really matured; this helps our relations with the socialist countries which fortunately are now excellent, better than ever. The socialist countries respect our country, the USSR and the others, taking into account the merits, revolutionary spirit, internationalist awareness, and determination of our country, which is threatened but does not get down on its knees, a country which neither surrenders nor sells out. Of course, we could never sell ourselves out, because the day we do so the values which are the strength of the revolution would disappear.

Why Washington Fears Cuba's Example

Conclusion of Speech to Federation of Cuban Women

There's been a great deal of talk, the imperialists talk a lot about the Cuban cooperation workers in Nicaragua. Of course they have the habit of inflating the figures. We never gave out any figures. We don't have to account to the imperialists for the number of cooperation workers we have in any country. [*Applause*] nor do we ask them how many they have, how many soldiers, officers, military personnel, CIA agents, even the Peace Corps, as they call it. But we have noticed their custom of interfering in the affairs of other countries, and the habit, the method of conjuring up, of falsifying with political motives in order to justify you-know-what crimes.

On occasion, in talking with journalists, even with U.S. visitors, I've spoken to them more than once about our teachers and their merits. It's unbelievable that our teachers should arouse fear, but the fear is not totally unfounded. Is it the number of teachers and civilian cooperation workers or even a number of military cooperation personnel that incites fear? No, it's not the number, nor could it be, but rather the strength they reflect, the strength of our ideas that these teachers and cooperation workers can generate.

Yes, and this is much more powerful than all the tanks, all the battleships, aircraft carriers, bombers, strategic missiles, and deadly weapons that the enemies of human progress can create. Much more powerful! First of all, because the men and women who uphold these ideas do not experience any fear at all in the face of sophisticated technology, military might, battleships, aircraft carriers, and the threats of extermination and death. [*Applause*] Who are more courageous? Those who manufacture these weapons with which they assume the privilege of threatening revolutionaries and all the world's progressive people, the peoples and the patriots, or those who feel absolutely no fear, but instead

---

This speech was given March 8, 1985, to the closing session of the Fourth Congress of the Federation of Cuban Women, held in Havana. It is excerpted here from the March 24, 1985 Granma Weekly Review.

contempt for all that might, for all those weapons, and for all those threats? [*Applause*]

I think that it is this spirit that really frightens the reactionaries and the imperialists, because this spirit is simply invincible. [*Applause*] And it's not the spirit of a handful of men and women; it's the spirit of an entire people. [*Applause*] And that's why we have asked, why didn't others send teachers to live in those conditions in the most remote places, together with the families, eating what the families ate, sleeping where the families slept, under circumstances such that in many cases the family, the entire family, the domesticated animals, and the teacher all lived in one hut? There were even circumstances when the Ministry of Education, concerned for the health of these teachers, decided to send them some foodstuffs, powdered milk, chocolate, etc. But that didn't solve anything nor could it, because none of our teachers were capable of drinking a little milk in the morning when there were children with no milk at all. [*Applause*] Those items they were sent didn't last at all because they shared them immediately.

I've spoken about this to visitors and journalists as irrefutable proof of the strength of our ideas, of the triumphs of our revolution, not only material but also moral. I've mentioned in passing some of the countries that the imperialists hold up as models in this hemisphere, some, even, with many resources that have been recklessly squandered, and I've asked: Could 2,000 teachers leave from these model countries to go to Nicaragua and work under those conditions? No. Could they send 1,000 under those conditions? No. Could they send 500 under those conditions? No. Could they send 100? No. But if they do not have enough teachers to send a few kilometers away from the capital of the republic, how are they going to send them thousands of kilometers away, far from their homeland, to work under those conditions?

I have asked other questions also. I've said, could all these model countries together in the hemisphere, these perfect models, incredibly democratic, incredibly respectful of human rights including the extremely human right of free enterprise and capitalism, do it? We know how long they can talk about human rights and democratic models over there, where the brightest students of the professors of the Pentagon and the CIA learn the techniques of death, murder, torture, disappeared persons, and all kinds of repression. That talk lasts until these bright students begin to solve the social conflicts, in their way, to impose order and protect the sacrosanct status quo and prevent that terrible, phantasmal, and ominous thing — communism — from propagating and advancing. The people must be made to disappear so that they do not become communists; they must all be executed, exterminated if necessary, and called on to withstand hunger, poverty, disease, the deaths of millions of children due to disease and hunger, ignorance, unemployment, prostitution, drugs, all the vices and all the defects of this society in order to conserve that order without quarter. All to prevent that terrible thing which is socialism, communism, Marxism-Leninism! And I have asked: Could all those model countries together be capable of sending 2,000 teachers to Nicaragua to work under those conditions? No.

How hard, how terrible! What are human values? What do human values or human rights mean where people are forced to live under such conditions of inequality and social injustice and are educated in such forms of egoism and individualism that it would be hard to expect an act of solidarity or even the supreme act of solidarity which is to give one's life for another people, for another country, not just one's own country? I don't mean that there's not a tremendous potential among the sister nations of Latin America. There is tremendous moral potential and solidarity like that which we have and, moreover, it is a potential which has not developed because the models block the morality and human values from developing. And of course I don't doubt that there are millions among our sister nations of Latin America capable of solidarity and sacrifice. I'm not talking about the human potential of our sister nations; I'm talking about the potential of the imposed system. And I ask: Can that system appeal to and call on the teachers to carry out this task under such difficult conditions? Two thousand teachers? No. One thousand teachers? No.

Nicaragua was criticized and Cuba was criticized for having teachers in Nicaragua, but those teachers didn't go there to teach Marxism-Leninism. We met with them more than once and told them to be completely respectful of the feelings of each family, to limit themselves strictly and give classes using Nicaraguan programs and texts, not to interfere in the least in the people's political convictions and religious beliefs, to have complete respect, and to preach by their example. That's what they did and that's how they won the affection and respect of everyone. Thus I've told people, we not only had 2,000 teachers in Nicaragua, but when we requested volunteers for that mission, 30,000 volunteered and when they killed two or three teachers, 100,000 more volunteered. [*Applause*]

So you can see the comparison and whether or not the values our revolution and our ideas represent are frightening. And when our party can speak about these values, and this strength, it is truly admirable to be able to state that half are women and in many cases, mothers who are capable of separating themselves from their children and families for a year or two years. [*Applause*] This is the work of the revolution.

I cited one example, although I can cite many others in many other places, but I wanted to cite this one alone in the framework of our solidarity with a sister people and in the framework of our hemisphere. The imperialists are right to harbor fears about our teachers, our cooperation workers, our men and our women, because of their example and banners, because of the invincible ideas they symbolize. [*Applause*]

There are around 150 delegations from other countries among us here for this congress. I'm not going to call them foreign delegations, but rather sister delegations. [*Applause*] They express the struggle of all the peoples and of women, who throughout the world are fighting against the same injustices against which our women fought for years and are striving for the same goals for which we are striving and for which we will continue to strive. Above all, they express the world's concern for peace, the people's concern about the madness of the arms race and the aggressive policies which threaten not only peace, but even humanity's survival. I am sure that as much as their presence encourages us, the work of our comrades and their successes have also encouraged them in their struggles. [*Prolonged applause*]

Among the guest delegations are those which represent women of the sister nations of Latin America. [*Applause*]

In the last few months we have had contact on several occasions with representatives of Latin America's women. The most recent was on the occasion of an event held in our country. Now we are again honored by their presence. We have also had contact with Latin American doctors, filmmakers, writers, and numerous delegations. We are witness to something new that is growing in the spirit of Latin America's peoples, something felt deeply by those who represent women, men, workers, and the members of the most diverse social sectors. And that's an awareness of the crisis that afflicts our hemisphere. This was made evident by the more than 1,500 Latin American pediatricians who participated in the [pediatrics] congress here, because they know better than anybody else how many children in those countries die before they are a year old and why they die. And the number of deaths is not counted by hundreds or thousands, but rather by hundreds of thousands, that is, almost a million deaths a year at that early age.

And as UNICEF's director said here, if those countries had the rates Cuba has now, 750,000 of those children under one year old would be saved every year. [*Applause*] These doctors know how many children between one and four years old and between four and sixteen years old die; what the life expectancy rate is and why; how many hospitals there are and how many others are needed; and how many children have medical care and how many don't and why. They don't have to be Marxist-Leninists or socialists to realize these things. All they need is their eyes. In these congresses, attended by persons of diverse ideologies and creeds, it becomes evident that writers, filmmakers, women, and workers are becoming increasingly aware of the tragedy. Many delegations representing diverse parties speak about the terrible crisis they face, the worst in history.

People still talk about the crisis of the 1930s, but the economic and social crisis that exists today is still worse. Many of the products exported by Latin America's countries are now worth less than in 1930, but those countries now have much larger populations than in the 1930s — around twice as large — and many more economic and social problems than they had then, and more political capacity. At that time they were not burdened by a $360 billion foreign debt. Now they are faced with a worse crisis, multiple problems, and an astronomical debt whose payment is being demanded. They are faced with the implacable demand for the payment of interest running to almost $40 billion and there's nowhere to get the money to pay for it, because the peoples of Latin America have been bled dry, and no matter how much they're squeezed they just can't take much more.

Right now, they are being charged colossal interest rates running to 12, 13, 14 percent, according to the whims and the sovereign will of the colossus to the north, whose currency is overrated, whose interest on loans grows according to its fancy. Sure, they lend you a dollar, and when the value of the dollar increases you have to pay for a dollar that is worth much more than the one you got on loan. You don't pay 8 percent for that dollar; you pay 10, 11, 12, 13, 14 percent. Moreover, the dollar that was lent to you circulated and returned to the United States, was spent in the United States, and not just the dollar. With it went the products, the raw materials, but sold at increasingly lower, withering prices, in line with the inexorable law of unequal trade. This is why the peoples of Latin America are paying increasingly higher prices for what they buy and obtaining increasingly lower income for what they sell.

Those over there who make bolts, nuts, or equipment are paid $1,000 to $1,200 a month or more, while those who produce sugar, cacao, coffee, cashew nuts, peanuts, iron ore, or copper in Latin America and the Caribbean are paid $60, $80, or perhaps $100 a month. Over there they always need more coffee, cacao, sugar, beef, nuts, and minerals for the payment of industrial equipment, bulldozers, tractors, or medicines, whose prices are constantly being raised. This has been going on for fifty years. How long can anybody stand this? On top of that, there are the protectionist laws enacted by the empire and the capitalist nations allied with the empire. You must pay, but you can't sell your industrial products there regardless of how cheap you want to sell them. The whole thing boils down to this: "I'll buy your coffee and cacao, but if you manufacture anything, even a single square meter of cloth, I won't let it in. But you must pay me and you must do it on the basis of my overrated dollar and also pay for the multiplied interests."

These are the real facts, these are the rules that the system of domination, now in crisis, has imposed. And as I stated recently, the situation is intolerable. And I've said publicly how we see the situation. If the imperialists insist on payment of that debt and those interests, the Latin

American societies will explode. You don't have to be an expert or a specialist to realize this. Only a blind person could fail to see it.

This brings to mind, after some twenty-odd years, the Alliance for Progress, when there was talk of some reforms — designed to prevent revolutions — economic aid in the form of $20 billion within a period of ten to fifteen years. This emerged after the Cuban revolution. Nobody had thought about it before. When a revolution took place here, there were some who immediately started thinking about what they were going to do: maybe loosen up a bit in order to prevent more revolutions, maybe some reforms and a little aid. More than twenty years have passed, and what do we have? A debt of eighteen times that $20 billion and the industrialized countries, especially the United States, are demanding that they be paid $40 billion every year. How can anybody put up with that?

We've talked about this problem before, and we have talked about it with all those from the industrialized countries we have met with. That is why when this congress is being held and we are visited by representatives of Latin America it's a special moment, a different moment, as the crisis in the hemisphere continues to develop.

In times of crisis, problems that cannot be solved in fifty or even 100 years can be solved one way or another. In this case, either they forget all about the debt and its onerous interests and put an end to their extortionist practices — what they have taken away through the mechanism of unequal trade, interests, and profits, the exploitation of natural resources, and the efforts of the peoples of Latin America amounts to much more than the debt — or there'll be revolutions!

Either they forget all about the debt and in addition put an end to injustice, exploitation, theft through trade, protectionism, and the brutal methods through which our peoples are exploited — because I don't believe that settling the debt problem is sufficient — or there'll be revolutions!

When crises arise, problems are solved one way or another!

I hope they don't start saying that we're preaching subversion. We're only predicting what is going to happen. Twenty-six years have not passed in vain, and we have seen many things, but never what we're seeing now, phenomena that are reflected in the delegations that visit Cuba. Not only is there an enormous, monstrous crisis, but also a growing awareness of the situation created by that crisis, and this awareness is reflected by all those who visit Cuba. That's why the coming years, the next five years of work for the Federation [of Cuban Women] will be very interesting years. For the peoples represented here by these Latin American delegates the coming years will be both interesting and decisive.

Our country has set its course and this is evident. We have come of age, for we are twenty-six years and two months old. [*Applause*] We have accumulated a great deal of experience, the revolution has matured and with it our cadres, organizations, and the party, and this enables them to conduct the process with much greater assurance and efficiency. We have worked tirelessly in the past few months, working out new ideas and concepts on development and planning their implementation. In these difficult moments, in these times of crisis, we're moving forward full speed ahead, [*Applause*] supported by our sound, fraternal, and indestructible relations with the socialist countries.

These countries neither rob us, nor exploit us, nor buy from us at increasingly cheaper prices, nor sell to us at increasingly higher prices, nor make us victims of financial extortion, nor charge us growing and arbitrary interests, but rather lower interests. Moreover, when our debts pile up on account of expenditures typical of a developing country and investments in such major projects as the nuclear power plant, the refineries, the nickel processing plants in Moa, Punta Gorda, and Camarioca, and so forth, for which we were granted credits, instead of overcharging us they have made things easier. They've said, "We'll postpone payment for five, ten, and even fifteen years — and without interest!" [*Applause*]

We invite the developed capitalist countries, particularly the United States, to practice the same policy with their Latin American model countries. If not, they'll lose their model countries. [*Applause*]

Thanks to our revolution, to these fraternal and solidary relations, to our ideas, our policy, the seriousness of our revolution, and our firmness as well as our experience — something we neither had at the beginning nor could anybody have transmitted to us — our course is clear and sure.

All these things have been said and discussed, and you have expressed your approval in the struggle for efficiency, economizing, discipline, and a demand for good work and a sense of responsibility.

Rallying around our beautiful revolutionary banners we must go on building the future, a better future that will enable us to overcome even the objective conditions that are now blocking our struggle for a society with an even greater sense of justice toward women.

Shadows may appear, but we're not afraid of shadows. Dangers may appear, but we're not afraid of danger. Threats may be hurled at us, but we've never been afraid of threats.

We are moving forward, confident and assured, with our course well charted.

We will reach our goal. However, should insanity and stupidity prevail, should the warmongers set this planet afire, then we will fall. But we'll never falter! We will fall, but we'll never take one single step backwards! [*Applause*] We will fall, but we will fall with our banners and our ideas held high! [*Applause*]

Patria o muerte!

Venceremos! [*Ovation*]

Latin America's Foreign Debt
Must Be Canceled

Interview with Mexican Daily 'Excelsior'

Regino Díaz: Can there be unity among such dissimilar governments in Latin America?

Fidel Castro: I think so.

The economic crisis and the debt will unite the Latin American countries, much more than the Malvinas War did. In that case, the Latin American peoples were united by a problem which we might call one of family relations — sentiment, morals, and politics; it was a struggle against a sister people caused by colonial pretensions, historic plunder, an act of injustice dating back to the period when England was the most powerful empire in the world. The Malvinas War was a war waged by a European country against a Latin American nation, but it wasn't something that affected the Latin American countries' vital economic interests — except for the Latin American patriotic aspect and the political aspect of the matter, they had nothing to win or lose economically. That solidarity was truly selfless. In the case of Latin America's economic crisis and foreign debt, however, the solution of that problem is a matter of survival for the Latin American countries.

There is talk of the crisis of the 1930s. The present crisis is worse than the one in the 1930s. Except for oil, Latin America's export products have less purchasing power than they had during the crisis of the 1930s. Even if we don't go so far back, referring to the prices our products had twenty-four years ago, the purchasing power of our main traditional export products, including sugar, is in many cases only a third or a fourth of what it was at that time.

Let me give you an example. Twenty-four years ago, it took 200 tons of sugar to buy a 180-horsepower bulldozer. Now, it takes 800 tons of sugar at the world market price to buy that same bulldozer. And, if you

The following interview was conducted March 21, 1985, by Regino Díaz, editor of the prominent Mexican newspaper Excelsior. *It is reprinted here from the April 7, 1985,* Granma Weekly Review.

analyze coffee, cocoa, bananas, and the minerals Latin America exports, the amount of products needed to buy a bulldozer or other piece of construction, transportation, agricultural or industrial equipment imported from the developed countries is three or four times as great now as it was then. Compared to 1950, the deterioration in trade relations is much greater.

What is the difference between the 1930s and the present situation? At that time, Latin America's population was less than a third of what it is now. Today's social problems are incomparably greater than the social problems in the 1930s; these problems have been accumulating. That is, we now have three or four times as many people, and social problems have multiplied since the 1930s.

The most important thing, though, is that, at the time of the crisis of the 1930s, Latin America had practically no foreign debt. Now we have a bigger crisis, incomparably greater accumulated social problems, and a debt of $360 billion. A mathematical analysis of this situation shows that this debt cannot be paid, and this is so whether you analyze the situation as a whole or whether you consider the individual situations of the countries; in some cases, it's more serious than in others, but it is serious in all, without exception.

According to the latest official data gathered by the United Nations Economic Commission for Latin America and the Caribbean (ECLAC), Brazil owes $101.8 billion; Mexico, $95.9 billion; Argentina, $48 billion; Venezuela, $34 billion; Chile, according to calculations that, in my opinion, are very conservative, $18.44 billion; Peru, $13.5 billion; Colombia, $10.8 billion; Costa Rica, a small country with a population of around 2 million, $4.05 billion; Panama, with a similar population, $3.55 billion; and Uruguay, $4.7 billion. And these are conservative figures, since, according to reports by distinguished Uruguayan and Chilean friends, Uruguay's real debt is $5.5 billion, and Chile's is $23 billion. That is, the official figures are lower than the real level of the debt. In many cases, it isn't easy for the international agencies — or the governments of the countries themselves — to know the real amount of their debts, because, in addition to the controlled debts, there are other ones, to private bodies, that aren't reported.

Díaz: Are the debts of the countries with the most indebtedness, such as Brazil, Mexico, and Venezuela, really greater than is said?

Castro: I'm not sure. A figure of $105 billion is mentioned for Brazil, around $100 billion for Mexico, and $35 billion for Venezuela, but none of the figures that are mentioned frequently are lower than the ones given in the official data of the international economic agencies.

Some countries, such as Argentina, are using 52 percent of their exports to pay the interest on their debts. Bolivia is using 57 percent of its exports for this purpose; Mexico, 36.5 percent; Peru, 35.5 percent;

Brazil, 36.5 percent; and Chile, 45.5 percent — and this when it is considered practically impossible to keep going when 20 percent of exports are absorbed by payments on foreign debts.

What do these figures mean? That it is impossible for any country to develop under these conditions. This has been expressed in the fact that the Gross Domestic Product (GDP) of the Latin American countries as a whole dropped between 1981 and 1984. In Uruguay, for example, it dropped by 13.9 percent; in Argentina, by 6 percent; in Chile, by 5.4 percent; and in Venezuela — in spite of that country's enormous economic resources — by 6.1 percent.

Since the population has grown during these years, the per capita GDP has dropped even more — in Bolivia, by 24.6 percent; in Costa Rica, by 14.1 percent; in Chile, by 11.2 percent; in Mexico, by 6.3 percent; in Argentina, by 11.8 percent; in Venezuela, by 16.2 percent; and in Uruguay, by 16.2 percent. In the case of Venezuela, the per capita GDP dropped not only between 1981 and 1984, but also in the last seven consecutive years, plummeting by 24 percent. The incidence of the economic crisis and of the foreign debt, especially in the last few years, may be seen in the fact that each country's production has not only stopped developing, but has even declined. Some countries are making truly impressive efforts to confront the situation. Here, I will cite three of the largest, most important ones:

In 1982, Brazil exported $20.172 billion worth of goods; in 1984, it exported $26.96 billion worth. In 1982, it imported $19.395 billion worth of goods; in 1984, its imports were reduced to $14.36 billion worth.

In 1982, Mexico exported $22.081 billion worth of goods; in 1984, it increased its exports to $23.5 billion worth. It reduced its imports from $14.434 billion worth of goods in 1982 to $10 billion worth in 1984.

Argentina increased its exports from $7.622 billion worth of goods in 1982 to $8.7 billion worth in 1984, and reduced its imports from $4.859 billion worth in 1982 to $4.27 billion worth in 1984.

By making great efforts to increase their exports and by cutting their imports drastically, to levels that are nearly untenable for their economies, these countries obtained favorable balances of trade. Brazil obtained a positive balance of $12.6 billion; Mexico, one of $13.5 billion; and Argentina, one of $4.43 billion. All of these balances — the results of tremendous efforts, using and practically exhausting their stocks of raw materials and possibly adversely affecting the maintenance and replacement of productive installations — have been used exclusively in all three countries to pay the interest on their debts.

As a whole, the Latin American countries paid $37.3 billion for interest and profits in 1984 — nearly $3 billion more than in 1983 — and they received $10.6 billion in loans and investments.

In 1984, Latin America's net transfers of financial resources abroad for interest and profits rose to $26.7 billion. In just two years, 1983 and 1984, the net flow of financial resources from Latin America amounted to $56.7 billion. That is, the Latin American underdeveloped countries are financing the economies and development of the richest industrialized countries in the world with impressive sums of money. These are the facts. And that money has gone forever; there is no possible way of getting it back.

The growth rate of the debt has declined and fallen far below the record 24 percent reached in 1981. This is only logical: now, nobody dares to lend those countries any more money. But, even so, for one reason or another, their debt grew by 5.5 percent. It is expected that in the next ten years the interest on it — even if it is held at more or less the same level — will average $40 billion a year.

Twenty-four years ago, when the Alliance for Progress was created, Kennedy proposed a program of economic cooperation for meeting Latin America's social problems and development needs, calling for $20 billion to be invested over a period of ten to fifteen years. That idea arose during the period of obsessive trauma over the Cuban revolution and sought to avoid the creation of objective conditions that would be propitious for new revolutions. Now, the economically underdeveloped countries of this hemisphere, with twice the population and triple the social problems, will be giving the industrialized countries $40 billion a year as interest on their debts. In ten years, they will have to pay $400 billion — twenty times as much as Kennedy suggested investing over ten to fifteen years as economic cooperation for solving Latin America's economic and social problems, when there were half as many people and incomparably fewer accumulated social problems, the international economy was advancing full speed ahead, there were no crises and the prices of their basic export products had much greater purchasing power.

The political, economic, and social situation of Latin America is such that it can't hold up under any more restrictions and sacrifices.

In recent months, when the International Monetary Fund's measures began to be applied, there were repercussions in the Dominican Republic, a country that had a relatively stable political situation, with a constitutional regime. Rising prices, triggered by the devaluation of the Dominican peso, which had been at par with the U.S. dollar but was reduced to a rate of three pesos per dollar, applied to the foreign currency that was invested to import medicines and other articles of popular consumption, caused an uprising. The government's reply was to order the army and the police into the streets to put down the protest demonstrations. The result, according to the official figures, was fifty dead and 300 wounded. Many people say that the real figure of victims was larger. A few weeks ago, new demands by the IMF led to the application of a rate of exchange of three pesos per dollar on all import products, including fuel. The government, acting before the people, once again ordered the army and the police to occupy the cities and try to crush the people's protests. This has created a situation of great desperation and tension in the Dominican Republic.

Another recent example of this occurred in Panama, after the new government was inaugurated. A 7 percent tax on certain services and the postponement of wage increases for doctors and teachers that had been agreed on previously caused a similar situation. Hundreds of thousands of people took to the streets, but there was no repression and no victims, due to the attitude of the National Guard, which has played a progressive role, has struggled for the recovery of sovereignty over the canal, and has close ties with the people. It doesn't want to fire on the people. As a result, the measures had to be annulled. And these weren't measures for solving Panama's serious economic difficulties, which are similar to those of the rest of the Latin American countries. Rather, they were simply attempts to balance the budget to a certain extent and thus create the minimum conditions that the International Monetary Fund requires for beginning to renegotiate the debt.

In Bolivia — where the preliminary report of ECLAC had predicted that inflation would be 1,682 percent in 1984, and where it really, according to the latest figures, rose to 2,300 percent in one year — an economic situation has been created that, in the last thirteen days, has completely paralyzed the country, with tens of thousands of miners armed with sticks of dynamite, workers, students, and other people in the streets, and farmers mobilized in the countryside blocking the highways and demanding wage increases, price controls, supplies of provisions, and other measures in a real state of desperation, making the situation almost unmanageable. Nobody knows how the country can emerge from the serious economic crisis that is afflicting it.

The curious thing is that these things that I've mentioned have come about practically spontaneously, in response to the objective situation.

Díaz: Why hasn't there been a coup d'état?

Castro: I should talk about this later on, when I go into how I think events in the various countries will develop as a result of this situation. I am simply pointing out things that have taken place spontaneously as a result of the economic crisis and the debt.

The economic situation has the most serious characteristics in Bolivia. There, as I've already said, the GDP dropped by 16.1 percent between 1981 and 1984, and the per capita GDP dropped by 24.6 percent in just three years.

The value of Bolivia's exports dropped from $828 million to $730 million between 1982 and 1984. Its modest imports increased from $429 million in 1982 to $460 million in 1984 — very meager figures. It is practically impossible for a country with Bolivia's population, problems, and needs to keep going with just $460 million worth of imports.

The $270 million in its favorable balance of trade for the last year had to be used to pay the interest on its debt.

That is, in the three countries mentioned the International Monetary Fund's measures, or attempts to apply those measures, have caused serious political and social conflicts, based on a situation in which the people are totally opposed to the imposition of new measures to lower the standard of living and to making new sacrifices.

A democratic opening has been created in the South American countries, and this has awakened enormous interest and great support in Latin America and the rest of the world.

Almost simultaneously, democratic openings have appeared in three important countries: Argentina, Uruguay, and Brazil. With regard to Uruguay, this is important not so much because of the country's size or resources as because of the symbolism involved in its return, after long years of military oppression, to a constitutional regime, since this is a country that had been a model of democratic institutions for a long time. Uruguay, like Chile, used to be called the Switzerland of the Americas.

The U.S. administration declares — almost presenting it as a result of its policy — that democracy is making advances in Latin America. What is really making advances is the crisis.

These democratic openings have come about, of course, partly because of the people's struggles and resistance to the military dictatorships. But the fact that the economic crisis is so serious that the military men — who are demoralized and bewildered — don't feel capable of handling the situation has contributed a great deal.

The military men are withdrawing from public administration. If the economic situation had been less serious, they would have resisted, would have tried to remain in government longer. Now, they have turned state administration over to the civilians and have left them a terrible inheritance, to be sure.

If the economic problems stemming from the debt aren't solved, those democratic processes, too, will inevitably enter into crisis.

In Uruguay, as people close to the new government have said, the foreign debt amounts to $5.5 billion; exports amount to only $1 billion. Such important markets as the textile market in the United States have just been hit by protectionist measures, and important meat markets have been seized by the European Economic Community, whose meat production is subsidized. The standard of living dropped by 50 percent during the years the military government was in power. How can the government of a country in those conditions — where civilians have just taken control, thanks to the people's support, after years of savage repression — apply the International Monetary Fund's measures and demand new sacrifices by the people? The democratic processes in Argentina and Brazil are confronted with similar situations.

It is impossible to conceive of the new leaders of those countries, who headed the democratic processes during the long years of military dictatorship, ordering the army and the police into the streets to fire on the people in order to apply the International Monetary Fund's measures and pay every last cent of their debts.

These leaders have stated three things perfectly clearly: that they aren't about to burden the people with the consequences of the debt, that they aren't about to apply recessionary policies, and that they aren't about to sacrifice their countries' development. That is, they have stated these three basic premises. What hasn't yet been said is how these premises can be applied if no solution is found for the problem of the debt.

The first thing the IMF demands is a reduction in the rate of inflation, a reduction in the budgetary deficit, and restrictive measures of a social nature that increase unemployment and aggravate the problems that have been accumulating and multiplying for long years.

Consumer prices in Latin America as a whole rose by 130.8 percent in 1983 and by 175.4 percent in 1984. With these levels of inflation, it is practically impossible to manage the economy.

I wonder how it is possible, in these circumstances, to demand that this group of Latin American countries — whose economies have not only stagnated but regressed in the last few years, while the population has continued to grow at a high rate — extract $40 billion from their economies each year and, in ten years, turn over $400 billion just for the interest on their foreign debts. What new sacrifices would these countries have to demand and what restrictions would they have to apply in order to pay that fabulous amount of interest, plus reduce inflation and promote development? What prospects and hopes do they have with which to stimulate this epic, costly effort? What arguments can they use to move the people and obtain the consensus, unity, support, and spirit of sacrifice required by such an enterprise? It is a practically impossible task.

In some cases, the levels of inflation are truly astounding — as in Bolivia, where it was 2,300 percent; Argentina, where it was 675 percent; Brazil, 194.7 percent; and Peru, 105.8 percent. How can anyone ask that, in a single year, those countries reduce their inflation, balance their budgets, and also pay astronomical amounts as interest on their debts?

Moreover, the figures on the transfers of resources to the industrialized world that I've already mentioned refer exclusively to what has left those countries officially, as interest payments and profits. The flight of capital should be added to this — a figure that, because of the way this capital leaves, is practically impossible to estimate. It is known, however, that tens of billions of dollars were sent from Venezuela to the United States in the last few years and that the same thing happened in Argentina. The Mexicans know that when economic difficulties arose and a devaluation was seen to be inevitable — there are always many indicators that make it possible to guess when a devaluation has become inevitable — tens of billions of dollars were also sent from Mexico to the United States.

I have referred to just three countries, but this has happened throughout Latin America, because of a very logical, very simple, and perfectly understandable mechanism: when the money of a Latin American country — any Latin American country — begins to be devaluated at an accelerated rate, people lose confidence in it.

Díaz: And in the government?

Castro: People usually lose confidence in the government, but it isn't always right to do so; sometimes new governments come along and inherit this situation. It could be said that not even men can be blamed for this crisis; it is the result of a crisis of a system of domination and exploitation that has been imposed on the underdeveloped world. Later, I will go into this idea further; I have tried to be orderly in setting forth my points of view.

The economic crisis has hit, and the brunt of it has been passed on to the economies of the least developed countries. It may be said that this is a process that has been developing for some time and has had more or less serious consequences, depending on each country's economic resources and also on the greater or lesser efficiency with which it has defended itself against or tried to overcome the crisis; there is a wide range of cases.

Doubtless, the policies followed in Chile, Argentina, and Uruguay — the official policies of the military regimes — have had terrible consequences.

I remember that in the last few months of Allende's administration, for example, Chile was importing $100 million worth of meat a year. Nevertheless, a few months after the coup, Chile began to export meat. How? On the basis of the dead, the people who were made to disappear, the thousands of people who disappeared, the thousands of dead, the thousands of victims of torture and other horrible means of repression, the massive firing of civil servants, the drastic cutting back of social services, massive layoffs of factory workers, wage cuts, and the drastic lowering of the people's standard of living. Logically, many people who used to eat meat stopped eating it, and in a few months, Pinochet was able to begin exporting it.

That wasn't the only thing Pinochet did. He presented himself as a champion of Western principles, Western values, capitalism, and free enterprise. As a result, economic advisers, economic specialists, and professors of the Chicago School immediately appeared and showed him how Western interests and the interests of capitalism really had to be defended. They expounded the theory that if he wanted to have efficient industry he would have to open the doors to foreign competition and place Chilean national industries in competition with European, U.S., and Japanese industries and those of such countries as South Korea, Taiwan, and Singapore, where the big transnationals had taken their technologies and imposed their discipline — for which, of course, they also needed authoritarian regimes based on force. The principle that is axiomatic for any developing country and has been accepted for a long time — that the nascent industries of the developing countries have to be protected against the competition of countries with more resources, more technology, and more development — was abandoned. As a result, industry was ruined, the number of the unemployed increased, and the debt shot up.

In Chile, where the most sophisticated economic principles of the Chicago School were applied rigorously, the foreign debt, which had been only $4 billion when Allende was president, rose to $23 billion — of all the figures that have been mentioned, this is the one that seems most realistic to me — and unemployment reached a record high for the Latin American countries: 18.6 percent of the work force. You know that in addition to the unemployed there is always a large number of the underemployed, who work only a few hours in various activities trying to subsist.

The same economic policy that was applied by the military dictatorship in Chile was also applied in Argentina and Uruguay. You can imagine what it meant to place Argentina's automobile, truck, and tractor industries, which produce high-quality vehicles — as we know, because we have Argentine trucks, cars, and other equipment here — that meet the Argentines' needs perfectly well and that meet our needs for transporting sugarcane and providing taxi service, in competition with the Japanese truck and automobile industries, which have highly automated plants that employ robots in many operations and use Japanese steel made with high-technology, high-productivity industrial processes. In short, they were placing Argentine skilled workers in competition with the robots of Japanese industry.

I asked an emissary of the party that won the election in Uruguay, who visited us recently, if the military men in Uruguay had done exactly what the military had done in Chile and Argentina. He said, "Yes, exactly the same thing." He even mentioned the case of an industry that produced hair curlers or something like that: when the same — but cheaper — South Koreans articles appeared, the Uruguayan industry was ruined. That is, the same economic formula was applied in the three countries, though the political formula of a military coup, the overt use of force against the people, and the most ruthless methods of oppression was applied first in Chile, Argentina, and Uruguay. You can appreciate the disastrous consequences of those political methods and economic measures.

The paradox of all this is that the United States, the most industrialized country in the world, uses all kinds of tariff and other formulas to jealously protect not only its industries, which are far from competitive in many branches, but also its agricultural products, such as beet sugar and even corn syrup for sweetening soft drinks. Yet its professors come to teach us how to tear down our tariff barriers and make our industries competitive.

I don't have enough information about Brazil, about what the military men did there in the economic field and how they did it — which formula they used and what gave rise to its enormous debt. Rather, I have the impression that Brazil didn't follow the exact same policy as Chile, Argentina, and Uruguay, that it may have protected its national industries more against foreign competition and that what it did was fling open its doors to the transnationals so they could make big investments there and set up plants, attracted by cheap labor, offering them all the advantages, guarantees, and securities that a strong-arm regime could. But I have the impression that the Brazilian military men were more concerned about protecting their national industries than the Chileans, the Argentines, and the Uruguayans were.

Díaz: Commander, weren't some corrupt public officials to blame for the creation of this foreign debt?

Castro: I'll tell you. That is an element to take into account, because it was a factor, and I've tried to explain how the policies of the governments of those three countries that I've mentioned aggravated the crisis in each of them. It's an example of how the governments' actions can be better or worse and, of course, have an influence on the situation.

Several factors had a bearing on the creation of that debt. They included the policies mentioned: if you open your doors to foreign competition and ruin your national industry, you will have to pay fabulous amounts each year for imports and, as a result, will be forced to ask for loans.

Díaz: Or if the money is misdirected, commander.

Castro: I'm trying to explain things in an orderly way.

Those countries' foreign debts — which are a result of their increased imports — are one of the factors. Also, much of that money went for weapons and other military expenditures. Another part served to make a lot of people rich — that is, much of that money was stolen — and a lot of it was sent abroad in various ways. The moneylenders didn't care what was done with it. That period coincided with an enormous accumulation of funds, much of which came from the surpluses that were created in several big oil-exporting countries and deposited in banks in the United States and Europe. There was so much money that the moneylenders, the banks, went running after debtors, offering them loans. The usual situation was reversed. Generally, it's the debtors who go to the banks to ask for loans, but, in many countries in Latin America, the bankers went around looking for debtors in order to lend them money at interest rates that were much lower than they are now — that is, money was lent at lower interest rates, and much higher interest is charged now. I can say more: a dollar that had a certain value was lent, and now a dollar that is overvalued by nearly 40 percent, according to some experts, is collected. It's as if I lent you a kilogram of gold and then asked you to return 1.4 kilograms of gold, apart from the higher interest charged for those 1.4 kilograms of gold.

In short, a part of that money may have been invested in a more or less useful way; another part was squandered on various things, apart from arms — it served to support absurd, antinational policies that were ruinous for local industries or was stolen or was sent abroad or was misspent on arms or squandered on other things — and some of it, in theory, may have been invested in something useful.

Díaz: Such as?

Castro: Well, some industrial equipment may have been purchased and installed somewhere, or perhaps it was used to pay for an infrastructure project or a road or a hydroelectric power plant was built — investments of that sort. But, in fact, that enormous debt didn't result in development for Latin America.

When I was talking about inflation associated with the flight of capital, I tried to explain that the 175.4 percent rate of inflation for the group of countries in 1984 — which is quite generalized inflation that affects all of Latin America, to a greater or lesser degree — resulted in loss of confidence in national currencies. The natural tendency of everybody who has an amount of money and wants to protect it is to change it for dollars and deposit them in U.S. banks. Even though various measures have been taken in different countries to protect their foreign currency income and keep it from being sent abroad, there are always many ways of getting dollars. In nearly all countries, in addition to the official exchange rate, there is a parallel exchange rate. I talked with some Dominicans, and they said that anybody who has money in national currency could obtain dollars without any great difficulty, either through the banks or in the street, though you always get a little more in the street.

Anyway, when confidence is lost in a national currency — which is the case in the Latin American countries — many people who want to make their money more secure — usually they belong to higher-income sectors and have the equivalent of $50,000, $100,000, $500,000, or a million dollars in national currency — exchange it, deposit it in the United States at a high interest rate, and have their money and interest guaranteed.

Even though, in this situation of inflation, countries tend to pay higher domestic interest rates, precisely in order to attract money and prevent the flight of capital, the present high levels of inflation in several Latin American countries practically make it necessary to use a computer to get weekly estimates (daily estimates in the case of Bolivia) of how much the national currency has been devaluated, so you can know what the interest paid by the local banks really means and what is happening to your money. On the other hand, people have the alternative of exchanging their money for the foreign currency of a country that pays high interest rates so that, far from being devaluated, it will rise in value, and they exchange it and deposit it in a safe place. Latin American countries with underdeveloped economies don't have an easy time of it, and they are beset by traps on all hands.

I am pointing this out because, as I told you, to the figures given on interest payments and profits — to all those figures — we must add the money that leaves those countries every year, because all countries are affected, to a greater or lesser degree, by the flight of capital, mainly to the United States.

You are Mexican. Just today, I read an international wire service report that contained information issued by the National Bank of Mexico, stating that the Mexican economy had lost more than $7.6 billion through the negative flow of foreign currency in the first nine months of 1984, not only for interest on its debt (which accounted for 67 percent of the nearly $13 billion that left the country), but also because, between January and September, the flight of foreign currency rose to more than $2 billion. In contrast, income from loans amounted to only $5 billion or so, with $192 million coming in as foreign investments. At least the central bank of Mexico has a clear view of the foreign currency that is leaving the country.

Well, I was talking about the flight of capital. This has occurred not only in Latin America but in Europe and Japan, as well. In 1983, $40 billion flowed to the United States, partly in response to the policy of high interest rates paid there. I understand that $4-5 billion were transferred from the Federal Republic of Germany [FRG], which is a great industrial power, to the United States last year because interest rates there are 4.5 points higher than in the FRG. With that kind of monetary policy, money flows toward the United States from all quarters. During that same year, 1983, $170 billion in foreign capital was invested in stocks and bonds in the United States. In order to be able to support a budgetary deficit of nearly $200 billion and a trade deficit of another $123 billion, you have to drain money away from the rest of the world.

And, if there is a flight of capital from such highly industrialized countries as Japan and the FRG [Federal Republic of Germany] (not to mention Spain, Italy, France, and England, all of which unquestionably have industrial development — some more, some less — but which fall short of the levels achieved by the FRG and Japan), what can you expect to happen in countries with weak economies that are struggling for development and have a lot of economic and social problems, such as the countries of Latin America? What could happen? How could the Latin American countries defend themselves more successfully against a policy that is adversely affecting the rest of the more developed industrial powers?

Other factors have also contributed to this crisis and to this debt, and I'm going to mention them to you. One of them — a really decisive one — is unequal terms of trade. This phenomenon has existed throughout history and can be traced precisely during the last four decades. I believe that economists should study and analyze this phenomenon more deeply in order to understand its essence and mechanisms better. It is a kind of law that operates in trade between the developing and the industrialized countries. I've already mentioned this: the constantly rising prices for the equipment, machinery, and other finished products we import from the industrialized countries, together with the declining purchasing power of the developing countries' basic exports.

The purchasing power of those products as a whole, including oil, dropped 21.9 percent — almost 22 percent — between 1980 and 1984. This means that if you take these products as a whole, some of whose prices dropped more than others, if with a given amount of those products you could buy 100 units of something in 1980, in 1984 you could buy only 78 with the same amount.

This is a very important element. If Latin America's exports in 1984 were worth $94.79 billion, the near 22 percent drop in their purchasing power, in itself, meant a loss of nearly $20 billion just because of the deterioration in the terms of trade.

To this must be added what we have lost through high interest rates — rates that are higher than the ones that were in effect when the debt, or a large part of it, was contracted and which remain artificially, arbitrarily high. Because of this, we have already lost more than $10 billion — in the interest that is superimposed each year.

To this we must add the loss consisting of the real increase in the debt and its corresponding interest caused by the overvaluation of the dollar. If you received $100 billion, and dollars are now overvalued by 30 percent — I'm going to say 30, not 40, percent here — your debt objectively increased by $30 billion, plus the interest on that $30 billion.

Then, in just these four ways — because of our being charged extra for their products and being paid less for ours, compared to the situation in 1980; because of the artificially high interest rates, a consequence of United States monetary policy; because of the flight of capital; and because of the fact that we are paying with more expensive dollars, inflated ones, that have been overvalued — the Latin American countries' economies were illegitimately stripped of more than $45 billion in 1984; $20 billion for the deterioration in trade relations, $10 billion for excessive interest, $10 billion for the flight of capital, and $5 billion (a conservative estimate) for the overvaluation of the dollar. Adding it all up, including what can be considered normal interest on the debt, in just one year the Latin American countries have turned values equal to around $70 billion over to the rich, developed world. And $50 billion of that was in cash.

Can the Latin American countries' economies withstand that drain? Can they continue to withstand it? Can anyone think about political and social stability in the Latin American countries, when they are subjected to such unheard of, ruthless extortion? Can such demands be upheld from the moral point of view? Is this policy — of overvaluated dollars; of exorbitant interest rates; of the unfair trade relations that are imposed on all of us; of the promotion of and support for repressive, bloody governments, which has happened in several states; of the economic theories and formulas and the monetarist formulas that advisers recommended be applied in those countries; and of the irresponsible lending of fabulous sums without any concern about what that money was invested in or what it was used for — is this policy fair or defensible?

If you consider and analyze the fact that this phenomenon of the deterioration in the terms of trade has occurred, historically, for decades and that it is a problem that has been discussed in the Third World, in the Movement of Nonaligned Countries, and in the United Nations when the need for the new international economic order or a new world economic order was expressed, and if, to this and to everything else I have already pointed out, you add the protectionist policies of the richest industrialized countries, plus the dumping and unfair competition with subsidized products which those same industrialized countries habitually engage in, how can you fail to understand the difficulties and the terrible crisis to which Latin America is now subjected?

Alfonsín isn't to blame for those problems, nor are Sanguinetti, Tancredo Neves, the leaders who will be chosen in the upcoming election in Peru, [Venezuelan Pres.] Belisario Betancur, [Ecuadoran Pres. León] Febres Cordero, and Siles Zuazo, because they simply inherited those problems. Pinochet can be blamed for a large part of them, because of his fratricidal coup and his enthusiastic contributions to and cooperation with that policy for nearly twelve years. The government of Panama and the government of Costa Rica aren't to blame, nor is the government of Mexico or the government of Venezuela. In short, as a rule, I should honestly say that all these aspects make for a situation that escapes the control, the desires, and the wishes of governments.

I believe that it is of decisive importance and absolutely necessary to solve the problem of the debt — and to do so without delay. If this isn't done, none of the democratic processes that have been initiated can be consolidated, because the same economic crisis that made the military withdraw from public administration, practically in flight, in such countries as Argentina, Uruguay, and Brazil, will drag the democratic processes that have been inaugurated in those countries into the whirlwind of insoluble difficulties, social tensions, and economic problems.

Pinochet's methods and even the Dominican Republic's methods for imposing the International Monetary Fund's draconian measures cannot be applied in the political, economic, and social conditions in many Latin American nations — nor are their new leaders about to accept them.

The crisis is advancing and will continue to do so. It is nothing but an illusion to believe that it can be solved with mere palliative, debt renegotiations, and traditional formulas. I can see that many Latin American politicians of all kinds have changed their attitude. I would even say that there are fewer and fewer conservatives in this hemisphere, because many who have traditionally been considered on the right and organizations and parties that have been called conservatives are aware of how deep and serious these problems are. Who can talk to them now of the Chicago School, of tearing down tariff barriers, of letting those countries' nascent industries compete with the industries of the most developed countries, with high productivity and high technology? Who can persuade them to promote free competition in their own domestic markets between their countries' industries and those of the United States, Japan, and Europe? They feel very bitter and defrauded. I am speaking now of conservative politicians and individuals, not of the many intellectuals, filmmakers, artists, writers, other professionals, and representatives of a broad range of political parties, running from the center to the left, or of workers, women, students, doctors, and teachers.

Therefore, I have maintained — and I have said this to U.S. citizens; to visitors from Japan, Europe, and many other capitalist and socialist countries; and to many journalists who have visited us — that the problem of the debt must be solved and the economic crisis overcome, or there will be a social upheaval in Latin America. And, if you ask me what kind it will be, I would say that there will be quite generalized revolutionary social outbreaks.

Díaz: Not right-wing ones?

Castro: I think not. I'm convinced that the process of democratic opening won't be threatened by right-wing military coups, and I'll tell you why. That has already happened; it was the last recourse employed to confront earlier crises that were only a pale reflection of the present situation. That was the recourse first used in Brazil more than twenty years ago, then in Chile, then in Uruguay, and still later in Argentina: strong-arm military regimes that made tens of thousands of people disappear — if you add up all the people who have disappeared, all over, they come to tens of thousands. And tens of thousands more were murdered, tortured, or forced into exile. Never before, anywhere, had such horrible repressive methods been used.

Díaz: What if the people vote for the right-wingers?

Castro: The people in several of those countries are now emerging from a veritable inferno. Their main concern is to leave that inferno behind and they often choose formulas that make it most probable, feasible, and rapid for them to emerge from the inferno. We shouldn't be deceived about the development of events.

The formulas of repressive fascist military coups have already been used, and the military themselves are getting out of public administration in those countries, because they can't handle the situation. The only one left is Pinochet, and he's ever more isolated, both at home and abroad — a kind of Somoza in the Southern Cone, building up the pressure in the boiler. If he does this too long, Chile may explode with such force that it will cause more damage than has been known anywhere else. Don't you think that, in normal situations, in countries such as Bolivia, with a tenth of the problems that have occurred in the last few weeks, there would have already been enough pretexts for ten military coups?

Díaz: But, commander, there might be a vote for the right wing, a democratic vote for the right wing, protesting without knowing why against the progressive governments.

Castro: Well, I know what you're thinking about.

As a rule, in any crisis situation the party in power loses support rapidly, and the people move to the opposition parties. Wherever you have a government — if you like we'll use the classical definitions — of the Left or of the Right, conservative or liberal (thought these words no longer imply any great differences), in stable societies, the people move to the opposition party because they tend to blame the one in power for their serious problems and difficulties. This is a general rule, as may be seen in Europe, even though those societies are more stable.

Apart from the exceptions, if the present economic and social situation in Latin America continues to deteriorate, I don't believe that future developments are going to take place through idyllic electoral, constitutional, and political processes. This may happen in some countries; not all countries have the same situation. The situation in Venezuela and Ecuador isn't as serious as in Bolivia. This isn't a principle that can lead you to deduce that the same thing is going to happen in all countries. No.

But there is no doubt that this crisis is already affecting all governments, to a greater or lesser extent. None can be excluded from this reality.

How do I view the situation in general, particularly in South America? I'm not speaking about Central America; these problems have been causing outbreaks in Central America for some time now. I believe that if a solution isn't found for the economic crisis — and above all for the crisis of the debt — South America is going to explode. I am deeply convinced of this. The old formulas for avoiding those outbreaks have already been applied; the instruments used throughout history have already been exhausted. The present crisis is more serious, deeper, and more generalized than ever before. The military are withdrawing from their positions in state administration; they cannot manage the countries; and they have left the civilian governments a fearsome legacy. Now the civilians have the responsibility of finding solutions.

I'm not making inflammatory, subversive statements — far from it. That isn't my intention. I'm simply analyzing what is happening and what is going to happen, as serenely as possible.

If you ask me — as one journalist already did, "As a revolutionary, aren't you glad that this is so?" — I'm going to tell you what I think. Right now there is something more important than social change, and that is our countries' independence. This situation has brought the Third World countries to such a state of dependence, exploitation, extortion, and abuse that independence and the struggle for the new international economic order have become the main issue for the Latin American and other underdeveloped countries. Social changes alone are not the solution. Social changes may bring greater justice, speed development, and make the efforts and sacrifices of all more equitable and more humane. We have effected these changes and are satisfied that we have done so, but the considerable progress that our country has made in economic and social development wasn't exclusively due to them. It is also due to the fact that within our sphere we have — to some extent — achieved a new international economic order in our relations with the other socialist countries. Eighty-five percent of our trade is with countries of the socialist community, and, while the terms aren't the same with all of them because they have different levels of development and availabilities of resources, our relations are based on truly fair principles of cooperation and trade.

For example, in our economic relations with the USSR and other developed socialist countries, we have overcome the tragic law of unequal terms of trade that has historically governed the relations between the Third World and the developed capitalist powers. We receive fair prices for the products we export, satisfactory prices that are protected by agreements against deterioration in the terms of trade — the phenomenon through which the Third World's exports (except in unusual market conditions) have ever decreasing purchasing power, while its imports grow ever more expensive.

We aren't affected by protectionist measures in our trade with the other socialist countries. We don't suffer from dumping or unfair competition by socialist countries. Our financial problems, which stem from our need for development credits, have been solved without delay or difficulty. We have been able to postpone payment of our debt for ten, fifteen, and even twenty years without interest. If the industrialized capitalist countries employed the same forms of trade and economic and financial relations that we have with the socialist community, the problems I have mentioned would be solved and the Third World countries' development would be guaranteed.

I believe that this is of enormous importance, because, I repeat, we have solved our problems not only through social changes but also because, as a Third World, developing socialist country, Cuba has established a form of new international economic order with the rest of the socialist community. Without these foundations, our great economic and social successes — our tremendous achievements in public health, education, physical education and sports, the elimination of unemployment and malnutrition, and the raising of our people's material and cultural standard of living wouldn't have been possible. Nor would we be able to offer the technical cooperation we do to dozens of other Third World countries. That requires resources, large investments and credits, technology, and a great deal of international cooperation over a long period of time. Many poor countries with scanty resources couldn't make those advances without the new international economic order and without a lot of international cooperation.

Social changes can bring about a better distribution of social wealth; more justice; and more concern for the poorest, neediest classes in the country, but social change alone is not enough. Therefore, we consider that the fundamental premise for the Third World countries' independence, sovereignty, and development — and even for their right to make social changes — is the disappearance of the iniquitous system of exploitation through which the Third World countries are victimized. That is, we consider the struggle for the new world economic order — that economic order that was talked about and agreed to at the United Nations ten years ago, largely thanks to Mexico's initiatives, support, and participation — to be the most essential thing in the short term. Marx himself always considered economic development to be a premise for socialism. Experience forced a number of countries, Cuba among them, to take the socialist road of development. Each people should decide for itself what it wants to do. I am absolutely convinced that for the peoples of the Third World, who have a great variety of systems and forms of government, different degrees of development of their productive forces, and the most diverse forms of political and religious beliefs, development is their most important current task and a vital priority for all, without exception, in which they can unite in a common struggle.

We must get to the bottom of the problems that have created underdevelopment, that adversely affect our countries' development, and that are widening the gap between the industrialized countries of the Third World. It has often been said that the gap should and must be closed but, far from being closed, it continues to widen. Now it is wider than ever.

Some industrial countries already have production figures equal to $15,000 per person. Compare them with Africa's per capita production figures of barely a few hundred dollars a year and with the figures for Latin America. The ratio was ten to one some time ago, but now it is fifteen, twenty, thirty, and (in some cases) forty or fifty to one. That is, the gap between the industrialized world and the underdeveloped world is widening.

The per capita income gap is also widening. Far from making progress, we are regressing; instead of developing, we are growing more underdeveloped. We have been going through a process of underdevelopment, not development. When the differences between you and the industrialized countries are increasing and you are farther and farther away from them, you are growing more underdeveloped — even if a mathematical index says that you have grown by 2 percent or 3 percent, for the gap has grown even more and your world is becoming poorer in comparison to the developed world. The situation is even worse because, while the population in the industrialized countries is growing by 0.6 percent, 0.7, or 0.8 percent, the population in the Third World is growing by 2 to 3 percent, which means that within the next fifteen years 80 percent of the world's population will be living in the Third World. This is why I say that a new system of international economic relations that will really make development possible is of paramount importance.

It is understandable, then, why I think that if the new world economic order isn't achieved the terrible problems affecting our countries won't be solved just through social changes. I repeat: even in a poor country, social changes can bring about better distribution and solve important problems (among other things, by promoting respect for human life by ending the horrible injustices and inequalities that may exist, in both very rich and very poor countries), but I consider the struggle for the new world economic order to be the most important thing the Latin American and Third World countries can do now, because it can lead to the creation of conditions needed for real independence, real sovereignty, and even the right to carry out social changes — and not only the right but the objective possibility of doing so.

There is one essential thing: the cancelation of Latin America's foreign debt in itself won't solve our problems; it would only offer a few years' respite.

There are several countries in Latin America in which if you canceled their debts tomorrow you'd have solved practically nothing. Problems have become so serious in some countries — Bolivia, for example — that canceling their debts wouldn't have any impact. They might be able to count on an additional $200 million, or $250 million, or $270 million, which was their favorable balance of trade last year, but the problems that have accumulated in those countries are so serious that $270 million wouldn't even give them a "breather." I've been told about installations at which it costs $16 to produce a pound of tin, while the present world market price is $5 a pound.

There are some countries where canceling the debt would undoubtedly provide a respite; it would give a respite to Argentina, Uruguay, Brazil, Venezuela, Colombia, Ecuador, Peru, and — yes — Mexico. Mexico isn't one of the countries with the most difficult situations but it would surely provide a respite for Mexico, too.

Now then, we should be aware of the fact that there can be no final solution for our problems as long as the ominous law of sustained deterioration of the terms of trade remains in effect, as long as the industrialized capitalist powers continue to impose the protectionist policies, as long as the practice of dumping subsidized products in order to grab markets and depress the prices of the exports on which many Third World countries depend continues, as long as monetary policies are imposed by means of which a powerful industrial country determines the interest to be paid and we are lent money at one value and expect to repay it at a higher value, as long as the capital we need for development is drained away, and as long as models and methods such as the ones recommended by the Chicago School are imposed.

Just yesterday, in a note to the government of the United States, the Andean Pact countries expressed their deep concern over the drastic reductions that are being made in their sugar quotas on the U.S. market. The United States — which in 1981 was still importing 5 million tons of sugar — reduced its sugar imports to 2.7 million tons in 1984, and, in the near future, its imports won't go over 1.7 million tons. The countries involved described the situation as terrible. These protectionist measures by the United States will reduce Latin America's revenues by hundreds of millions of dollars and will create surpluses that will further depress the world market price.

A little over twenty years ago, Cuba had a quota of over 3 million tons on that market. One day it was taken away and parceled out among other countries in this hemisphere. The pretext then was the Cuban revolution, which had to be crushed without mercy. Now, when the debt amounts to

$360 billion, what pretext will the United States give for eliminating the Latin American countries' sugar quotas?

If we don't overcome these problems, we will obtain only a respite; a few countries will get a respite, but the real causes of our difficulties won't be solved. I believe that this is the time to wage this struggle. Such a serious crisis situation has been created that the Third World countries are being forced to think, to unite, and to seek solutions, regardless of their political stands and ideologies, as an elementary matter of survival.

I believe that the Latin American countries need to wage that struggle and that, fortunately, they have excellent conditions for waging it. The struggle to solve the problem of the debt will benefit all the Third World countries — not just the Latin American countries, but all the developing countries in Asia and Africa, as well. I feel that the debt should be canceled. Mathematically it can be shown that it is unpayable.

The problem no longer involves the amount of the debt, but the interest that is paid on it.

I base my view on four hypotheses, all based on the assumption that the debt won't grow.

First hypothesis: that a ten-year grace period is granted for paying the capital; that, during that period, the interest will continue to be paid, as it has been thus far; and that ten years will then be given for the amortization at an interest rate not exceeding 10 percent. Latin America would have to pay $400 billion in the first ten years and an additional $558 billion in the next ten years. In twenty years, Latin America would have transferred $958 billion — nearly $1 trillion in U.S. terms, or $1 billion in English terms — to its creditors. That is, nearly a trillion dollars would leave these countries, in spite of their enormous accumulated social problems, their enormous economic problems, and the development they will have had to forgo. In twenty years, they would have to extract nearly $1 trillion from their modest economies and send it to the industrialized capitalist countries. Is this possible? Is it conceivable? And this, I repeat, is assuming that the debt won't grow and that the interest rate doesn't go over 10 percent during the amortization period. Is this conceivable, especially if the other problems I have mentioned— unequal exchange, protectionism, dumping, and so on — are taken into account? No.

Second hypothesis: that the formula of paying a maximum of 20 percent of the value of each country's exports and each year is applied and that interest rates don't go over 10 percent. The exports of Latin America as a whole are already close to but haven't reached $100 billion. Let us even assume that even if those exports surpass that figure, no more than $20 billion will be paid each year. In that case, we would pay $400 billion in twenty years, and, at the end, we would have a debt of $1.16185 trillion — that is, after we had paid $400 billion, our debt would be triple what it is now.

Third hypothesis: that a ten-year grace period is granted, including the interest; an additional ten years is granted for its amortization; and the interest doesn't go over 10 percent in any given year. This would undoubtedly mean a ten-year respite. In twenty years $1.44731 trillion would have to be paid.

Fourth hypothesis: that the interest rate is lowered to 6 percent; a ten-year grace period is granted, including the interest; and an additional ten years is given in which to pay. This would certainly be the kindest of the four formulas, but in twenty years $857.471 billion would still have to be paid.

I have put forward four hypotheses. In all, I have assumed that the debt would never exceed 10 percent, and all of them show that the debt and its interest cannot be paid.

Based on reality, on all the problems I've mentioned, it is simply impossible to pay the debt. It can't be done from a practical standpoint — our economies couldn't survive it — and it could never solve the problem of development. The debt is an economic and a political impossibility. It is also a moral impossibility. The immense sacrifice that would have to be demanded of the people and the blood that would have to be shed to force them to pay that immense sum of money — which, to a large extent, was drained away, misspent, or embezzled — would be unjustifiable. The debt has already taken its first toll in blood in the Dominican Republic, where dozens of poor people were killed. Any attempt to pay the debt under the present social, economic, and political circumstances in Latin America would cost our suffering and impoverished nations rivers of blood, and it could never be done. Our peoples are not to blame for underdevelopment or for the debt. Our countries are not to blame for having been colonies; neocolonies; banana republics; or coffee, mining, or oil republics whose role was to produce raw materials, exotic products, and fuel at low cost and with cheap labor.

Economic specialists and historians tell us that the fabulous amounts of gold and silver that were extracted from the entrails of our nations and amassed over the centuries thanks to our peoples' sweat and blood financed the development of the industrialized world that is now the creditor demanding payment of the debt. The amount wrenched away from our peoples in just the last few decades through unequal terms of trade, high interest rates, protectionism, dumping, monetary manipulations, and the flight of capital is much greater than the total amount of the debt. The riches and well-being of which we have been deprived through the imposition of economic dependence and underdevelopment cannot even be estimated, let alone measured. It is our peoples who, by right, are the creditors of the rich and industrialized Western world, both morally and materially. The FRG has been paying Israel cash compensation for the

Nazis' genocide against the Jews. Who is paying compensation for the deliberate destruction of our peoples' lives and riches throughout the centuries?

As a result of all these mathematical calculations and moral, historical, political, and economic reflections, I have come to the conclusion that the Latin American debt is unpayable and should be canceled. It has been said that failure to pay the debt would destabilize and sink the international financial system. This isn't necessarily so. I suggest that the industrialized creditor countries can and should make themselves responsible for the debts to their own banks.

As a rule, the public debts of the industrialized countries increase; it is a historic fact that they tend to increase. All that the industrialized states make themselves responsible for is the interest on their increasing public debts.

In 205 years the public debt of the United States has reached $1 trillion — when I say "trillion," I'm referring to the U.S. trillion, which is equal to the English billion — a million million. The U.S. public debt reached that figure in 1981; but from 1981 to 1984, in just three years, it increased by another $650 billion; and it is estimated that it will reach or surpass $2 trillion by 1986. This is almost never mentioned in the United States, however. It doesn't seem to be much cause for concern. Rather, it stresses the growth of the economy — and, as a matter of fact, the economy was reported to have grown by 6.8 percent in 1984. So, if we follow the theories and concepts of official economics, we see that the increase in the public debt hasn't ruined the economy or impeded its growth; nor has it hampered the optimism with which some U.S. economists talk about future economic growth and development. If the federal government of the United States, plus the governments of other industrialized powers, were to make themselves responsible to their private banks for the debts of the Latin American and other Third World countries, this would imply added increases in their public debts.

Where could they find the resources with which to pay the interest on the increases in their debts without affecting their countries' economies? That's easy: from military expenditures — and not all military expenditures, just a small percentage of them: 10 percent or, if interest rates remain as high as they now are, a maximum of 12 percent.

With this modest percentage of their military expenditures, the industrialized powers could make themselves responsible to their own banks for the foreign debts of the Latin American and other Third World countries — and military spending would still be fabulously high and cause for concern.

Military spending throughout the world now amounts to a million million dollars (a trillion, according to U.S. nomenclature, or a billion in English). And, if the arms race (which world public opinion considers absurd and unacceptable in a world in which there are more than 100 underdeveloped countries and billions of people who lack food, health care, housing, and education) isn't ended, that spending will continue increasing until it unleashes a nuclear catastrophe, which would be more dangerous than the economic catastrophe from which a large part of humanity is suffering. If the former were to take place, talking about the latter would make no sense at all.

It would be very sensible and wise if the reduction in military spending were associated with the beginning of a solution for international economic problems. All economists have stated that with a fraction of the money now spent for military purposes the problems of underdevelopment and poverty that beset the world could be solved.

This problem of increased military spending and the danger it poses to mankind was the subject of a recent meeting held in New Delhi, in which individuals of such international prestige and authority as [Indian Prime Minister] Rajiv Gandhi, [Tanzanian Pres.] Julius Nyerere, Raúl Alfonsin, [Mexican Pres.] Miguel de la Madrid, [Greek Prime Minister] Andreas Papandreou, and [Swedish Prime Minister] Olaf Palme participated.

By issuing ten-year treasury notes and treasury bonds, the United States could make itself responsible to its own creditor banks for all the credits given to the Latin American and other Third World countries. This wouldn't affect U.S. citizens' current contributions to the budget. The banks would recover the capital they have invested, U.S. export companies would increase their exports, and U.S. investors abroad would increase their profits.

More important, such a solution would create jobs in all the industrialized countries; their industries would use a large percentage of their installed capacities, and international trade would increase.

It should be kept in mind that the main problem confronting the industrialized countries isn't their domestic public debts or foreign debts. It is rather the scourge of unemployment, which is steadily increasing in most of the Western countries, with figures in the order of 3 million in Britain, despite its new oil resources; 2.6 million in the FRG, a postwar record; 3 million in France; 2.8 million in Spain; and so on.

Solving the problem of the underdeveloped countries' foreign debts could be an important step toward emerging from the prolonged international economic crisis — which is far from over, despite the optimistic forecasts that some would make.

The economy of the European Economic Community grew by a mere 2.4 percent in 1984, and better results aren't expected this year. What is growing — constantly — is unemployment. According to very recent data, the U.S. economy had growth difficulties during the first quarter of this year.

Even though solving the Third World's foreign debt problem would doubtless provide relief for many countries, it would fall far short of solving the problems of development. Within a few years, if unequal terms of trade, protectionist measures, dumping, monetary policies based on the economic clout of a few countries, excessive interest on loans, and the other elements in the unjust system of econmic relations and exploitation that is imposed on the countries of the Third World; if these aren't eliminated once and for all — that is, if a new world economic order isn't firmly established — the situation would be the same as or worse than it is now.

Díaz: How should this be handled? Could the pressure that the creditor banks bring to bear on the countries be somehow turned around so that we can demand that they take a series of measures to avoid their own financial crisis?

Castro: Because of their political importance, their political weight in the world, their enormous debts, their terrible economic and social crises, and the dangers of a social upheaval of unforeseeable consequences, their deep community of interests and their potential for joint action, the Latin American countries, in my opinion, are in a better position than those of any other region in the world to tackle this problem seriously. Many of their leaders have already set forth the premises concerning the foreign debt, which would be the first step in that struggle, clearly and precisely.

Yet, it is inconceivable at this stage that the first thing that is proclaimed and solemnly pledged is that the countries of this hemisphere that are affected by this situation will not form a debtors' club — even though the creditor countries are closely joined in the International Monetary Fund and the Paris Club. A club, a committee, a group, or whatever you want to call it is indispensable. Acting on their own, our countries cannot achieve any kind of lasting solution for our problems; all they can hope for are more palliative formulas that only mitigate their difficulties: a brief grace period on the payment of capital or a small reduction in the percentage of interest paid in addition to the Libor rate.*

As I've already said, the problem no longer concerns just the payment of capital. Even if a four-, six-, eight- or ten-year grace period of and a similar — or longer — period after that for payment of the total debt are granted, the problem would still get worse and worse. The current renegotiations will solve absolutely nothing. The problem resides in the enormous amounts of interest that must be paid each year, religiously and punctually, accompanied by inapplicable political measures; exaggerated, unrealistic goals related to inflation; the reduction of the budget-

---

*The London Inter-Bank Rate is the rate at which banks borrow from each other.

ary deficit; the limitation of social expenditures in countries riddled with problems in education, health care, nutrition, housing, unemployment, etc.; and other measures demanded by the International Monetary Fund which become impossible to apply when the country is forced to make enormous disbursements simply to pay the unfair interest on its debt. The people don't understand this, nor can they understand it. There is no other message for them but the message of fruitless sacrifices. They've been promised a lot of things for a long time, and they see that things are getting worse and worse. They don't understand the technical aspects. Technical aspects mean nothing to them for they offer them nothing when they get up in the morning to look for work or when they see their wages shrinking while products grow more and more expensive. Remember what Lincoln said: "You can't fool all of the people all of the time."

Membership in the Cartagena group was limited to eleven countries.

I met Enrique Iglesias, the director of ECLAC, who is now minister of foreign affairs of Uruguay. He is an economist who is highly esteemed in our hemisphere and has excellent relations with many heads of state. The prevailing view at that time was that the group shouldn't be increased, because a larger number of countries would make negotiations and analyses more difficult. The principle wasn't at all democratic. No clear explanation was given of why some had the privilege of being members while others didn't. This principle seemed more applicable to a social club than to the idea of how to face a serious, crucial situation involving each and every nation in Latin America. I believe that this criterion doesn't make any sense. All the Latin American countries should be included in the group. Even such countries as Guyana, Trinidad and Tobago, Jamaica, and others with a lot of weight and long standing as independent nations in the Caribbean could be included if they were ready and willing to cooperate loyally; their debts are also considerable.

Probable disloyalties aren't to be feared. I don't believe that any self-respecting Latin American government would be capable of betraying the feelings and interests of the Latin American family in these critical circumstances. In any circumstances, the dissenters would never be anything more than individual cases or isolated groups. Cuba would be willing to exclude itself from those activities if this were advisable, if the other countries didn't want to displease the United States, as is already traditional. But I don't think it would be good tactics, in this situation, to display excessive caution or cowardice to the "colossus of the north" — which must, of course, be persuaded to cooperate. Moreover, undignified, irresponsible attitudes (which not even the United States respects) shouldn't be adopted in order to achieve its cooperation.

I'm not saying this so Cuba will be included or to reflect some Cuban problem. Cuba is now the only Latin American or Caribbean country that is immune to the crisis. Its foreign debt in convertible currency is minimal, barely $300 per inhabitant. We don't have any problems in our financial relations or in our trade with the rest of the socialist community — with which, as I said, we have 85 percent of our foreign trade. Between 1981 and 1984 our Gross Social Product increased by 24.8 percent, and the per capita GSP grew by 22.6 percent; our economic and social development programs for the next fifteen years are guaranteed — something that is a privilege for any country at a time like this.

If it weren't for the principles of the new economic order which we have attained with the rest of the socialist community, as I explained, our annual sugar exports of over 7.5 million tons — at the current price of sugar on the so-called world market and supposing that there were markets for that volume of exports — wouldn't be enough to pay for even 25 percent of our fuel imports.

If the Latin American countries want to tackle the problems of their foreign debt they must reach a consensus in order to attain the goal of engaging in a political dialogue with the creditor countries, as many of their leaders have suggested, because, as has been correctly pointed out, the problem is political, not technical, and, at the rate things are developing, it's beginning to be a revolutionary problem.

I'd like to add something about the intermediate formulas that have been mentioned or similar ones that may crop up.

From the mathematical calculations that I showed you, you can see that the payment formula involving only 20 percent of each country's annual exports, limiting those figures to $20 billion, solves nothing. Without considering new loans, they would have to pay $400 billion over twenty years and wind up, with interest at 10 percent, by owing $1.16185 trillion. Even reducing the interest rate to 6 percent and having a ten-year moratorium including interest, in line with the kindest formula, they would have to pay $857.471 billion in the next ten years.

Such intermediate formulas as reducing payments to 20 percent of annual exports or simply reducing the interest rate without a moratorium of at least ten years wouldn't even give them a respite. Such intermediate formulas don't attract, don't rally, don't persuade, don't motivate, and they don't mobilize anyone, simply because they can't solve the problem.

One very important question would be what to do with those resources. I believe, on the basis of the austerity measures already established by many governments, that most of those resources would have to be used for economic development, to create a solid, essential base from which to attack unemployment, hunger, and many other social calamities.

No matter how pressing the problems are, you can't just think of distributing and consuming those resources and of immediately raising the standard of living. Rather, a percent of them — 20 or at most 30 percent, depending on the circumstances — could be used to meet the most pressing health, education, and housing needs. You can do a lot with 20 percent of $400 billion to complement the resources now being used for those purposes.

All this would require great awareness and great national consensus equal to the challenge posed by the circumstances.

The solution of the debt would simply be a first step; we have to get at the real, root causes of this debt, of the economic crisis that has been unleashed, reaching the elements that gave rise to it. Solving the problem of the debt would be no more than the beginning. We would have to demand an end to unequal terms of trade; an end to protectionist policies; an end to the practice of dumping and to unjust, abusive monetary policies, excessive rates of interest, overvaluation of the dollar, and other diabolical procedures that make our countries' development impossible.

We should demand fair prices for our export commodities. We can't go on supplying coffee, cocoa, bananas, sugar, meat, minerals, and other essential raw materials, produced on the basis of starvation wages that often are less than $80 a month, to purchase merchandise, equipment, medicines, and other industrial articles that are processed in the industrialized nations on the basis of huge profits for the enterprises and wages of more than $1,000 a month — that is, twelve, fifteen, and sometimes twenty as high as the wages that the workers and technicians in the Latin American countries receive. Our unemployed don't usually have any kind of subsidy, and a large part of the population doesn't even receive medical and educational services.

Paradoxically, this crisis is providing the Latin American and other Third World countries with the first real opportunity they've had of receiving due consideration of their demands. We have spent dozens of years in the United Nations, in the Movement of Nonaligned Countries, and in all the other international agencies demanding a fairer economic order and requesting better prices for our products, loans, and resources for development. It wasn't long ago when, speaking on behalf of the Movement of Nonaligned Countries, following the Sixth Summit Conference, I expressed the need for the Third World to have $300 billion in development assistance during this decade.

Now, it isn't a matter of our getting on our knees and imploring the industrialized countries to supply us with funds or to assign a modest 0.7 percent of their Gross National Products to development — a commitment which only a few states have made. Now, when they are demanding that the Latin American and Caribbean countries turn over $400 billion in ten years, the decision making has passed to us. We have the power to simply declare that we won't accept this plunder and won't hand over the $400 billion. They couldn't even threaten us with suspending future loans. Well used, that $400 billion that they are demanding we produce from the sweat and sacrifices of the Latin American peoples could finance Latin America's development in the next ten years. Every country can lend itself what it's paying in interest.

If the industrialized countries are rational, not only will they benefit from our increased exports, but even their own banks will benefit through a formula such as the one suggested, which will guarantee them the availability of their credits, and they can make new loans — which, when you get right down to it, is their purpose in international finances and trade. If the new world economic order is really achieved, new loans can be received and paid on solid bases.

Since the OPEC countries managed to raise the price of oil from around $2.50 to $30 a barrel, the industrialized countries — the European ones, the United States, Japan, and others — have paid more than $1 trillion to cover these higher oil prices in just eleven years. This was much more than the entire accumulated foreign debt of the Third World, and it didn't ruin their economies or even affect their enormous military expenditures. Ninety percent of this money ended up in the banks of the same countries from which it started out. They also collected the money that the non-oil-producing Third World countries spent on oil imports. The prices of their exports soared. Many Western companies — including arms manufacturers — made fabulous deals, thanks to the new purchasing power of their oil-purchasing clients. Many technological innovations were made, and scores of measures were adopted to save fuel. New and old sources of energy were used. Waste decreased considerably. Only the non-oil-producing developing countries suffered from the catastrophe in all regards and were subjected to new unequal terms of trade.

The cancelation of the Third World's foreign debt would be much fairer and economically more beneficial for all countries, much more vital and much less costly than was agreement to the oil exporters' demands in their day — demands that, with regard to most of the Third World countries, will be fully justified and balanced only when the branches of their basic exports are given the same treatment.

The new world economic order should mean fair trade relations for all the Third World countries, which will mean that the rich industrialized powers will have to stop wasting so many resources on arms. Nobody has the right to pay starvation wages for the cocoa, tea, coffee, cashew nuts, peanuts, coconuts, and fibers that are gathered leaf by leaf and grain by grain, the minerals, and other raw materials in order to manufacture aircraft carriers, battleships, strategic missiles, and nuclear submarines and to pay for star wars weapons. Those resources should be invested in the war on hunger, here on earth.

If the Latin American and Third World countries take a firm, united stand, they will, for the first time, have a real opportunity to reach these goals, beginning with the question of the foreign debt. If total lack of understanding should force them to make a unilateral decision with regard to the debt, they cannot be threatened with a suspension of trade. Since the other countries wouldn't be able to survive without trade with the Third World, they can't do without our fuel and other raw materials, and they wouldn't be happy without our coffee, tea, cocoa, shrimp, lobsters, and other tropical delights.

It is absolutely impossible for them to blockade the Third World economically or take over our countries because of the debt, as they did in Haiti, the Dominican Republic, and other countries in the first few decades of this century. They can't divide up the world again to assure their supplies of raw materials and markets, as they did in other eras.

The new Latin American leaders have an immense responsibility. I reiterate my conviction that if the problem of the debt isn't solved, if efforts are made to pay it no matter what the cost, if the disastrous formulas of the International Monetary Fund are promoted, great social upheavals will be produced.

I don't see any danger of a return to the wave of right-wing repressive, fascist coups — which may occur only in exceptional cases, in some countries, on an isolated basis. Rather, I think it is possible that in the case of great social upheavals in some countries, leaders imbued with a patriotic spirit and a realistic sense of the situation who are ready to promote social changes along with the people will arise from among the military.

In much less critical circumstances, figures who arose from the ranks of the military, such as Omar Torrijos in Panama and Velasco Alvarado in Peru, held high the banners of national demands and social reform.

The struggle for demands as rational as the solution of the problem of the foreign debt and fair economic relations between the Third World countries and the industrialized world is so essential for the survival and future of the Latin American peoples that it would doubtless be supported by all social strata and would generate great internal unity in all the countries. It would also strengthen the unity among all the Latin American countries and would receive the unhesitating, enthusiastic, determined support of all the developing countries in Asia and Africa.

I have no doubt that many industrialized countries would also support these demands. Nor do I doubt that the ideal, most constructive thing is for these problems to be solved by means of political dialogue and negotiation, which would promote essential solutions in an orderly manner. If this is not done, desperate situations will doubtless force a group of countries to take unilateral measures. This isn't desirable, but, if it occurs, I am sure that all the countries in Latin America and the rest of the Third World will join them.

Appendix
Cuban Government Response to
'Radio José Martí'

As a result of the cynical and provocative decision of the government of the United States to start subversive broadcasts against Cuba as of May 20, a grim and shameful date which recalls the military occupation of Cuba by the United States, the plunder of its best lands and other natural resources, the neocolonization of our country, and the pseudo-republic accompanied by an amendment to its constitution which gave the United States the right to intervene in Cuba, to which must be added the gross insult of using the glorious name of José Martí for these broadcasts, deeply wounding the feelings of the Cuban people, the government of Cuba wishes to communicate to the government of the United States the following statement:

It is the government of Cuba's understanding that going on the air with these broadcasts, a decision taken years ago but not implemented until now, when it is done in a strangely secretive and surprise manner, without prior notice to the U.S. press or the government of Cuba, save the laconic, hypocritical, and justificatory message sent twelve hours before by the U.S. Interests Section and information made public shortly after — all at a time when various kinds of constructive steps had been taken to reduce existing tension between the two countries — has no possible explanation other than that of a clear intent to respond basely to the solid and irrefutable charges and statements made by the government of Cuba on the critical economic situation of Latin America and the Third World, and on the immoral, unpayable foreign debt and the ruthless economic plunder that the unjust system of international relations has imposed on those countries.

Unquestionably, the government of the United States clearly intends,

---

This May 19, 1985, note delivered to the U.S. Interests Section in Havana was published in the May 26, 1985, Granma Weekly Review. *The date of the start of "Radio José Martí" was the eighty-third anniversary of the imposition of a formally "independent" U.S.-dominated regime in Cuba.*

with this measure, to create tension and conflict around Cuba that will divert the attention of international opinion on this grave problem, divert our country's efforts in the struggle for an adequate solution to this critical and explosive situation, and silence Cuba's charges.

Taking into account, moreover, the fact that this downright act of provocation shatters and ruins the bases for communication and relations which have been established over years between citizens of Cuban origin resident in the United States and citizens of our country, and in view of the perfidious position of the government of the United States in its relations with Cuba and the contempt for our people reflected in these shameful, dishonest practices, the government of Cuba has decided:

First, to suspend all proceedings related to the implementation of the agreement on migratory questions signed between the delegation of the two governments on December 14, 1984, in the city of New York.

Second, to suspend all trips by citizens of Cuban origin living in the United States to Cuba, except for those authorized on strictly humanitarian grounds.

Third, the goverment of Cuba plans to adopt additional measures regarding communications between the United States and Cuba.

Fourth, the government of Cuba reserves the right to reconsider the cooperation it has been unilaterally providing to the government of the United States in the struggle against illegal exits from the country and other activities in which the United States benefits from the spontaneous and selfless cooperation of Cuba.

Fifth, the government of Cuba reserves the right to transmit medium-wave radio broadcasts to the United States to make fully known the Cuban view on the problems concerning the United States and its international policy.

The government of Cuba wishes, therefore, to notify the government of the United States that it is not at all concerned by the warning in today's note to the effect that a strong Cuban reaction would make relations with the United States more difficult for a long period of time and block any possibility of progress on bilateral issues. Such unscrupulous methods of blackmail and force on the part of the government of the United States make any improvement in relations with Cuba, or any other self-respecting country, impossible.

Cuba will continue developing its relations with other Latin American and Third World countries. It will continue advocating the need for the cancelation of the foreign debt in these countries and continue fighting for an end to protectionism; the ruinous dumping of many of their basic export items; the brazen theft of their natural resources by way of unequal terms of trade, exorbitant interest rates, the unethical and arbitrary overvaluation of the dollar, and other brutal and abusive methods of exploitation and plunder of their economies; and fighting for a new international economic order. If the price we must pay for this and for the defense of our dignity and sovereignty is to make relations with the United States more difficult for many years and prevent any possiblity of improvement or any other price, we will gladly pay it. The government of the United States bears the sole responsibility for this option.

The people of Cuba have withstood over twenty-five years of arrogant policy, economic blockade, and threats and aggressions of all kinds from the United States. The current administration in that country should harbor no doubts as to our resisting as long as is necessary. One day, the people of the United States themselves will put an end to such a sterile, blind, senseless, egotistical policy.

Other Titles from Pathfinder Press on Cuba, Central America, and the Caribbean

Che Guevara Speaks

Cuba for Beginners
  by RIUS

Fidel Castro at the UN

Fidel Castro on Chile

Fidel Castro Speeches:
Cuba's Internationalist Foreign Policy 1975-80

Fidel Castro Speeches Vol. 2:
Building Socialism in Cuba

Fidel Castro Speaks to Trade Unionists:
The U.S. War Drive and the World Economic Crisis

Maurice Bishop Speaks:
The Grenada Revolution 1979-83

Nicaragua: The Sandinista People's Revolution
  Speehes by Sandinista Leaders

Sandinistas Speak
  by Tomás Borge, Carlos Fonseca, Daniel Ortega, et al

Second Declaration of Havana
  by Fidel Castro

Selected Speeches of Fidel Castro

Women and the Cuban Revolution
  Speeches and Documents by Fidel Castro, Vilma Espín, and others

Women and the Nicaraguan Revolution
  by Tomás Borge

Index